THE POEMS OF CICERO

THE POEMS OF CICERO

Edited with Introduction
and Notes by
W.W. Ewbank

Bristol Classical Press

To D.M.E.

This impression 2003
This edition published in 1997 by
Bristol Classical Press
an imprint of
Gerald Duckworth & Co. Ltd.
61 Frith Street, London W1D 3JL
Tel: 020 7434 4242
Fax: 020 7434 4420
inquiries@duckworth-publishers.co.uk
www.ducknet.co.uk

First published in 1933 by University Press of London Ltd.

© 1933 by W.W. Ewbank

All rights reserved. No part of this publication
may be reproduced, stored in a retrieval system, or
transmitted, in any form or by any means, electronic,
mechanical, photocopying, recording or otherwise,
without the prior permission of the publisher.

A catalogue record for this book is available
from the British Library

ISBN 1 85399 529 0

CONTENTS

Preface vii

§ Introduction. Cicero the Poet 1

Attitude to Poetry—To the Ennian School and the Alexandrines—The Aratea—Poetry and Education—Romanticism—Compound Adjectives—Archaism.

§ The Poems 10

De Consulatu—Marius—De Temporibus Meis—Caesar and the Expedition to Britain—The Aratea—Miscellanea.

§ Criticism of the Poems 27

Ancient Criticism—Modern—Conflict of Opinions—Influence of Rhetoric on the Poems—Original Work—Translations—Cicero the Translator—Summary.

§ The Ciceronian Hexameter 40

Caesura—Composition of the First Foot—Of the First Four Feet—Cicero's Use of Rhythm, some Examples—Pauses — Final Pauses — Elision — The Fifth and Sixth Feet — Miscellaneous, Rhythm, Alliteration, Rhyme, Homoeoteleuta—Synizesis and Hiatus—Suppression of Final ' s.'

§ The Text 72

§ The Poems 75

§ Commentary 109

Appendix 264

PREFACE

THE present edition has been designed to meet the needs of the general student who may wish to read the poems of Cicero, but who has been unable to do so owing to their inaccessibility and to the absence of any modern work dealing with them. In compiling the commentary I have been at pains to avoid including any information which might be termed elementary, and have purposely omitted such bogeys as long quotations in the original, the multiplication of references, and the extended discussion of textual difficulties, except in so far as such discussion has been considered indispensable for the elucidation of the author's meaning or of his translation of the original Greek—for throughout the commentary it has been my object to lay especial stress on Cicero's merits and demerits as a translator.

Of late years the study of Astronomy has become increasingly popular. Assuming that the general student is unlikely to be a skilled astronomer, I have not hesitated to treat this part of the work as simply as possible. The notes on the relative positions of the constellations are intended only for the reader's convenience, and it would be well to supplement them by reference to some suitable star atlas.

In dealing with the metre of Cicero, no account has been taken of the dramatic iambic senarii, as the importance of this metre is not commensurate with that of the hexameter so far as our present author is concerned. But the extent to which he improved and popularised the hexameter as a medium of national expression merits our serious attention and respect.

The bibliography appended to the commentary is

intended to acknowledge the help gained from those whose works have been found especially useful. My indebtedness to the translation of Aratus by A. W. Mair and G. R. Mair and to S. E. Winbolt's *Latin Hexameter Verse* is considerable. I hope that all other books not mentioned in the bibliography, and to which reference has been made, will be found acknowledged in their respective places in this edition.

Finally, I wish to thank all those who have helped me in any way whatsoever, and to record the assistance received from the University of London Publication Fund which has helped to defray the expenses of publication.

W. W. E.

HARROW, 1933.

§ INTRODUCTION. CICERO THE POET

Attitude to Poetry

Apart from aesthetic considerations, the composition of verse fulfilled for Cicero a twofold purpose. By it he felt that he was helping to elevate the Latin language to that level already attained by Greek, and from it he derived a very real intellectual pleasure. He realised that many preferred to read what had been well done in Greek to an indifferent translation of the same work in Latin ; but he once went so far as to say that his own feelings, which he had constantly urged, were that the Latin language not only was not deficient, so as to deserve disparagement, but that it was even more copious than the Greek (*De Fin.* i. 3)—an exaggeration, but significant as exhibiting his own strong nationalist tendencies in literature. In the second chapter of the same work he cogently remarks that " although Sophocles has composed an Electra in the most admirable manner possible, still I think the indifferent translation of it by Atilius worth reading too . . . for to be wholly unacquainted with our own poets is a proof either of the laziest indolence or else of a very superfluous fastidiousness."

To the Ennian School and the Alexandrines

The last century of the Republic witnessed the rise of the ' neoteroi,' adherents of the new school of Alexandrinism. Indeed, traces of this movement are to be found in a work as early as Laevius's *Erotopaegnia,* and during the next sixty years Alexandrinism enjoyed a rapid rise to popularity in certain quarters in Rome. Short odes, epyllia, and sketches in miniature were the order of the day : a long work was indeed a big bore, and

I

form was more important than content. Carefully polished diction, the introduction of a variety of Greek metres, frequent mythological allusions, careful insistence on the erotic element, and a studied scorn of the old Roman poets were some of the characteristics of this modernist school. Its members were young men of advanced ideas who, like the Parnassians in France towards the end of the nineteenth century, were destined to become affected and precious.

The early poets of Rome, on the other hand, whilst basing their metre and technique on Homer and the Greek dramatists, were, nevertheless, in many ways very Roman in tone. Naevius drew upon the history of Rome for his subject ; Ennius did likewise in his Annals ; the authors of the ' fabulae praetextae ' and the ' fabulae togatae ' and Lucilius with his farrago of contemporary satire all struck an intensely national note. But their technique was rude and rough, although not without power.

Cicero stood half-way between the old and the new. His sincere affection and respect was given whole-heartedly to the early Roman poets, but there is no evidence that he despised the ' neoteroi ' in consequence of this. He laughed at them, no doubt, but he himself translated Aratus with much of their technical skill. He was older than they, and stood outside a movement which in actual fact, if not in historical truth, belonged to the next generation. He freely admitted the beneficial effect of Greek culture upon Roman thought, and had nothing but unqualified praise for the works of the classical Greek poets ; but, as he remarked quite often, there was no valid reason why Latin should not take its place by the side of Greek as a language eminently suited to the expression of universal thought, provided that it was as an individual language, and not as one slavishly aping the form and content of its sister tongue.

It was with this attitude that he approached his work

of translation, and the care with which he avoided, on the one hand, an ' ad verbum ' rendering, and on the other a mere paraphrase, is at once evident. An interesting remark occurs in *De Fin.* i. 3 : . . . " although if I were to translate Plato in as bold a manner as some poets have translated the Greek plays, then, I suppose, I should not deserve well at the hands of my fellow-countrymen for having brought these divine geniuses within their reach. . . . But I imagine some people have become accustomed to feel a repugnance to Latin writing because they have fallen in with some unpolished and inelegant treatises translated from bad Greek into worse Latin. And with these men I agree, provided they will not think it worth while to read the Greek books written on the same subject." And here is the sum of the whole matter when he concludes : " I can never sufficiently express my wonder whence this arrogant disdain of everything national arose among us." Much more in similar strain is to be found in his works. His affection for the early school led him to conscious imitation in the elision of final ' s,' the use of compound adjectives with an old-fashioned ring, the deliberate introduction of archaisms, and the employment of the hexameter which he re-fashioned and improved out of all recognition. It is often forgotten that when Cicero first handled this metre he had little more than the work of Ennius and Lucilius upon which to model it. A moment's reflection will show the extent of his achievement in this direction.

The Aratea

Cicero was quite ready to use a Greek original as the basis of his own work. Indeed, it was expedient, for he possessed no expert knowledge of astronomy, only the interest of the amateur, of the philosopher who " has learnt to survey the stars, not only those that are fixed, but those which are improperly called wandering ; and the man who has acquainted himself with all their revolutions and motions is fairly considered to have a soul resembling the soul of that Being who has created those stars in the heavens " (*Tusc. Disp.* i. 25). Hence the fact that he did not attempt an original poem on astronomy was due to his youth and lack of technical knowledge. Such originality as he possessed lay in his translation itself. Indeed, originality in its narrowest sense was almost an impossibility for any Roman poet. Lucretius, for example, based his philosophy on Epicurus, and derived many of his ideas from Empedocles ; Virgil's borrowings were recognised and admitted by his contemporaries. But the works of both poets continue to live as unique productions stamped by an originality of insight and treatment which no amount of borrowing can obscure.

At first, in matters of minor importance, Cicero was undoubtedly influenced by the ' neoteroi,' as is shown by his partiality for detail. This led him to insert phrases not paralleled by anything in the original (amongst other passages cf. *Ph.*, 20, 21, 54, and 414). But he later came to realise their inherent affectation, which led him to regard them with an amused tolerance, as his famous jest on the line " Flavit ab Epiro lenissimus Onchesmites " shows. This was written to Atticus on November 26th, 50 B.C., and reveals his attitude to these ' Graecissantes ' in his later years.[1]

POETRY AND EDUCATION

The arguments expressed in the *Pro Archia*, that poetry can be defended on the grounds of its utility or of the pleasure it provides, must be regarded as springing from the needs of the moment. At the same time there is no doubt that Cicero did recognise the fulfilment of a definite educational need by poetry. He argues that the poet is privileged to commemorate nations and the deeds of great men. The Annals of an Ennius perform this function, at the same time giving

---

[1] Cf. p. 244, Fr. xi.

pleasure to the reader. The 'utility' of Cicero's own work is obvious. The *Aratea* are wholly didactic, the poem on Marius historical, most of the fragments translated into verse are quoted solely to illustrate some particular point in his prose works, whilst the *De Consulatu* is admittedly history in verse. The reference to it, cited in the introduction to the poems (*De Cons.* p. 10), and taken from the *Letters to Atticus* i. 19. 10, concludes : " If there is any more fitting subject for eulogy, then I am willing to be blamed for not choosing some other subject. *However, my compositions are not panegyrics at all but histories.*"

Romanticism

Although the classicism of a Sophocles appears to have little in common with the romanticism of a Wordsworth, ancient poetry, especially that of Rome, was not entirely devoid of the romantic spirit. Through Cicero's poems runs a vein of romanticism so primitive in conception as to be little more than a conscious realism. The juxtaposition of these two terms may give rise to some misunderstanding. It is desirable, therefore, to state at the outset that no more is meant by realism or romanticism in Cicero than his love of animating the inanimate, his sympathetic attitude towards animals, his use of picturesque epithets, his description of nature as represented by the majestic grandeur of the universe, his realisation of the comparative insignificance of man in the face of this grandeur. The nature of his work debarred any introduction of eroticism, whilst, except in his reference to the story of Orion and Diana at the end of the *Phaenomena*, he seldom makes any extensive use of mythology—other than that necessitated by the constellations.

The tendency of regarding the constellations as living entities is attributable to Cicero's outlook on life. Nowhere can we picture him accepting the Epicurean conception of a lifeless universe, of a human race in whose concerns the gods had no share. On the other hand, Stoicism, which recognised the immanence of a divine spirit in all things material, was undoubtedly acceptable to Cicero. Mankind may have been, at times, the sport of the gods owing to its own folly, but it was also closely under their protection. This general feeling of humanism is reflected by Cicero, when he deals with animals, in a manner strangely anticipatory of the future sympathy shown by Virgil towards the same subject. Indeed, in the *Prognostica* we find verses which might well be from Virgil's own pen. The coot flying far inland

"nuntiat horribiles clamans instare procellas
    haud modicos tremulo fundens e gutture cantus"
(F. iv.)

Talking of the frogs as weather prophets, Cicero writes :

"Vos quoque signa videtis, aquai dulcis alumnae,
    cum clamore paratis inanes fundere voces
    absurdoque sono fontes et stagna cietis." (F. v.)

In F. vi we see the ' acredula ' (cf. n. *ad loc.*) which—

". . . pertriste canit de pectore carmen
    et matutinis . . . vocibus instat."

And again later in the same fragment we read of the chattering crow on the seashore who " demersit caput et fluctum cervice recepit," a description as delightful as that of the ambling oxen who " . . . spectantes lumina caeli/naribus umiferum duxere ex aere succum " (F. vii.).

Although instances of this realism, or romanticism, of Cicero are noted in the commentary, a few of the more striking passages may be mentioned here. The description of Leo, " tremulam quatiens e corpore flammam," owes nothing to Aratus, who has merely ὕπο καλὰ φαείνε : the Latin seems all the more apt to one who has observed

Leo on a clear night with Regulus flashing out its brilliance. (Cf. n. *Ph.* F. xxiii., and further references there given and verses 187–8.) Speaking of Pegasus (F. xxxii. 4), Cicero, adds the happy phrase " iubam quatiens fulgore micanti " (cf. n. for possible borrowing from Ennius).

More will be said shortly about the use of compound adjectives by Cicero, and the employment of epithets not appearing in the original is so frequent as to make any examples here unnecessary. In the meantime it will be well to glance at a certain aspect of the *Phaenomena* which the reader will not fail to notice for himself. This is the feeling of awe evoked by the mysteries of the universe. Cicero is far removed from the somewhat prosaic attitude of Aratus. Typical is the description of the four zones (*Ph.* 237–9) :

> " Quattuor, aeterno lustrantes lumine mundum,
>   orbes stelligeri portantes signa feruntur,
>   amplexi terras caeli sub tegmine fulti."

The insignificance of man compared with the power of the elements is vividly portrayed in *Ph.* 62–8, the passage culminating with the vindication of man's determination to defy the forces of nature, 69–71. On the other hand, man's fear of the supernatural is admitted in such passages as :

> " Nos autem timidi stantes mirabile monstrum
>   vidimus in mediis divom versarier aris " (*Iliad* F. i.
>   20–21).

Instances of similar terror abound in the *De Consulatu.*

COMPOUND ADJECTIVES

Longinus once wrote that " lovely words are in very truth the real light of the soul " (φῶς γὰρ τῷ ὄντι ἴδιον τοῦ νοῦ τὰ καλὰ ὀνόματα). Whilst Latin never acquired a poetic vocabulary which could match that of the Greeks, there is no doubt that the Roman ear demanded verbal felicity. Even in the days of Lucilius, who satirised the diction of Pacuvius as " monstrificabile " (Bk. xxvi), we see evidences of that discrimination in the choice of words which the Augustans were later to pursue with such assiduity. Now, the compound adjective can be a thing of beauty or a sheer barbarism. Early Latin freely admitted its use, and so Cicero deliberately affected it, as being a part of the old native tradition. In this he approached close to the borders of Alexandrinism, which also still further developed the compound under Greek influence. The ' Graecissantes ' did not scruple to adapt Greek words to suit their purposes, and Lucretius himself used many Greek terms forced upon him by the exigencies of his subject. The Augustans, however, seem to have discarded most of the new compounds which appear in Lucretius and Catullus. This was due partly to metrical difficulties, partly to the feeling that the compound was a literary device too closely akin to Alexandrinism to be welcomed by the national poets of Rome. Horace's *Odes* are almost devoid of compounds, in spite of his dicta about coining words when necessary (*A.P.* 52 *et sqq.*). Virgil rarely uses any but familiar words, such as ' armipotens ' or ' horrisonus ' : he seldom adventures upon new or striking forms. Some of the compounds found in Cicero were probably of his own invention, and perished with him, although worthy of a longer life. The note on ' tristificas ' (*Prog.* iii) should be consulted for a full list of these and other compounds appearing in the poems.

ARCHAISM

Reference has already been made to the consciously archaic style assumed by Cicero in his earlier work. He was as ready to insert archaisms as to admit neologisms in the form of new compounds, so catholic was his taste. He was anxious to " recover beautiful words once spoken by Cato or Cethegus," and so " endow Latium with a rich language " (Hor. *Ep.* ii. 2. 115; *A.P.* 70). Macrobius summed up Cicero's position, long after the orator's death, when he wrote " vetustas quidem nobis semper, si sapimus, adoranda est " (*Sat.* iii. 14. 2). Below is appended a list of references to passages of the poems in which archaisms are to be found[1] : a fondness for the Gen. Sing. in -ai, and the Pres. Infin. in -ier, are marked characteristics. The periphrasis formed by using ' vis ' with the Gen. of the noun (i.e. ' equi vis ' for Pegasus) has been noted in the commentary (cf. n. *Ph.* 57 and references there given). For elision of final ' s,' cf. Essay on Metre, pp. 70 and 71, where references to the seven (or eight, including that emended by Orelli) passages in which this occurs are given.

Despite these archaisms, the *Phaenomena* has a much more modern ring about it than the *De Rerum Natura.* A contemporary of Cicero would feel them to be less harsh than we moderns do ; he would also be aware of the poet's attempt to " wear the crown of unfading leaf which Ennius first brought down from Helicon." As we shall endeavour to show in the following discussion on Criticism, the right to adopt or discard such devices as neologism or archaism is, after all, the poet's own. It is scarcely the province of a modern critic to acquiesce in, or to dissent from, such expedients. The final criterion is the reader's personal taste, and in such matters the " beauty is in the eyes of the beholder."

---

[1] *Ph.* F. ix. 1 mŏdō; F. xv. 2 ēius; 5 Nepai; 26 magno sub culmine, Abl. for Acc.; 33 dicier; 57 terrai; 77 Indic. emergit; 106 potesse; 179 aquai; 216 Nepai; 226 labier; 231 metirier; 243 cf. n.; 269 convertier; 278 Nepai; 304 possiet; 324 Nepai; 327 inde loci; 372 Aquilai; 418 Nepai. *Prog.* v. 1 aquai. *Iliad* F. i. 9 divom; 10 aquai; 21 versarier; 27 exanclabimus. *Od.* i. 1 Argolicum. *De Cons.* 41 divom; 43 Mavortis.

§ THE POEMS

De Consulatu

Cicero laid down his consulship in the year 63, at a time when his political supremacy was unchallenged, his successful career patent to all. His anxiety to have the story of his consulship—his apotheosis as Curio called it (*Ad Att.* i. 16. 13)—permanently recorded amounted almost to an obsession. In his defence of the poet Archias, delivered in 62, he mentions that his client had promised to compose a poem, and had even begun it (*Pro Archia* xi. 28 ; xii. 31) ; later, in the letter referred to above, comes the mournful cry, "Archias has not written anything about me," whilst its author goes on to complain that the epigrams which Atticus had composed on famous men—one of which was concerned with Cicero —were too trifling to win him the immortality he coveted.

He accordingly set to work himself, and at the beginning of 60 composed in Greek a ' commentarium ' on his consulship, which he sent to Atticus on March 15th, with the further promise of a Latin version so soon as this should be completed ; he continues : " *In the third place, you may expect a poem, not to let slip any method of singing my own praises.* . . . If there is any more fitting subject for eulogy, then I am willing to be blamed for not choosing some other subject " (*Ad Att.* i. 19. 10 ; cf. also Plut. *Crass.* c. 13 ; *ib. Caes.* c. 8 ; Dio. Cass. xlvi. 21. 4).

Little is known about the Latin version ; it seems never to have been published, and was probably never finished. The suggestion has been made that it may have been Cicero's letter to Pompey (Tyrrell and Purser,

Epp. Cic. i., 3rd ed., 1904, p. 238), described by a scholiast (Or. *Cic.* vol. iv. pt. i. p. 567) as " epistulam non ad mediocris instar voluminis scriptam," which Cicero himself mentions in *Pro Sulla* xxiv. 67. This contained a detailed account " de meis rebus gestis et de summa rei publicae."

In May 60 we read in a further letter to Atticus (i. 20. 6) : " I have sent you one of my works, a history of my consulship in Greek. . . . I fancy you like my Latin compositions, but being a Greek, envy this Greek one. If others write about it, I will send you copies ; but I assure you, as soon as they read mine, they somehow or other don't hurry themselves about it." In the following month Cicero wrote to Atticus (ii. 1. 1) acknowledging the receipt of his last letter, which had been accompanied by the returned ' commentarium.' He was glad that he had despatched his account before reading his friend's (Atticus had also composed a similar work), for, had he not done so, Atticus would surely have accused him of pilfering ! In the next letter a request is sent to Atticus, " tu, si tibi placuerit liber, curabis ut et Athenis sit et in ceteris oppidis Graeciae : videtur enim posse aliquid nostris rebus lucis afferre "—with reference to the copies which Atticus would have had made of his friend's Greek version.

A significant passage occurs in a letter (ii. 3. 4) dated December 60 : " *But my blood is still stirred by the finale I laid down to myself in the third book of my poem :* ' Interea cursus . . . laudesque bonorum.' Since Calliope herself dictated these verses to me in a book full of passages of lordly vein, I ought not to have the least hesitation in holding ' no omen better than to right one's country's wrongs ' (*Iliad* xiii. 243)." This last letter, taken in conjunction with that written in March of this year (i. 19. 10), allows us to date the *De Consulatu*, with a considerable degree of accuracy, as having been composed in the year 60.

The exact title of the poem is unknown, but that it was *De Consulatu* or something similar is shown by Quintus's reference, in *De Div.* i. 11. 17, to " in secundo de consulatu," and by Nonius, p. 202, M. Linds. p. 298, who writes " Cicero in consulatu suo."   The work appears to have been divided into three books, of the first of which all trace has been lost, except for a note of Servius on *Ecl.* viii. 105, which attests its original existence, describing the omen which befell Terentia : " (corripuit tremulis altaria flammis sponte sua . . . cinis ipse) : hoc uxori Ciceronis dicitur contigisse, cum post peractum sacrificium libare vellet in cinerem : quae flamma eodem anno consulem futurum ostendit eius maritum, sicut Cicero in suo testatur poemate."   This incident would have been quite out of place in any but Book i.   The same book seems to have contained an episode describing the admission of Cicero into the assembly of the gods, where Jupiter told him of the danger threatening Rome, and Minerva showed the means whereby it might be averted.   Cf. Ps-Sall. *in Cic.* ii. 3 : " Cicero se dicit in concilio deorum immortalium fuisse, inde missum huic urbi civibusque custodem " and again iv. 7 : " sed quid ego plura de tua insolentia commemorem ?   Quem Minerva omnes artes edocuit, Iuppiter optimus maximus in concilium deorum admisit."   (Cf. too Quint., xi. 1. 24, who refers to a similar occurrence in similar language— he appears to have used the account in Ps-Sall.—cf. iv. 1. 68 and ix. 3. 89—and explains that, in introducing the gods in this way, Cicero was following certain Greek authors.)

The second book contained our long Fragment in which the Muse Urania details the omens foretelling the Catilinarian conspiracy (cf. *De Div.* i. 11. 17 ; *ib.* ii. 20. 45 ; Lact. *Inst. Div.* iii. 17. 12 *et sqq.*).   The existence of a third book is proved by the passage quoted above from *Ep. ad Att.* ii. 3. 4.   The pompous style in which the poem was written, the boast that he had suppressed the conspiracy by peaceful methods, whereas he had really employed force in having the ringleaders illegally executed, his own growing unpopularity in certain quarters by the end of the year 60 lead one to suppose that Cicero made no very wide appeal with the *De Consulatu*. In fact, he himself attempted a defence of the famous verse, "Cedant arma togae, concedat laurea linguae," on more than one occasion (cf. *In Pis.* xxix. 72 *et sqq.* ; *Phil.* ii. 8. 20 ; *De Off.* i. 22. 77, as quoted in the n. *ad loc.* ; cf. further Ps-Cic. *in Sall.* ii. 7). Quintilian's criticism is quoted elsewhere, but what one remembers best is the terse remark of a scholiast : " De consulatu suo scripsit poetico metro, quae mihi videntur opera minus digna talis viri nomine " (*Schol. Bob. pro Planc.* xxx. 74).

THE POEM ON MARIUS

That the poem was entitled *Marius* is attested by three passages : *De Legg.* i. 1. 1 ; *ib.*, 47. 106 ; *Ad Att.* xii. 49. 1. Little is known of the circumstances in which it was written, or of the work itself. It was a tribute from Cicero to his fellow-townsman, Marius, and the extant verses describe the omen which befell the latter at Arpinum, their native place, after the latter's flight from Rome in 88.

The date of composition has been put as early as 86 and as late as 52 ; but a review of the available evidence, scanty enough, as well as the extant verses themselves, incline one to the belief that it was a late work. A conversation between Atticus, Quintus, and Marcus at Arpinum, recorded at the beginning of the *De Legg.*, has considerable bearing on this question, and is of interest as expressing certain views about poetry. The three friends meet, whereupon Atticus remarks, " This must be the oak of Marius."

" Yes," replies Quintus, " it will always exist as a nurseling of genius : as long as Latin is spoken, this

place will always have an oak known as ' Marius's oak.'
This tree, as Scaevola says about my brother's poem,
Marius, ' canescet saeclis innumerabilibus ' : it is at
present the genuine tree, but in later years an oak of
Marius will still be found here."

Atticus then asks the speaker whether the tree owes its
celebrity to Marcus's verses alone, or whether the events
narrated ever really happened in the history of Marius.
Thereupon Marcus interposes :

" Are all fables believed to be true ? One must not
inquire into them too closely."

" But," retorted Atticus, " *strict accuracy is expected
from you, Marcus, for not only are the events described fresh
in men's memories, but you speak as a native of Arpinum
about a fellow-townsman.*"

" A reputation for inaccuracy is certainly undesirable,"
answered Marcus, " but you cannot expect the historian
to treat a subject in the same manner as a poet."

" Then," suggested his brother, " you assume that the
laws which bind an historian are different from those
which bind a poet ? "

" Certainly," said Marcus, " for the object of an
historian is truth in all its relations, whilst that of the
poet is amusement."

To date the poem, we must start with Scaevola's
criticism of it. But who was this Scaevola ? He is
generally assumed to be the pontifex who died in 82. If
one admits that the last five verses of the Fragment (when
read in connexion with *De Div.* i. 47) suggest that the
work was composed after Marius's return to Rome in 87,
the poem must be assigned to some period between 87 and
82. But this Scaevola was an ardent supporter of the
optimates, and had incurred the hatred of the Marians
to such an extent that he was finally murdered by them
near the temple of Vesta in 82. Hardly the sort of man
to lavish such high praise on this poem !

Another suggestion has seen in the Scaevola mentioned

above the augur of that name who was born *c.* 160 (cf. *De Rep.* i. 12. 18, where he is said to be " iam aetate quaestorius " in 129, the year of this dialogue). Val. Max. iii. 8. 5 tells how, as an adherent of the Marian régime, he, Scaevola, refused to vote for his leader's outlawry in 88. The date of his death is unknown, but probably occurred before 80. This would still allow the *Marius* to be dated approximately within the same limits, but with more justification than in the first case. However this may be, publication was unlikely to have occurred after 83, the year of Sulla's triumphant return from the East. Any eulogy of Marius could hardly have found a more inauspicious moment for its appearance !

The conjecture of Haupt (*Opusc.* i, 1875, pp. 211–13) appears far more probable. He argues that the whole of this period, from 87 to 80, was fraught with far too much danger and turbulence to admit of any such publication. Moreover, the remark of Atticus italicised above implies a degree of publicity and criticism quite unlikely to have been accorded to verses written as youthful exercises thirty years previously. And it is improbable that Cicero would insert in the *De Legg.*—written in 52—a fragment from such an early work. Now, this presupposes the possibility of the poem being a very much later work. Support of a valuable kind would be gained if one could point to a Scaevola contemporary with the later years of Cicero's life. The son of the augur at once suggests himself as the man referred to by Quintus. Significant are the facts, that not only was this Scaevola one of Quintus's personal friends (he was with him in Asia in 59) and a poet (probably Pliny refers to him in *Ep.* v. 3), but also *Quintus* is the one to introduce his name into the conversation. That people had considerable familiarity with the *Marius* by 52 is clear from Atticus's words, " lucus quidem ille et haec Arpinatium quercus agnoscitur *saepe* a me lectus," quoted in the note on

Fr. i.   These considerations point to the inevitable conclusion that the poem was published (and therefore presumably written) after Cicero's return from exile and before the year 52.   One is tempted to suggest 56, the year in which Cicero was outwardly converted to the Caesarian party, as being an appropriate time at which to send forth the new work !

In spite of attempts to show that this was a youthful effort at versification (amongst others Ribbeck, *Gesch. d. röm. Dichtung* i., 2nd ed., 1894, p. 300 ; Grollmus, *op. cit.* 18–27), most of which place it as early as 86, one is led to regard it as late, not only by the foregoing considerations, but also by internal evidence.   The style shows powers more matured than those which wrote the *Aratea* : greater mastery over metre is apparent, and one looks in vain for the abnormalities by which the earlier work is characterised.   That the *Marius* attracted considerable attention is certain : Virgil availed himself of it (see n. *ad loc.*), and this borrowing infers further plagiarism by him of those parts no longer extant (cf. too Hor. *Odes* iv. 4. 11 ; Ovid *Met.* iv. 361 *et sqq.*); *Schol. Veron. Aen.* v. 255, quotes the first verse of the longer Fragment as coming from the *Marius* of Cicero, all of which goes to prove that the poem was well known and regarded seriously by the poet's successors.

De Temporibus Meis

There are no extant verses which can be ascribed to this poem, which was written by Cicero to describe his exile and return to Rome in 57.   He was again anxious to secure to posterity a permanent literary record of his vicissitudes, and in 56 approached the historian, Lucceius (*Ad Fam.* v. 12), imploring him to narrate the story of the Catilinarian conspiracy, and continue it so as to include Cicero's return from exile.   Let him transgress the limits of strict veracity, if necessary !   His refusal would compel Cicero to do what many censured—write an autobiography. But this method has many draw-backs : one has to employ more self-restraint in passages redounding to one's credit whilst ignoring entirely those incidents which do not ! The tone of this letter is interesting. By now Cicero had probably suffered con-siderably from adverse criticism of his two works on his consulship, namely, the prose account in Greek and his own poem. He was evidently anxious to avoid impli-cating himself in further controversy if possible. In April 55 (*Ad Att.* iv. 9) he writes : " I am most grateful to you for saying you will recommend me as a subject for a panegyric to Lucceius." It is clear that the historian had as yet done nothing for him, and it appears that he persisted in his refusal. History repeated itself, and again, as in 60, the unfortunate Cicero was compelled to be his own biographer.

Like the *De Consulatu*, the work was divided into three books, for we read in a letter written to Lentulus in December 54 (*Ad Fam.* i. 19. 23) : " With regard to your request that I should send you such works of mine as I have completed since your departure, there are some speeches. . . . I have also written three books of verse called *De Temporibus Meis*, which I would have sent to you long since if I had deemed them worthy of publica-tion." Lentulus had left for Cilicia as pro-consul in 56, and this letter is dated 54, so that the work was pre-sumably composed between these two years, probably in 55.

The story is carried a little farther for us by reference to a letter of Cicero's to his brother, written early in 55 (*Ad Quint.* ii. 7. 1). Marcus had probably sent him a copy of part of the MS. of which he says : " Placiturum tibi esse librum meum suspicabar." That this work was completed, at any rate in rough, by 54, is proved by the letter to Lentulus : in June of this year Caesar appears to have read and approved it (*ib.* ii. 15. 12) whilst in Britain. In the next letter (August 54) the author appears to entertain some doubt about Caesar's approval, when he says : " Now look you here, it seems to me that you are keeping something back from me. What, oh what, my dear brother, did Caesar think of my verses ? He wrote to me some time ago that he had read my first book, and of the first part he declared that he had never read anything better, even in Greek : the rest of it, as far as a certain passage, was rather 'happy-go-lucky,' that is the term he uses. Tell me the truth—is it the subject, or the style, that does not please him ? You needn't be afraid ; I shall fancy myself not a wit the less ! Write about this like a lover of truth, and, as you always do, like a brother."

That the work had not been finally completed by the autumn of this year is evidenced by another letter to Quintus, written in September (*ib.* iii. 1. 24), where we are told that Cicero intends inserting a fine episode in Book ii ". . . dicentem Apollinem in concilio deorum qualis reditus duorum imperatorum futurus esset quorum alter (*sc.* Piso) exercitum perdidisset, alter (*sc.* Gabinius) vendidisset." [1]

Heikel (*Adversaria ad Cic. de Cons. suo Poem.* 1912), following Voss and others, has attempted to show that there were not two distinct works at all, but that Cicero rewrote the *De Consulatu,* hitherto unpublished, after his return from exile, in order that the additional period 62–57 should be included. He then renamed this *De Temporibus Meis.* We have no direct evidence that this was so, and it is unlikely that Cicero failed to publish the *De Consulatu* directly it was finished. In any case, it was public property by the year 55, as is proved by the reference to the famous " Cedant arma togae, concedat laurea linguae " in the speech *In Pis.* (xxix. 72) which was

---

[1] Gabinius, whose province was Syria, had helped Ptolemy Auletes, and restored him to his kingdom for a bribe of 10,000 talents. Piso's indolence had allowed the Thracians to overrun his province of Macedonia and destroy the Roman army.

delivered in that year.[1]   Further, in the *De Div.* i. 11. 17, which introduces the extant Fragment of the *De Consulatu,* we find the following words : " Sed quo potius utar aut auctore aut teste quam te ?   Cuius edidici etiam versus et lubenter quidem quos *in secundo de consulatu* Urania Musa pronuntiat."   The *De Div.* was written long afterwards in 44.   If Heikel's theory were correct, surely Cicero would not have referred to his rewritten work under its former title.   Hence we may conclude with considerable certainty that there were two separate poems, the *De Consulatu,* which was composed in 60, and the *De Temporibus Meis,* which was written about the year 55.

Caesar. Expedition to Britain

It is necessary to say something of two works, an epic in praise of Caesar and a poem concerned with his expedition to Britain.   The first was written by Cicero ; in the second he probably collaborated with his brother, but whether he ever completed his share of the task is unknown.   There are no extant verses, no other reference to the poems is found in contemporary literature, and our only means of information is contained in Cicero's letters to his brother.

After the reconciliation between Caesar and Cicero had taken place, the latter was not slow in expressing his appreciation of Caesar's magnanimity.   We find him writing to Quintus in 54 (*Ad Quint.* iii. 1. 18) : " Ille mihi secundum te et liberos nostros ita est ut sit paene par."   Until 52 Quintus was himself in Gaul and Britain as one of Caesar's officers, where his efficiency and personality gained his leader's respect, by whom he was treated with marked courtesy.   Accordingly he wrote to

---

[1] " Qui modo cum res gestas consulatus mei conlaudasset, quae quidem conlaudatio hominis turpissimi mihi ipsi erat paene turpis, ' Non illa tibi,' inquit, ' invidia nocuit sed versus tui.   Nimis magna poena te consule constituta est sive malo poetae sive libero. Scripsisti enim, " Cedant. . . ." ' "

his brother in Rome requesting him to compose a poem in Caesar's honour (*ib.* ii. 15. 2), a task which Marcus was dilatory in performing. All this we gather from the preceding remarks in the above letter, which continues : " So I shall make up for my slowness [i.e. in paying court to Caesar] by galloping not only on a relay of horses, but also (since you write that my poem [i.e. the *De Temporibus Meis*] meets with his approval) by driving a four-horsed chariot of poesy. Only you people must give me Britain for a subject, so that I may paint it in your colours, but with my own brush " (June 54). But farther on in the same letter he seems to be assailed by doubts as to whether he will have enough time to complete this, for we read : " What am I to do ? What free time have I whilst in Rome ? " Indeed, things were far from easy for Cicero just now. He was hard pressed by much legal business, the summer was intensely hot (*Ad Att.* iv. 16. 1 ; *Ad Quint.* ii. 16. 1), scarcely a day passed without some call being made upon his time (*ib.* iii. 3. 1), he was preoccupied with his work on the Republic (*Ad Att.* iv. 16. 2 ; *Ad Quint.* iii. 5. 1) and he foresaw the danger threatening the State, which he himself, now in comparative obscurity, had formerly done so much to save.

That his doubts were only too well founded is evident from another letter to Quintus in September, when he says : " That poem to Caesar which I had put together for final arrangement I have broken off." Quintus was obliged to tell Caesar of this delay in the projected work, and was asked to write again with a further request that his brother should complete it. To this an answer was despatched in November as follows (*ib.* iii. 8. 3) : " You bid me finish the poem addressed to him [Caesar] that I have begun ; well, in spite of the distractions of work and far more of my thoughts, still, now that Caesar has got to know better from a letter that I sent you that I have something on the stocks, I shall return to what I have

begun, and shall finish it during these leisure days of the
' supplicationes '." By December (*ib.* iii. 9. 6) the poem
was completed. " As to your urging me to finish my
job, I have now finished my epic to Caesar, and a charm-
ing one it is, in my opinion."

In this same year, 54, Quintus appears to have been
meditating an epic on the expedition to Britain. He
asked his brother's assistance, and a reply was sent in
August, in which Cicero told his brother that he had
" glorious subject-matter for his pen " and continued :
" I shall willingly assist you, as you ask me, in any way
you wish, and shall send you the verses for which you
ask, though it is ' coals to Newcastle ' " (*ib.* ii. 16. 4).
As in the case of the epic upon Caesar, this work, too, was
laid aside, and two months later comes the excuse, with
the plea that Marcus considers Quintus his superior in
this kind of composition : " About the verses you wish
me to write for you, as a matter of fact I lack the neces-
sary energy, which requires not only leisure, but a mind
free from all anxiety (cf. Juv. *Sat.* vii. 53–8) ; but the
divine ' afflatus ' is also wanting, for I am not altogether
without anxiety as regards the coming year, though I do
not fear it. At the same time, there is also the fact (and
on my oath I am speaking without a touch of irony) that
in this style of composition I assign a higher rank to you
than I do to myself " (*Ad Quint.* iii. 4. 4).

This letter was quickly followed by another at the end
of the month : " As to your asking me about writing
some verses, you couldn't believe, my dear brother, how
pressed I am for time, and I really lack the necessary
inclination to write the poetry you want. But come now,
is it you who seek suggestions for what I myself do not
succeed in attaining, even in imagination—you who have
surpassed everybody in that kind of fluent and graphic
expression ? I would do your bidding to the best of my
ability, but (as you are the last man to forget) *the composi-
tion of a poem demands a certain sprightliness* (alacritas)

of mind which I have been completely robbed of by the times we live in."

The silence maintained by contemporary and succeeding writers about these two works makes it very doubtful if either was published. Indeed, we do not know if the second was ever written, but the evidence here summarised is useful, in so far as it proves that Cicero was actively concerned with the writing of poetry during this period.

ARATEA

There remain of Cicero's translation 554 verses of the *Phaenomena* and 27 of the *Prognostica*, totalling 581 as compared with 1,154 in the Greek. Aratus was later translated by Germanicus and Avienus : of the former's work only the *Phaenomena* is extant. Amongst others who used Aratus in their work are to be counted Varro Atacinus, Virgil, and Ovid.

The Stoic Aratus wrote his poem about the year 275 B.C., and based it on a prose treatise by Eudoxus. This he subsequently named Φαινόμενα. Grammarians later subdivided this into three parts, of which the first two were entitled Φαινόμενα, the third being called Διοσημεῖαι. Traces of the nomenclature adopted by Cicero for this third part are found in one of the lives of Aratus.[1]

Whether Cicero ever wrote a complete translation is doubtful.[2] At first he left this translation unnamed, for

---

[1] Westermann Βιόγραφοι, p. 56 ; Ar. ed. Buhle ii. p. 443, has the following : ἔστι δὲ τριχῶς Φαινομένων αὐτοῦ πραγματεία· καταστέρωσις καὶ συνανατελλόντων καὶ συνδυόντων καὶ προγνώσεις διὰ σημείων.

[2] Grollmus (*De Cicerone Poeta*, Königsberg, 1887, pp. 11–12) says : " Neque praetermittam quod Lupus, abbas Ferrariensis (Lupi *opera ed. St. Baluz.*, Antverp 1710, epist. 69, p. 112) Ansbaldo, monacho Prumiensi, scribit : ' Tu autem huic cursori Tullium in Arato trade, ut ex eo, quem me impetraturum credo, quae deesse illi Eigil noster aperuit suppleantur,' quae verba Fabricius (*bibl. Lat.* i. lib. 1, c. 8) monet. Verisimile igitur est Prumii in monasterio (apud Augustam Trevirorum sito) etiam saeculo nono integrum exemplar Ciceronis Arateorum fuisse : fortasse autem id quoque fieri potuit ut Lupus erraret."

he nowhere refers to it as ' Phaenomena ' but by some periphrasis such as ' carmen Arateum '[1]; others always write ' Cicero in Arato,' or some similar phrase, and Hyginus (*Fab.* xiv) seems to have been the first to use the present title. But the Weather Signs are always referred to by Cicero himself and his successors (Prisc. i. p. 196. 9; ii. p. 105. 8; p. 287. 6) as Prognostica (cf. *Ep. ad Att.* ii. 1. 11 ; xv. 16b ; *De Div.* i. 13, and ii. 47).

If a second edition of the Weather Signs appeared in 60 B.C., as is assumed below, it was probably given the title of *Prognostica* then. This would account for the second part of the poem having a title, whilst the first, which was not republished so far as we know, remained as *Carmen Arateum.* We are therefore justified in assuming the original existence of one unnamed translation which included the two works of Aratus : that Cicero regarded them as distinct is shown by his use of the plural ' carminibus Arateis ' in *De Nat. Deor.* ii. 41. 104, and by the second edition of the *Prognostica* as compared with one only of the *Phaenomena.*

The approximate date of translation can be fixed with some certainty from Cicero's own words in the passage referred to above. " Utar," inquit, (*sc.* Balbus) " carminibus Arateis quae a te *admodum adulescentulo* conversa ita me delectant, ut multa ex eis memoria teneam." The style of the *Phaenomena*, its archaisms and occasional harshness of metre, the errors in subject-matter due to a misunderstanding of the original, all go to show that it was an early work. The exact year of its composition is unknown, but it can be assigned to a period prior to Cicero's journey to Greece in 79–77 with some degree of certainty. Mayor, in his edition of the *De Nat.*

---

[1] Cf. *De Legg.* ii. 3. 7 ; *De Nat. Deor.* ii. 41. 104; *De Rep.* i. 36. 56. Cf. too Serv. *Ad Aen.*, iii. 22 ; *Georg.* i. 111 ; Priscian i. p. 210. 21 ; p. 211. 11 ; p. 247. 17 ; p. 285. 4 ; p. 351. 2 ; p. 504. 15 ; ii. p. 55. 25, ed. Hertz.

Deor., places it as early as 89, but quotes no evidence for this, whilst Leo (*Hermes* 49. 1914, 191, n. 3) suggests 86.

A letter to Atticus (ii. 1. 11), written in June 60, in which we read, " Prognostica mea cum oratiunculis propediem exspecta," has given rise to much conjecture. Some believe that, after translating the two poems in his youth, Cicero later wrote some Prognostica of his own, as original work, to which reference is here made. They claim support for this theory by his use of ' mea ' above, and by ' Prognostica tua ' (*De Div.* i. 8. 13). But this is evidence hardly worth consideration, and why does he quote in the *De Div.*, written in 44, a translation done some forty years earlier rather than his own verses composed within the last eighteen years ? Others have arrived at the conclusion that Cicero wrote a version of the *Phaenomena* only in his youth, not attempting the *Prognostica* until the year 60. But Pease (ed. *De Div.*) thinks it most unlikely that so long a time intervened between the two versions. There is, too, the use of the plural ' carminibus Arateis,' implying more than one translation—to say nothing of the fact that Cicero would hardly spend time at the age of forty-six on a poetical ' exercise,' and at the very period when he was busy with the *De Consulatu.* In his later years he seems, also, to have modified his opinions on the value of Aratus, as is seen from the criticisms passed in 55 and 54 in *De Or.* i. 16. 19, and *De Rep.* i. 14. 22.

Much more likely is the opinion of Leo (*loc. cit.*) that a new edition of the *Prognostica* was issued in 60 (cf. notes on *Prog.* F. vi) which was a revised version of the early translation. Grollmus admits this to be a possible solution, but thinks that if Cicero rewrote the one poem he would certainly have revised the *Phaenomena* as well in order to remove its errors. This appears to be his only objection to Leo's contention : as a refutation of the theory it is surely very inadequate.

Miscellanea

Of the remaining verses amongst these poems we have seven short translations (of which the longest contains 29 lines) from the *Iliad*, two from the *Odyssey*, eleven miscellaneous fragments which include those named *Alcyones*, *Limon*, and *Thalia Maesta* (?), six verses of doubtful authenticity, two fragments translated from Aeschylus, one from Sophocles, and nine from Euripides. These are dealt with in the introductions prefixed to the notes relating to each fragment.

From Plutarch's testimony (quoted in the essay on Criticism), we know that Cicero wrote a poem entitled *Pontius Glaucus* in his youth. He may have been imitating some Alexandrine poet : the work was in trochaic tetrameters and dealt, presumably, with the legend of the fisher who became a sea-god. The fact that the hexameter was not used and the use of the word Ποιημάτιον by which Plutarch designates the work suggest that it was little more than a short lyrical poem.

Two more titles have come down to us, but no verses are extant. There seems to have been a poem called *Nilus* (if that be the correct title ; cf. intro. to *Misc. Vv.* i), of which nothing is known. This too may have been an early excursion into the realms of Alexandria, as the name seems to suggest. Lastly, there was a work called *Uxorius* (?) (cf. *Misc. Vv.* i. intro.). Grollmus (*op. cit.*, p. 10) suggests that this may have been a translation of part of some comedy of Alexis or Amphis, who were contemporary with Alexander the Great, and whose plays were styled Γυναικοκρατία. That the comedies of Alexis were translated into Latin is testified by A. Gellius, *N.A.* ii. 23. ' Uxorius,' in the same sense as the Greek γυναικοκρατούμενος, is used by Horace, *Odes* i. 19–20 : Virg. *Aen.* iv. 266 ; Macr. *Sat.*, vii. 3. 19.

The only point of interest or importance arising from

these titles is the indication they give that in his early days Cicero paid some attention to Alexandrinism (cf. essay *Cicero the Poet*, p. 4). It was only a passing phase, however, and in his later years he never refers to the ' neoteroi ' without some gibe at their expense.

§ CRITICISM OF THE POEMS

APART from references to the poems in Cicero's own works, there exist certain isolated remarks in ancient writers, remarks interesting in themselves perhaps, but deficient in any real critical penetration. In the preface to Book iii of the *Controversiae* we read that Seneca, upon asking Cassius Severus why his faculties deserted him in set declamation, was thus answered : " What great wit has ever been good at more than one thing ? *Ciceronem eloquentia sua in carminibus destituit.*" The younger Seneca contributes a further remark in the *De Ira* iii. 37 : " Te Ennius quo non delectaris odisset et Cicero, si derideres carmina eius, inimicus esset." Quintilian, *Inst.* ix. 4, warns would-be poets with this caution : " Videndum ne syllabae verbi prioris ultimae et primae sequentis sint eaedem. Quod ne quis praecipi miretur, Ciceroni in carmine excidit, ' O fortunatam . . .' " Later, in xi. 1, he reminds us that Cicero, when attacked by opponents, justified his actions and then continues : " In carminibus utinam pepercisset quae non desierunt carpere maligni," quoting the foregoing verse together with the notorious ' Cedant arma togae. . . .'

In the course of his remarks on orators, Aper, in the *Dialogus*, asserts that some may have admired speeches by Caesar and Brutus. They also composed verse and " in bibliothecas rettulerunt, non melius quam Cicero, sed felicius, quia illos fecisse pauciores sciunt." Martial continues the series of gibes by the well-known couplet :

> " Carmina quod scribis Musis et Apolline nullo
> Laudari debes : hoc Ciceronis habes " (ii. 89. 3).

And Juvenal thus :

> " ' O fortunatam natam me consule Romam ! '
>   Antoni gladios potuit contemnere si sic
>   omnia dixisset ! " (x. 122).

In Petronius 118, Eumolpus is represented as saying that the composition of verse appears to present little difficulty, for anyone thinks that he can become an expert so soon as he has learnt the rules, " sic forensibus ministeriis exercitati frequenter ad carminis tranquillitatem tanquam ad portum feliciorem refugerunt, credentes facilius poema exstrui posse quam controversiam sententiolis vibrantibus pictam." Although unnamed, the victim of this sarcasm is probably not far to seek.

Amidst this adverse criticism one voice is raised in defence of Cicero. Plutarch, in his *Life* (sec. 2, Langhorne trans.), says : " He had both the capacity and inclination to learn all the arts, nor was there any branch of science that he despised ; yet he was most inclined to poetry, and there is still extant a poem, entitled *Pontius Glaucus*, which was written by him, when a boy, in tetrameter verse. In process of time, when he had studied this art with greater application, he was looked upon as the best poet, as well as the greatest orator, in Rome. His reputation for oratory still remains, notwithstanding the considerable changes that have since been made in the language : but, as many ingenious poets have appeared since his time, his poetry has lost its credit and is now neglected." Farther on, in sec. 40, Plutarch informs us that, after Rome had ceased to offer any political scope for Cicero's talents, the orator withdrew from public life and, devoting himself to the composition and translation of philosophical dialogues, rendered many Greek technical terms into Latin. " His ready turn for poetry afforded him amusement : for, we are told, when he was intent upon it, he could make five hundred verses in one night."

Although it is well that the reader should have these references quoted above for his convenience, he will at once realise that they are of little practical use. The elder Seneca is judging Cicero by his oratorical standards ; the younger Seneca presumably has in mind Cicero's defence of ' Cedant arma togae, concedat laurea linguae,' which its author attempted to justify no less than three times—*In Pis.* xxix. 72 ; *Philipp.* ii. 8. 20 ; *De Off.* i. 22. 77. Neither of Quintilian's references is definitely hostile ; indeed, the second seems to be tacitly assuming that Cicero wrote much that was good, but that even he nodded sometimes. Aper at least gives Cicero credit for some notoriety, whilst Juvenal only concerns himself with the one verse which caused annoyance to others than him. That fragments of Cicero's verse are found preserved in the works of writers so varied as Hyginus, the elder Pliny, Quintilian, Servius, Macrobius, Suetonius, Probus, Augustine, Priscian, Isidore—all of whom together embrace a period of some six hundred years—is ample proof that the poems of Cicero were read and known long after his death, and were regarded as being of importance.

It is interesting to see that modern criticism is as contradictory as ancient. The following opinions, collected more or less at random, will show this. Ellis, in his ed. of *Catullus* (Oxford, Clarendon Press, 1876, p. xvi), writes : " Between the comedies of Terence and the poems of Lucretius and Catullus nothing is left us in anything but a fragmentary state except the *Aratea* of Cicero. *We pass at a bound from this prosiest translation of a prosaic original* to the delightful grace of the Catullian hendecasyllable and the sublime exaltation of the Lucretian hexameter." On p. xix we read : " Whether Catullus had, like Lucretius, studied Cicero's *Aratea* is uncertain ; but the coincidence in both poems of the same recurring rhythm is at least remarkable, though we may feel sure that *Catullus would have held Cicero a very sorry versifier.*"

Munro (*Lucretius* 1908, reprint, 4th ed., p. ix) shows more appreciation : " Many years before Lucretius wrote his poem Cicero in boyhood had translated the works of Aratus. *This translation, of which large fragments are preserved, shows much spirit and vivacity of language.*"

Nettleship (*Lectures and Essays*, Oxford, Clarendon Press, 2nd series, 1895, p. 56) discusses Cicero's outlook upon poetry in general, lamenting the fact that we have little from him on this subject but detached utterances. After giving Cicero's opinions on individual poets, Nettleship concludes the paragraph thus : " It is much to be wished that we had more of this kind from the hand of a man of genius who *was a considerable metrist himself, and only fell short of being a poet.*"

Prof. G. Saintsbury (*Hist. of Criticism*, Blackwood, 1908, Bk. ii, pp. 214–15), describing Cicero's criticism of the *De Rerum Natura*, writes : " Cicero, who would fain have been a poet, and *who sometimes could hammer out a tolerable hexameter*, could not, as a mere craftsman, as a mere student of Rhetoric, fail to appreciate something of the art of Lucretius." The following remarks are appended as a footnote : " It has been urged upon me that my judgment of Cicero's verse is rather harsh, and that he at any rate made some progress towards the Lucretian hexameter before Lucretius. It may be so : tolerably careful and tolerably wide students of literature know that these things are always ' in the air,' and that, some time, if not always, you find them in the poetaster before you find them in the poet. But after reading all Cicero's extant verse two or three times over, seeking diligently for mitigation of judgment, I am still afraid that ' Cousin Cicero, you will never be a poet,' would have been, and justly, the verdict of Lucretius, had they stood to one another in the relations in which Swift and Dryden stood."

In his *Roman Poetry* (Methuen, 1923, p. 32), Mr. Sikes remarks : " As a matter of fact, Cicero's verse has been unduly belittled, since the time when the wits of the Empire fastened on his least felicitous line. For a short time—between Accius and Lucretius—he was even acknowledged as the chief poet of Rome. . . ."

German commentators are hopelessly at variance with one another in their estimate of the poems. Guendel (*op. cit.*, pp. 40–2), discussing the worth of the translation of the *Aratea*, considers that Cicero displays ignorance of astronomy and of particular passages of the original (cf. Maybaum, *De Cic. et Germ. Arati Interpretibus*, 1889, pp. 15–16; Moll, *Ciceros Aratea*, 1891, pp. 12 *et sqq.*, both of whom agree with Guendel in severely criticising the *Aratea*). On the other hand, Sieg (*op. cit.*, pp. 8 and 13) holds that Cicero translated faithfully and well a difficult work. " Itaque si leviter modo versionem Tullianam cum Arato contuleris, miram esse Ciceronis diligentiam facile intelleges." Again, on p. 13 : " Cum iam satis monstrasse mihi videar Tullium magnam in vertendo Arato adhibuisse diligentiam. . . ." (Cf. too Ribbeck, *Gesch. d. röm. Dichtung*, i. 1887, p. 301.)

CRITICS DIVIDED IN OPINIONS

It is not without relief that one turns from the above criticisms to a consideration of the poems themselves. The first thought which suggests itself is the extraordinary lack of unanimity on the part of these critics, ancient and modern. The reason is clear. In each case we find merely the personal reaction of the critic to the poems, not ordered criticism based on definite criteria. The personal element must necessarily vary in each individual. Indeed, this subjective criticism on the part of a modern reader is not only dangerous, but often actually misleading, for the attitude towards the poetry of to-day is necessarily different from that existing in the age of imperial Rome. The former tends towards the emotional, the latter towards the intellectual ; the necessity of realising this and of freeing our minds of modern conceptions is essential if we would come to a true understanding of ancient poetry. That this intellectualism was a marked feature of Aratus's work was clear to Quintilian, who wrote : " Arati materia motu caret ut in qua nulla varietas, nullus adfectus, nulla persona, nulla cuiusquam sit oratio : sufficit tamen operi cui se parem credidit " (*Inst.* x. 1. 55)—a pertinent criticism, and one which accounts fully for the lack of popularity from which the *Phaenomena* suffers at the present time. But this lack of popularity does not imply that the poem in question is valueless as a work of art. The object of the *Phaenomena* was admittedly didactic, and it was composed, as we shall shortly see, for a strictly utilitarian purpose. It contains no picturesque episodes and no digressions. Coupled with this austerity is the difficulty of subject-matter. To-day astronomy appeals to a limited class of readers, whilst the *De Consulatu* appeals to no one ; these, unfortunately, are the only two fragments of which enough is preserved to us to give them any intrinsic value. Add to this a metre inferior to the Virgilian hexameter, and one begins to perceive that real appreciation of Cicero's verse is by no means easy to experience at a first reading.

The Influence of Rhetoric on the Poems

Judged by the standard of his oratory, Cicero's poetry falls far short of his political speeches, but although his achievements in the field of oratory have inevitably had the result of belittling his work as a poet, the study of oratory which they necessitated reacted upon his poetry with beneficial results. In saying this one is exposing oneself to severe criticism, but it is said deliberately. Another shibboleth which the modern must discard is his instinctive reluctance to admit rhetoric within the confines of poetry. So far as ancient poetry is concerned there was never a greater mistake. Every poet of Augustan Rome was, to a more or less degree, under the domination of rhetoric. One need only instance Virgil and direct attention to almost any one of the speeches in the *Aeneid*—not to mention numberless points of detail—to show this. The practice may be abused, as it was later by Lucan, but that is the fault, not of rhetorical training itself, but of him who cannot use it wisely or well. The old objection, that the aim of poetry is not to persuade but to transport, is a generalisation as wholly false in the case of Cicero's poems as most generalisations are when applied to the particular. The very aim and object of didactic verse is to instruct, and instruction is wrought by persuasion.

The *Phaenomena* is certainly under rhetorical influence, which accounts for the frequent repetitions noted with such scorn by critics like Faguet, who assert that they detract from the verse and add nothing to the sense. But in didactic work the necessity of emphasising points of importance is obvious, whilst ' theme and variation ' can be worked out into an artistic form as beautiful in literature as it undoubtedly is in music. Parallelism of construction is not infrequent (cf. *Ph.*, 114 n.), and the origin of the Virgilian period, which fuses verse with sentence so that the end of the hexameter does not coincide with the end of the sentence, is apparent in Cicero, although he did not carry this development far enough, and left it to his great successor to perfect. Directly opposed to this is the brief ' one-line ' sentence, so many of which are discernible in the poems. In the *Aratea* they are partly due to the didactic nature of the original, partly to the poet's difficulty in handling the hexameter itself.

Enough has been said about the influence of rhetoric, and considerations of space forbid the multiplication of examples. Cicero's own dictum that the poet is akin to the orator, together with his own remarks on the subject, are to be found in *De Orat.* i. 70; *ib.* iii. 27; *Orator* 67. Cicero's use of dactylic and spondaic lines has been dealt with elsewhere, and shows that he paid considerable attention to rhythm. As M. Patin (*Etudes sur la poésie latine*, ed. 4, 1900, ii, p. 447) observes in discussing Cicero's translations of the Greek tragedians: " *Cicéron . . . pesant les mots au lieu de les compter* et plus jaloux de conserver l'esprit que la lettre de son modèle, me paraît avoir montré, dans ses traductions des tragiques grecs une louable flexibilité."

ORIGINAL WORK

Although the *De Consulatu* is interesting as an example of original work upon a subject so dear to the heart of Cicero, although technically an advance upon the youthful *Phaenomena*, the consciously archaic style of which has been replaced by one smoother but less virile in the later poem, this autobiography cannot command much interest to-day. Not only is the subject-matter tedious, but it is burdened with heavy passages of pompous narrative. The ten-verse introduction to our fragment is a prosaic summary of the Stoic theory of a divine intelligence permeating the universe : the omens described in verses 20–29 are employed only for dramatic effect— one cannot believe that Cicero himself regarded them seriously—and this kind of insincerity is as immoral artistically as it is ethically. Typical of the language of the *De Consulatu* is the following :

" Quid vero Phoebi fax, tristis nuntia belli,
   quae magnum ad columen flammato ardore volabat,
   praecipites caeli partes obitusque petessens ? "

(vv. 20–22).

One is irresistibly reminded of Lucan, and not of Lucan at his best, by this forced and unnatural piece of description. Adjectives are sprinkled into the poem with lavish hand ; they serve to weaken the force of many otherwise tolerable lines. Phrases such as " terribili . . . fulmine " (23) ; "luce serenanti vitalia lumina " (24) ; " variae . . . terribiles formae" (26–7); "perpetuis signis clarisque"(31); "tuus glomerans . . . annus"(35); "constanti voce"(51); " fixi ac signati temporis " (62); " cura . . . sagaci "(71) suggest an obvious straining after effect, and provide examples of the extent to which the schools of rhetoric could mar as well as help to make good poetry. The last four verses of the first fragment contain nothing to redeem the self-satisfied complacency which they so smugly express.

The poem, however, has compensations. The description of the Moon's eclipse, with the skilful " subito stellanti nocte perempta est," is worth many of the other verses. 'Stellanti' is used here with real meaning, whilst the elision in the sixth foot and the final monosyllable make an ending as effective as the famous " simul aureus exoritur sol " of Ennius. Charmingly realistic is the description of the statue of wolf and twins, occurring in verses 42–6, whilst the praise of true religion is expressively sung in verses 66–70.

Much better than the *De Consulatu* is the fragment from the poem to Marius. This is a vigorous piece of work which demonstrates beyond dispute its author's capabilities as a poet. The picture of the half-dead snake " varia graviter cervice micantem " (4), the bird which " se(que) obitu a solis nitidos convertit ad ortus " (8), the confirmation of the omen by Jupiter who " partibus intonuit caeli . . . sinistris " (12), and the quiet close of the whole incident by " Sic aquilae clarum firmavit Iuppiter omen " are all admirable examples of a picturesque simplicity far removed from the turgid bombast of the *De Consulatu*. The use of alliteration in " subrigit ipsa feris transfigens unguibus anguens " is especially felicitous, for it conveys a definite effect, unlike many of the seemingly pointless alliterations used by Cicero elsewhere.[1]

TRANSLATIONS

Of the translations, the *Phaenomena* and the dramatic fragments alone possess any intrinsic value, the other verses being too fragmentary to contribute much to our appreciation of Cicero the poet.   His reasons for choosing the *Aratea* for translation are easily discerned.   Just as he was a pioneer in popularising the hexameter, so he was the first, so far as is known, to provide the Romans with an ordered treatise on astronomy.   (This may account for the fact that he chose to translate the simple and unadorned work of Aratus rather than the later and much more elaborate poem, *Hermes*, of Eratosthenes, only a few fragments of which are now extant.)   The Stoic sympathies of Aratus, perhaps " the least Alexandrine of the Alexandrines," his love of detail characteristic of the Peripatetics, and his comparatively easy language would have made him especially acceptable to Cicero.

Added to this was the immense vogue enjoyed by Aratus amongst the ancients.   Ovid's famous pronouncement " Cum sole et luna semper Aratus erit," is well known [2] (*Amor.* i. xv. 16).   Mahaffy (*Greek Life and*

---

[1] No doubt his fondness for hunting the letter was due, in part, to influence exerted by the early poets.   Ennius's lines :

> " Haec omnia vidi inflammari ;
> Priamo vi vitam evitari,
> Iovis arcam sanguine turpari,"

aroused Cicero's enthusiastic praise, ' O poetam egregium ! ' (*Tusc. Dis.* iii. 44).

[2] Further references to Aratus are : *De Repub.* 14 ; *De Orat.* i. 15 ; C. Helvius Cinna (Müller, Baeh., p. 87, Fr. Rom. Poet) :

> " Haec tibi Arateis multum invigilata lucernis
> carmina, quis ignes novimus aetherios,
> levis in aridulo malvae descripta libello
> Prusiaca vexi munera navicula."

Cf. too Quint. *Inst.* x. i. 55.

Thought, Macmillan, 1887, pp. 227–34) maintains that Antigonus Gonatas of Macedonia originally induced Aratus to compose his treatise as a manual for sailors. With the spread of culture and luxury, navigation was no longer confined to the summer months (cf. Cic. *Ph.* 72–4), so that a plain enumeration of the constellations was a real need, and Mahaffy points out that Aratus omits all constellations invisible from Greek waters, although familiar to him from his sojourn in Egypt. Eudoxus himself may not have included these southern star groups, but " we can hardly conceive Aratus to have been so slavish a versifier as to mention no star except those found in his model. It would rather seem to me that he composed his book with special and deliberate exclusion of anything that might serve Egyptian trade. . . ."

Prof. Gilbert Murray (*Hist. of Greek Lit.*, Heinemann, 1917, pp. 386–7), speaking of Aratus, says : " The extraordinary influence and reputation enjoyed by Aratus in antiquity appear to be due to the fact that he succeeded in annexing, so to speak, as his private property, one of the great emotions of mankind. In the centuries following him it almost seems as if no cultured man was capable of looking long at the stars without murmuring a line from the *Phaenomena.*"

CICERO THE TRANSLATOR

Thus we see that a Latin version of Aratus was assured a hearing by Cicero's contemporaries. The works of Varro Atacinus (82–37 B.C.), Germanicus, Avienus, and the use made of Aratus by Ovid and Manilius, to say nothing of Virgil, testify to the impression made by Cicero upon the cultured class of Rome. As a translator he realised the danger of extreme looseness on the one hand, and of a word-for-word translation on the other. In general, he successfully avoided both extremes. He never departed far from the Greek if an adequate effect could be secured by a close translation. But if a passage required, in his opinion, further explanation, as, for example, when the use of Greek instead of Latin nomenclature necessitated such expressions as 'apud Graios' (F. v), 'quem claro perhibent Ophiuchum nomine Graii' (F. xiii), he did not hesitate to make additions of his own. Expansion (cf. n. *Ph.* 116, 317, 421 *et sqq.*) is far more commonly used than compression (cf. n. *Ph.* 155, 190, 245, 266, 332), and Cicero frequently inserts epithets and short phrases of his own, most of which are justified, some of which are instinct with real poetic feeling. He adopts various devices to secure vividness of description, such as rewriting the third person of Aratus in the second (*Ph.* 196–7), animating the constellations, and repeating similar ideas in slightly different settings. Sometimes he misunderstands his original (cf. n. *Ph.* 96–101, 250–2) : sometimes he fails to interpret the spirit of the Greek (cf. *Iliad* i. 13–16). The further detailed criticism, available in the notes makes additional examples here unnecessary[1] ; enough has been said to show that Cicero refused to acknowledge any hard-and-fast rules. His own taste was the standard to which he most often referred, and he practised, with considerable success, the precepts laid down in *De Fin.* iii. 4, where, in the course of some remarks to Cato on the difficulty of interpreting Greek philosophical terms, he says : " Nor will it be necessary for you to render what he [*sc.* Zeno] has said, word for word, as translators are in the habit of doing who have no command of language of their own, whenever there is a word in ordinary use which has the same meaning. *I, indeed, myself am in the habit, if I*

---

[1] But from many passages the following are noteworthy, either for some particularly happy turn of expression or for some fault in diction or translation : *Ph.* 32, 41, 62–71, 82, 113–19, 128–30, 147–8, 189, 237–9, 273–7, 280–1, 302–7, 320–31, 413–14 ; *Prog.* iii. ; vi. 1–3 ; vii. ; *Iliad* i. 6, 14–16 ; *Mar.* 5–8 ; Soph. 24–6.

cannot manage it any other way, of using many words to express what the Greeks have expressed in one."

SUMMARY

There is a remark once made by Anatole France which is especially applicable to Cicero. " Tous ceux," he said, " qui se flattent de mettre autre chose qu'eux-mêmes dans leurs oeuvres sont dupes de la plus fallacieuse illusion—*on ne sort jamais de soi-même* " [my italics].   In the same way we see that Cicero, whilst preserving the meaning and (in most passages) the spirit of the original, never sinks his own individuality in a word-for-word translation.   Cicero was an innovator in subject-matter (so far as the *Ph.* was concerned), and something of a pioneer in the more extended use of the hexameter. Special qualities are needed in the reader who would enjoy the *Ph.* to-day, but if an interest in astronomy (and perhaps an academic interest in the poem as being by a man who was, in other departments, the greatest representative of his age) is his, he will find much to repay his perusal.

In conclusion, we would insert one last criticism, a criticism from the pen of him whose works have been the delight and inspiration of so many.[1] " But it is gross injustice to treat his [*sc.* Cicero's] verse as if it were mainly jingling and bombast. The attacks read as if Cicero were judged by the standard of his own oratory, which overshadowed his poetry, or by that of Virgil, whose incommensurate superiority owed some debt after all to the poets of the Ciceronian age. There is an old-fashioned ring in Cicero's tragic adaptations which explains why some were for long attributed to Accius. Now this suggests the true view. Cicero is a vivacious and tasteful intermediary who transmitted to Lucretius and Catullus the ancient Latin versification enhanced in dignity and, still more decidedly, in technique."

[1] *A Literary History of Rome*, J. Wight Duff, Unwin, 1920, p. 372

§ THE CICERONIAN HEXAMETER

Caesura

$$\begin{cases} -\,\smile\,\smile\ /\ -\,\smile\,\smile\ /\ -\,\smile\,\smile\ /\ -\,\smile\,\smile\ /\ -\,\smile\,\smile\ /\ -\,- \\ -\,-\ /\ -\,-\ /\ -\,-\ /\ -\,-\ /\ -\,\smile\,\smile\ /\ -\,- \end{cases}$$

The principal caesuras occur in the hexameter verse as follows :

> Penthemimeral   (semiquinaria) at $2\frac{1}{2}$.
> Hephthemimeral (semiseptenaria) at $3\frac{1}{2}$.
> Trihemimeral   (semiternaria) at $1\frac{1}{2}$.
>   (tertia trochaica) at 3T.

This numbering assumes that each foot can be divided mathematically into two equal parts (Quint. ix. 4. 47), and for brevity reference will be made in future to each caesura by the above numbers. The last named falls after the third trochee in the verse. All secondary (1T. 2T. 4T) and tertiary ($\frac{1}{2}$. $4\frac{1}{2}$. 5T and apparent, i.e. those occurring in elision) caesuras are excluded from the statistics. They are subsidiary to the four principal and used for ornamentation only. The terms ' arsis ' and ' thesis ' are understood to denote the stressed and unstressed part of a foot respectively.

Of the principal caesuras the most important is $2\frac{1}{2}$. Four combinations exist in which it occurs, seven from which it is excluded. It is not proposed to consider the relative value of the principal caesuras, as this is largely a matter of personal taste. Who shall say, for example, where the main caesura falls in such a verse as ? —

" Italiam fato profugus Lavinaque venit."

The Ciceronian usage has been calculated, therefore, for the eleven possible combinations given below, irrespective of the most important caesura in any one group or of the secondary and tertiary caesuras.

For purposes of comparison the *Peleus and Thetis* of Catullus and the *Ciris* have been analysed, and the results placed side by side with the Ciceronian figures. The separate fragments of the *Phaenomena* have been kept distinct from the continuous poem. (This was found to be desirable in dealing with the question of Pauses and for greater uniformity has been retained throughout.) Likewise the Homeric translations have been treated in two parts. The following abbreviations are employed in all the sections :

De Cons.	.	De Consulatu.
Mar.	. .	Marius.
Ph. .	. .	Phaenomena, continuous poem.
Ph. ff.	. .	Ph. separate fragments.
Prog.	. .	Prognostica.
Il. .	. .	Iliad translations.
Ody.	. .	Odyssey translations.
Misc. Vv. .	.	Miscellaneous verses (including the elegiac couplets).
Cir. .	. .	Ciris.
P. & T.	. .	Peleus and Thetis.

The following results are to be understood, in each section, as percentages.

	De Cons.	Mar.	Ph.	Ph.ff.	Prog.	Il.	Ody.	Misc. Vv.	Cir.	P. & T.
1½. 2½. 3½	24·2	13·3	25·3	24·6	33·3	38·1	36·4	31·8	29·8	17·7
2½. 3½ .	24·2	40	22	17·4	14·8	7·1	18·9	18·2	20·4	14·3
1½. 2½ .	23	20	23·9	24·6	22·2	33·3	27·3	18·2	22·6	33·5
2½ .	19·6	26·7	17·4	23·2	14·8	19	18·2	27·3	15·1	25
1½. 3T. 3½	2·3	—	1·5	1·5	3·7	2·4	—	—	7·5	4·9
1½. 3½ .	2·3	—	3·5	1·5	—	—	—	—	1·5	1·3
3T. 3½ .	—	—	·6	2·9	—	—	—	—	·2	1·3
1½. 3T .	2·3	—	·8	—	—	—	—	—	1·1	1·1
3½ .	1·6	—	2·5	1·5	3·7	—	—	—	·8	—
3T .	1·6	—	·8	—	7·4	—	—	4·5	·2	·8
1½ .	—	—	1	2·9	—	—	—	—	·2	1·6

The average frequency of these combinations of caesura in Cicero *only* is :

$1\frac{1}{2}$. $2\frac{1}{2}$. $3\frac{1}{2}$	28·3
$2\frac{1}{2}$. $3\frac{1}{2}$	20·3
$1\frac{1}{2}$. $2\frac{1}{2}$	24·1
$2\frac{1}{2}$	20·8
$1\frac{1}{2}$. 3T. $3\frac{1}{2}$	1·4
$1\frac{1}{2}$. $3\frac{1}{2}$	·9
3T. $3\frac{1}{2}$	·4
$1\frac{1}{2}$. 3T	·4
$3\frac{1}{2}$	1·2
3T	1·8
$1\frac{1}{2}$	·5

Further calculation shows that the proportion of feet including $2\frac{1}{2}$ to those not containing this caesura is approximately 14 : 1. This proves Cicero's preference for a strong medial caesura, in accordance with what later became general usage.

Cicero does not employ a $2\frac{1}{2}$ caesura alone, and, when such caesura is implied in the foregoing table, it must be remembered that a minor caesura will be found supporting it. Thus in " sed tamen anni iam labuntur tempore toto " $\frac{1}{2}$ comes to the help of $2\frac{1}{2}$, whilst in " quidnam torpentes subito obstipuistis Achivi " similar support is provided by 5T. Likewise what appears in the table as $3\frac{1}{2}$ is often accompanied by $2\frac{1}{2}$ (apparent) in addition to other minor caesuras, as " quod quasi temoni adiunctam prae se quatit Arcton." Further examples *Ph.* 189, 310, 410, 430.

The rarer combinations can be found in the poems by the following table of verse numbers :

	1½.3T.3½	1½.3½	3T.3½	1½.3T	3½	3T	1½
De Cons.	39 67	53 84	—	41 70	73	40	—
Mar. .	—	—	—	—	—	—	—
Ph. .	36 120 230 276 302 453 480	15 39 49 74 87 140 154 174 194 354 357 382 388 407 450	138 372 470	35 207 241 469	11 135 173 182 189 287 310 343 348 430 449 479	31 76 201 278	22 82 188 254 375
Ph. ff. .	xi. 1	vii. 1	vii. 5 viii. 3	—	xvi. 2	—	xxvi. 1 xxvii. 1
Prog. .	vi. 1	—	—	—	vi. 3	v. 1 & 2	—
Il. .	i. 24	—	—	—	—	—	—
Ody. .	—	—	—	—	—	—	—
Misc. Vv.	—	—	—	—	—	ii. 2	—
Cir. .	41 examples	8 ex.	1 ex.	6 ex.	4 ex.	1 ex.	1 ex.
P. & T..	19 examples	5 ex.	5 ex.	4 ex.	—	3 ex.	6 ex.

No account has been taken in the above tables of the so-called 'bucolic diaeresis' (see Pauses, p. 55). Cicero has many unmusical verses, but there is no doubt whatever that he aimed at greater unification of the hexameter through a careful use of caesura—especially in his later work. Amongst points worthy of notice are the following. A clumsy use of 2½ tends, in some verses, to disconnect the sense from the rhythm, as in *Ph.* ix. 5 " obstipum caput a tereti cervice reflexum " which contains an unpleasant break after ' a.' Amongst other examples of this cf. *ib.* xxii. and verses 143, 243, 357, 385 and *De Cons.* 55. This is not so prominent in the later poems, and was probably due to Cicero's partiality, in common with the later poets, for the 2½ caesura of which at first he was not entirely master.

Again the second hemistich is somewhat violently separated from the first by a mannerism frequent in Cicero, namely, coincidence of verse ictus and word accent in the last three feet. In *Ph.* 101, for example, we have " viribus erumpit qua/summi/spiritus/Austri." Cf. too *ib.* Ff. ix. 3 ; xxii ; xxxii. 5 and in the first 100 verses of the *Ph.* 6, 50, 82, 100.

In a great many verses the same monotonous effect is produced by the first syllable of the word forming the fourth foot being placed in the thesis of the third, " et post, hiberni praepandens temporis ortus," *Ph.* 40. In the first 100 verses of the *Ph.* cf. 41, 54, 60, 61, 64, 67, 69, 76, 77, 90.

Disjointed rhythm is also noticeable in the first two feet of the verse for reasons similar to those mentioned above. In *Ph.* verses 100–200 cf. 127, 140, 143, 146, 164 (but note pause in second foot), 173, 174, 182. This was common in Ennius and Lucretius, but avoided by Virgil. In the *De Cons.* there are only four examples, 7, 39, 78 and the Fragment " nam quasi vos sibi dedecori genuere parentes," of which the first is discounted by the pause preceding the second thesis, as in verse 164 above. There are no instances in the *Marius*.

Composition of the First Foot

The 1½ caesura was of little real importance in the Greek hexameter, but in Latin it was frequently employed to support 3½ and 3T. This preference for 1½ caesura helps to explain why Roman poets were averse to first feet composed solely of a dactyl or a spondee. For the second foot must then necessarily begin with a mono-syllable if 1½ is to be obtained : this was considered harsh. In one hundred verses of the *Aeneid* taken at random (viii. 510–609) there are only five cases of such beginning. Furthermore, an initial spondee with the resultant diaeresis has the effect of slowing down the rhythm considerably cf. *De Cons.* 48, 49, *Il.* i. 23, 24 and examples in *Ph. passim.* This movement is, in cases where the subject-matter demands dignified and stately treatment, still further emphasised by a pause. The following verses of the *Ph.* provide instances, 12, 30, 53, 146, 172, 281, 356, 376, 445, 446. Consequently Latin hexameters tend to start with a dactyl or dactylic word— as Greek did—rather than with a spondee. In Virgil, as in Homer, spondaic to dactylic first verses are as 2 to 3 (Winbolt. *Lat. Hex. Verse*, Meth. 1903, p. 106). Later writers, like Ovid, raise the proportion of dactyls to spondees as 5 to 1. An initial spondee also anticipates the end of the verse : this was avoided whenever possible.

The following percentages are found in Cicero :

	De Cons.	*Mar.*	*Ph.*	*Ph.ff.*	*Prog.*	*Il.*	*Ody.*	*Misc. Vv.*	*Cir.*	*P. & T.*
Dactyl.	23	40	11·9	12·9	18·5	21·4	36·4	9	16·4	19
Dactylic ft.	41·4	40	38·3	34·3	33·3	52·4	45·6	58·6	50·4	46
Spondee	4·6	0	9·6	4·3	0	4·8	9·1	9	3·3	4·2
Spondaic ft.	31·1	20	40·2	48·6	48·1	21·4	9·1	22·5	29·4	31·7

(The first foot of Alcyones, verse 1, has been calculated as a dactyl.)

The average frequency of the four feet in Cicero *only* is :

Dactyl	21·6
Dactylic ft. . . .	43
Spondee	5·2
Spondaic ft. . . .	30·1

It will be readily seen that in the *De Cons.* Cicero had decreased the spondees and increased the dactyls considerably.

Plessis (*Traité de Metrique*, Paris, 1889, p. 50) who bases his conclusions on Drobisch (*Ein Statist. Versuch über die Formen des latein*) is incorrect when he writes : " Conclusions de Drobisch : 1° A l'exception d'Ennius, *de Cicéron* et de Silius Italicus, les poètes latins ont majorité de dactyles au premier pied."

Appended is a table showing verses beginning with a single spondee in the first foot. The preponderance in the *Ph.* is noteworthy.

De Cons.   48 49 and in ff. 83 85
Marius .   —
Ph.   .   3 12 28 30 33 53 93 96 100 105 131 138 139 146 156 171 172
            176 184 193 221 238 243 261 281 286 306 318 323 328 342
            346 347 356 372 376 381 384 398 419 435 445 446 459 463
            478
Ph. ff. .   viii. 3 xxxii. 5 8
Prog.   .   —
Il.   .   i. 23 24
Ody.   .   ii. 1
Misc. Vv.   ii. 4 ; iv. a 1

Composition of the First Four Feet

Having considered the proportion of dactylic to spondaic first feet, it now remains to examine Cicero's arrangements in the first four feet taken together. The possible combinations are sixteen in number :

		De Cons.	Mar.	Ph.	Ph.ff.	Prog.	Il.	Ody.	Misc. Vv.	Cir.	P. & T.
DD	DD	2·3	—	·2	3	3·7	—	—	—	2·4	·3
	DS	3·5	13·3	6·1	4·5	11·1	9·5	9·1	9	9	2·9
	SD	3·5	13·3	3·2	1·5	—	4·8	—	—	6·6	2·6
	SS	15	26·7	14·3	11·9	14·8	11·9	36·4	18	13·1	13·5
DS	DD	2·3	—	1·3	3	—	2·4	—	—	2	1·8
	DS	8·1	13·3	5·5	7·5	7·4	11·9	—	—	9·6	11·2
	SD	8·1	—	2·5	6	—	—	—	13·5	6·3	4·9
	SS	21·9	13·3	17·2	7·5	14·8	33·3	36·4	27	17·3	28·9
SD	DD	—	—	1·5	1·5	7·4	—	—	—	1·1	1·1
	DS	3·5	—	6·3	16·4	7·4	4·8	—	—	4·2	2·6
	SD	2·3	—	4	6	—	—	—	4·5	3·3	1·8
	SS	15	13·3	12·6	10·4	18·5	9·5	9·1	13·5	8·4	14·8
SS	DD	—	—	1·5	3	3·7	4·8	—	—	1·3	1·3
	DS	3·5	6·7	6·7	9	3·7	—	—	9	5·5	3·6
	SD	3·5	—	3·6	—	3·7	—	—	—	3·7	1·8
	SS	8·1	—	14·1	9	3·7	7·1	9·1	4·5	5·7	8·6

The average frequency of these sixteen combinations taken in the above order from DDDD to SSSS for Cicero's poems *only* is :

			SDDD				1·3
DDDD	. . . .	1·6	SDDD	. . . .	1·3
DDDS	. . . .	8·3	SDDS	. . . .	4·8
DDSD	. . . .	3·3	SDSD	. . . .	2·1
DDSS	. . . .	18·6	SDSS	. . . .	12·6
DSDD	. . . .	1·1	SSDD	. . . .	1·6
DSDS	. . . .	6·7	SSDS	. . . .	4·8
DSSD	. . . .	3·8	SSSD	. . . .	2·4
DSSS	. . . .	21·4	SSSS	. . . .	7

It is only natural that there should be found in Latin a preponderance of spondaic over dactylic feet. This is particularly noticeable in the early poets, and Ennius's favourite verse was SSSS. Winbolt (*op. cit.* p. 114) says of him : " He over-emphasises the contrast with Greek in the manner of pioneers."

Lederer in a pamphlet published at Leipzig in 1890 calculated the percentage of combinations for the whole *Aeneid*. A comparison of his results with those of Cicero obtained from the foregoing tables is interesting.

Cicero.					*Virgil.*				
DSSS	. . .	21·4	DSSS	. . .	14·3
DDSS	. . .	18·6	DDSS	. . .	12
SDSS	. . .	12·6	DSDS	. . .	11·2
DDDS	. . .	8·3	SDSS	. . .	9·5
SSSS	. . .	7	SSSS	. . .	7·1

The least frequent combinations show the following results :

DSDD	. . .	1·1	SDDD	. . .	1·9
SDDD	. . .	1·3	DDDD	. . .	2·2
DDDD	. . .	1·6	SSDD	. . .	2·6
SSDD	. . .	1·6	SSSD	. . .	3

It often happens that two or three verses occur in the Ciceronian poems of similar structure, generally consecutively, sometimes in close proximity to each other. This points to the fact that Cicero took no especial trouble to vary the composition of his hexameters, except for some particular purpose. This unconsciously close correspondence, therefore, which exists between the two poets goes to prove that Cicero's feeling for rhythm and arrangement was very closely allied to that of Virgil. Their favourite verse is also found to be the most frequent in the other poets. Plessis (*op. cit.* p. 49) gives a list of average arrangements for the Latin hexameter in general :

DSSS	.	.	.	. 15
DSDS	.	.	.	. 11·8
DDSS	.	.	.	. 11
SDSS	.	.	.	. 10

The least common are :

SSDD	.	.	.	. 1·9
SDDD	.	.	.	. 2

It will be seen that Cicero affects a spondaic fourth foot in the five most common arrangements. This helps to retard the rhythm and contrasts well with the succeeding dactyl. It was a device later adopted by Virgil with increasing persistence. (Drobisch shows the numerical superiority of spondees in the fourth foot to be: *Eclogues* 62·8, *Georgics* 71·5, *Aeneid* 72·5.)

Hence in this matter of the ' spondaic fourth ' Cicero, with unerring instinct, pointed the way for his great successor.

The rarest combinations may be ascertained from the following table :

	De Cons.	Mar.	Ph.	Ph. ff.	Prog.	Il.	Ody.	Misc. Vv.
DSDD .	39 73	—	7 48 227 240 465	ii. 1 xxv.	—	i. 1	—	—
SDDD .	—	—	11 33 121 134 258 276 303	xxvi. 2	i. 1 iii. 2	—	—	—
DDDD	65 84	—	141	ix. 3 xii. 1	vi. 3	—	—	—
SSDD .	—	—	3 14 46 97 187 337 421	vi. xxix.	viii. 3	i. 23 24	—	—

It is probable that the use of metre by ancient poets to express the imagery of any particular verse has been over-emphasised by modern writers. It is so easy to read more into a verse than was ever intended! Within certain limits, however, Cicero did undoubtedly adopt special rhythm to secure special effects, and there is no doubt whatever that he had perfectly clear ideas as to the cumulative effect obtainable by the use of spondees in contradistinction to that produced by dactyls.

From amongst many examples in the poems it is easy to select a number of spondaic rhythms illustrative of dignity, grief, extent of distance, physical strain, and cognate ideas. In the *De Consulatu* at the close of the introduction the importance of the apostrophe to Cicero is emphasised by the spondaic structure of verse 6. The reader's attention is, as it were, especially demanded. Similarly one can compare verses 33 and 47, both of which prelude new introductions to further parts of the poem. The dignity of sacrifice is suggested in 14 (cf. *Il.* i. 22), wisdom in 74, mystery and destruction in 17, 20, 27, 50 and 79. Dramatic force is imparted to the description in 62 and 63 by the use of spondees and, in the former verse, by elision. Appended is a brief list of references to verses in the rest of the poems remarkable for spondaic rhythm :

Ph. ff.	The dejection of Engonasin	xi. 1. (Contrast the dactylic origin of his name in xii. 1 and cf. *Ph.* 6.)
	Physical effort . . .	xvi.
	Disgust	xx. 1.
	Dignity and splendour .	xxvii. 1 ; xxxii. 2.
	Extent of space. . .	vii. 3.
Ph.	Effort	13 23 61 77 78 125 (in contrast with the four preceding dactylic verses descriptive of the Hare's flight) 127 131 132 264 415 471.
	Extent of space. . .	9 26 164 194 208 209 211 226 230 235 239 242 243 248 268 305 306 314 332 334.
	Dignity	34 38 391.
	The serpentine motion of Hydra's tail . . .	218.
	Orion's might . . .	81 102 149 291.
	Sorrow	146 148.
	Fear	158.
	Destruction . . .	199 (cf. the rushing of the wind in 198) 401 404.
Prog.	Muffled noise . . .	iii. 5.
Il.	Death	i. 5.
	Religious rites . . .	i. 22 (cf. *De Cons.* 14).
	Duration of the war .	i. 27.
Misc. Vv.	Death . . .	iv. c. 1.

From verses composed mainly of dactyls and denoting success, rapidity, freedom, lightness, peace, and similar ideas one notices :

De Cons.	The disclosure of the Catilinarian conspiracy . .	65 (cf. the spondaic verse 64).
	Religion and peace . .	70.
Mar.	The eagle . . .	1.
	The hissing snake . .	4.
	Success . . .	10 11 (cf. the spondaic verse 12).

Ph. ff.	Immortality	. . .	ii. 1 (cf. verse 2).
	Sparkling light	. . .	ix. 3 ; xxiii. 3 ; xxxii. 4.
	The floating beaks	. .	xxv.
Ph.	Reference to the Greeks is often dactylic	. .	6 (cf. xii).
	Wind	. . .	13 141.
	Grace and lightness	. .	42 354 (cf. 409).
	Light, heat	. .	51 112.
	Approach of night	. .	76.
	The Hare, the Dog	. .	121–4 276 (cf. 377 378 465).
	Smoothness, movement	.	134 414 (cf. 426) 456 461 469 476.
Prog.	The swelling sea	. .	iii. 2.
	A bird's flight	. .	iv. 1.
	Frogs	. . .	v. 1.
	The cries of a bird	.	vi. 3.
Il.	The fluttering sparrow	.	i. 15.
	Her young	. .	i. 17.
	Immortality	. .	iii. 3.
Ody.	Contentment	. .	5.

The quotations cited above are sufficient to show that Cicero's use of rhythm was by no means haphazard. Certain it is that he did not employ it for special effects so frequently or so skilfully as Virgil did later, but he fully realised the necessity for careful arrangement when such arrangement was desirable.

In reading through the poems, one is occasionally confronted by a verse wherein the rhythm appears to conflict with the sense. For example,

" ipse suum cor edens, hominum vestigia vitans " (*Il.* ii. 2).

and

" Mors mea ne careat lacrimis : linquamus amicis " (*Misc. Vv.* iv. b. 1).

This may be due to lack of studied care by the author at any particular point, or may be sometimes explained

by reference to the original which is often translated so
literally that the dactylic metre of the Greek is preserved
in the Latin :

ὃν θυμὸν κατέδων, πάτον ἀνθρώπων ἀλεείνων.
μηδέ μοι ἄκλαυστος θάνατος μόλοι, ἀλλὰ φίλοισι.

PAUSES

The location of pauses is, to some extent, arbitrary,
as it depends on the reader's own taste in many cases.
The following table takes account of pauses occurring
within the verse whilst to it are appended the statistics
of final pauses.   As the caesura affects a verse metrically,
so the pause affects it rhetorically, serving to break up
what would become a monotonous cadence if repeated
as a series of complete types.

The following calculations include amongst heavy
pauses : (1) Strong antitheses.   (2) Ends of interrogative
sentences. (3) Introductions to direct speech. (4) Heavy
stopping, i.e. full stops, colons.   They include amongst
light pauses : (1) That between an antecedent and its
relative clause. (2) Co-ordinating conjunctions. (3)
Light antitheses.   (4) Parentheses.   (5) Verbs like ' in-
quit ' used inside direct speech.   (6) A series of ques-
tions in quick succession.   No distinction has been made
between diaeresis and the more frequent pauses in caesura.
The upper set of numbers refers to light pauses : where
heavy ones occur they are printed immediately below the
light.   The percentage in Cicero is as follows :

De Cons.

– ˘ ˘ 10·3 / – ˘ ˘ / – 1·2 ˘ ˘ / – ˘ ˘ / – ˘ ˘ / – –
– 1·2 – / – 1·2 – / – 12·6 – 1·2 / – 1·2 – 1·2 /
1·2

Mar.

– ˘ ˘ / – ˘ 6·7 ˘ / – 6·7 ˘ ˘ / – ˘ ˘ / – ˘ ˘ / – –
– – / – – / – 26·6 – / – – /

Ph.
```
- ·2 ᵕ ·6 ᵕ 2·7 | - 1·9 ᵕ ·2 ᵕ ·8 | - 1·5 ᵕ ·8 ᵕ ·4 | - ·2 ᵕ ᵕ 1·7 | - ᵕ ·8 ᵕ ·8 | - ·2 -
         ·4      ·2        ·2                  ·2               ·2    1·1              ·2
- ·6   -   2·5 | - 1·5      -      | - 4·6     -    | - 1·5 - |
       1·1        ·2                  1·1                  ·6
```

Ph. ff.
```
- ᵕ 1·4 ᵕ | - 1·4 ᵕ ᵕ | - 1·4 ᵕ ᵕ | - 1·4 ᵕ ᵕ | - ᵕ ᵕ | - -
-   -   | - 2·7   - | - 2·7   - | - - 1·4 |
```

Prog.
```
- ᵕ 3·7 ᵕ | - 3·7 ᵕ 3·7 ᵕ 3·7 | - 7·4 ᵕ 3·7 ᵕ | - ᵕ ᵕ | - ᵕ ᵕ 3·7 | - -
-   -   | - 3·7      -      | - 7·4    -    | - - - |
```

Il.
```
- 2·4 ᵕ 4·8 ᵕ 7·1 | - 2·4 ᵕ ᵕ 2·4 | - 7·2 ᵕ ᵕ | - ᵕ ᵕ | - ᵕ 2·4 ᵕ | - -
                                     2·4
-     -     | -   -    - | - 7·1   - | -   -   - |
                            4·8
```

Ody.
```
- ᵕ ᵕ | - ᵕ ᵕ | - ᵕ ᵕ | - ᵕ ᵕ | - ᵕ 9·1 ᵕ | - -
-   -   | -   -    - | - 18·2 - | - 9·1 - |
```

Misc. Vv.
```
- ᵕ 4·5 ᵕ 4·5 | - ᵕ ᵕ | - 4·5 ᵕ ᵕ | - ᵕ ᵕ | - ᵕ 4·5 ᵕ 4·5 | - -
- 4·5 - | - 4·5 - | - 13·6 - | -   -   |
                                          4·5
```

<hr>

Ciris.
```
- ·6 ᵕ 1·5 ᵕ 4·4 | - 1·5 ᵕ ·9 ᵕ | - 2·9 ᵕ ·9 ᵕ ·4 | - ·8 ᵕ ᵕ 1·1 | - ᵕ 2·7 ᵕ 2·2 | - -
- ·8 - 1·1 | -   3·9   - | - 6·6 - ·2 | - 3·3 - ·6 |
              ·9            1·8               ·2    ·2
```

P. & T.
```
- ·3 ᵕ ·3 ᵕ 3·1 | - ·8 ᵕ ·5 ᵕ | - ·3 ᵕ 1·8 ᵕ | - ·3 ᵕ ᵕ ·5 | - ᵕ ·8 ᵕ 1·1 | - -
                  ·3
- ·3 - ·3 | -   2·7   - | - 4·2 - | - 1·3 - ·8 |
              ·5            1·7       ·8    ·3
```

A rare pause is that which occurs after the second
trochee : Greek in character, it is used of sudden action.

Cicero has two especially happy verses containing this pause :

" vocibus instat, et assiduas iacit ore querellas " (*Prog.* vi. 3).
" subrigit ipsa, feris transfigens unguibus anguem " (*Mar.* 3).

In 200 verses of *Aen.* vi. taken at random, there are three examples, viz. 630, 656, 705—all light.

The second dactylic pause is uncommon and used to arrest attention : this naturally produces an uneven effect.   Virgil ends this dactyl in a pyrrhic ; Ennius has four examples in some 600 verses (one assuming Virgilian form, i.e. ' perculit in latus ') ; the 1115 verses of Book i of Lucretius show seven instances, whilst Catullus resembles the *Iliad* in abstaining from this pause.   In the *Ph.* are to be noted verses 11, 33, 92 (the last Virgilian in form).   In the *Prog.* iii. 2 (also Virgilian).   In the *Iliad* i. 28 (Virgilian).

Cicero, in accordance with most Latin poets, made $2\frac{1}{2}$ his most frequent pause, for this break in sense coincides naturally with a strong caesura and provides a suitable resting place for the reciter.   Homer in the *Iliad* shows it in approximately 8 per cent. of verses, Ennius 11 per cent., Lucretius 8 per cent., Catullus (who prefers the Greek third trochaic pause) 6 per cent.   In the *Aeneid*, however, these numbers are considerably raised, the average being 15 per cent. : with this the *De Cons.* is in close agreement.   Ovid shows 50 per cent. ! (Cf. *Met.* vii. 34–45.)

The Greek 3T pause is produced by the presence of Greek words and is followed by a spondaic fourth foot. For Ciceronian examples, cf. *Ph.* 35, 36, 372, 453 ; *Prog.* v. 1.   The *Iliad* of Homer shows 10 per cent., whilst in Ennius it scarcely reaches 1 per cent. : Lucretius uses it even less, but Catullus under Greek influence increases to nearly 2 per cent.   Virgil agrees with the older poets and employs it very rarely. The Romans realised how unsuited to the heavy sounds of Latin this elegant pause was, and preferred rightly to give priority to 2½.

A pause after the third foot is extremely rare, and hardly ever seen after a spondee. The objection to it seems to have been that it divided the verse into two equal parts, this similarity of rhythm being disliked. There is one indisputable example in *De Cons.* 20, a possible second in *Prog.* iii. 5 (although if no punctuation be insisted upon after ' cum,' the verse runs on smoothly without it), two possible third dactylic pauses occur in *Ph.* 46, 139 (but I incline to the belief that both could well be omitted in reading), whilst the *Ciris* exhibits a third spondaic pause in verse 202. The 3½ pause is rare in Cicero when one considers how quickly it came into favour after Virgil's time. The latter shows 1½ per cent. in the *Eclogues* and *Georgics*, increases to 3½ per cent. in the first six, and exceeds that proportion in the last six, books of the *Aeneid*. Ovid 3 per cent.; Lucan 7½ per cent.; Claudian nearly 9½ per cent. For examples in the poems, cf. *Ph.* 8, 18, 157, 158, 171, 293 (heavy), 348 (heavy), 355, 363 (heavy), 456 (heavy), 470, 478 ; *F.* xxiii. 2 ; *De Cons.* 58, and the Fr.

" mors mea ne careat lacrimis : linquamus amicis."

Cicero shows no pause after the fourth trochee. Such pauses are extremely rare. (Cf. *Aen.* v. 167, 623, 871.)

The so-called ' bucolic diaeresis ' (from its frequent occurrence in the Greek pastoral poets) is employed after a fourth foot dactyl—rarely after a spondee in Cicero— and before some definite punctuation. Ennius's use was not quite 2 per cent. Lucretius 3 per cent., about one-third of his examples being heavy : he preferred a word composing a foot and a half before the pause, and in about half the cases the fourth foot is spondaic. Cicero avoids the Lucretian spondee, and places a pyrrhic before the pause, being influenced in this by the early poets. Virgil showed his appreciation of Cicero's rhythm by himself eliminating the spondee and slightly increasing Lucretius's percentage. Ovid, on the other hand, decreases to less than 2 per cent. and makes these pauses very light, but he supports the preceding pyrrhic in opposition to the spondee. The poems show the following examples :

After a spondee. *De Cons.* 83 ; *Ph.* F. xxxii. 5.
After a dactyl. *Ph.* 2, 89, 105, 121 (heavy), 158 (heavy), 196, 254 (heavy), 258 (heavy), 260 (heavy), 276, 381, 406, 462.

(The numbers underlined denote those verses in which a pyrrhic occurs.)

The 5T pause is almost non-existent in Homer : Ennius and Lucretius show approximately 1 per cent. each ; Cicero about 2 per cent., with which Virgil is again in close agreement, but the latter prefers a heavy to a light pause ; Ovid nearly 6 per cent. In the poems examples are found in :

Ph. 275, 364, 379, 444. *Il.* i. 23. *Ody.* i. 1 (both before vocatives).
Misc. Vv. ii. 1 (also before a vocative).

To what extent the existence of a pause after the fifth foot can be considered depends on the taste of the reader. Of the five verses in the *Ph.*, 121, 171, 187, 266 (heavy), 373, the one which cannot be disregarded is 266. Lucretius does not attain to ½ per cent., whilst there appear to be no examples in Ennius. Two more possible examples in Cicero are *Prog.* vi. 5 and *Misc. Vv.* v. 2. The latter, although somewhat unusual, has point as emphasising ' leto.'

No example of a sixth foot pause occurs in the poems, with the possible exception of *Ph.* 189. Even here, it is better to read the verse continuously as punctuated in the text. If the pause be retained, however, the comma must be inserted after 'curriculo' and deleted after 'nox.'

FINAL PAUSES

From an examination of the *Georgics* and *Aeneid* statistics have been compiled showing that Virgil allowed 60 per cent. of his verses to be ended by a pause (the light somewhat preponderating) and 40 per cent. to be 'run on' verses without pause. In this respect the Ciceronian hexameter is very different from the Virgilian. The difference arose partly because the hexameter in Cicero's hands was, as yet, imperfect, its sentences not being fused into one harmonious whole, but being allowed to stand as detached lines : partly because of the didactic nature of the verse, which demands a succession of precepts each distinct from the other.

	'Run on' verses.	*Light pause.*	*Heavy pause (including full-stopped endings).*
De Cons.	. 20·7	47·15	32·2
Mar.	. 20	53·3	26·7
Ph.	. 27	32	41
Ph. ff.	. 21	22	57
Prog.	. 11·1	48·1	40·7
Il.	. 19·04	33·33	47·62
Ody.	. 9·09	54·54	36·36
Misc. Vv.	. 36·3	18·2	45·5

ELISION

In the following table are included elisions arising from apocope and aphaeresis : examples of the latter in the sixth foot occur in the *De Cons.* 19 ; *Ph.* F. xx. 1 ; *Ph.* 74, 312, 354, 449.

```
                    –  ∪  ∪ / –  ∪  ∪ / –  ∪  ∪ / –  ∪  ∪ / –  ∪  ∪ / –  –
De Cons.  .  – 6·9 1·2 / 5·8 2·3 – / 3·5 – – / 1·5 – – / – – – / – 1·5
Mar. .    .  – 6·7 –   / 6·7 6·7 – / 6·7 – – / – – –  / – – – / – –
Ph. .     .  – 1·3 ·2  / 2·3 1·7 – / 2·7 1·1 – / ·4 ·2 – / ·6 ·2 ·6 / ·2 ·8
Ph. ff.   .  – 2·7 –   / 6·9 5·5 1·4 / 1·4 1·4 – / 2·7 – – / 1·4 – 1·4 / – 1·4
Prog. .   .  – 7·4 –   / – – – / – – – / – – – / – – – / – –
Il. .     .  – 2·4 –   / 7·1 2·4 – / – – – / 2·4 – – / – – – / – –
Ody. .    .  – – –     / – – – / – – – / – – – / – – – / – –
```

```
Ciris .   .  – 5·9 1·1 / 4·1 1·7 – / 1·7 ·6 ·4 / ·2 ·4 1 / ·6 ·2 1 / ·2 ·2
P. & T.   . [1]·5 2·9 1 / 3·6 – – / 1·3 ·3 – / 1·3 ·5 – / 1·8 – 2·6 / – ·5
```

```
                    –  – / –  – / –  – / –  – / –  – / –  –
De Cons.  .  – 2·3 / 6·9 1·2 / 1·2 – / 4·6 10·4 /
Mar. .    .  – 6·7 / 6·7 –  / – – / – 6·7 /
Ph. .     .  – 3·2 / 5·7 ·4 / 4·6 1·5 / 1·1 2·3 /
Ph. ff.   .  – 6·9 / 5·5 –  / 5·5 2·7 / 2·7 4·1 /
Prog. .   .  – –   / – –   / – – / – 7·4 /
Il. .     .  – 4·8 / 9·5 2·4 / 4·8 2·4 / 4·8 7·1 /
Ody. .    .  – –   / 18·2 – / 9·1 – / – – /
Misc. Vv. .  – –   / 4·5 4·5 / 4·5 – / 9 9 /
```

```
Ciris. .  .  ·2 [2] 3·5 / 7·7 ·8 / 2·4 1·5 / 2·4 4 /
P. & T.   .  – 2·1   / 6·5 ·5 / ·8 1·3 / 1·6 5·2 / ·5 ·3 /
```

The history of the hexameter shows a steady decrease in the elision of monosyllables. In the poems are to be found only nine examples in all, viz. *De Cons.* 75; *Mar.* 5; *Ph.* 62, 87, 243, 287; *Il.* vi. 2; *Misc. Vv.* iv. c. 1 and x. 1. Winbolt (*op. cit.* p. 177) prints the following table to illustrate the percentage decrease: Ennius 1·3 per cent.; Lucretius 1·3 per cent.; Cicero 1 per cent. (more accurately 1·19 per cent.); Virgil. *Ecl.* 2 per cent., *Georg.* ·96 per cent., *Aen.* 1·28 per cent.; Ovid *Met.* ·00 per cent. since he has but 12 of these elisions in 12,000 verses.

[1] Verses 306, 347 excluding refrain.
[2] Cir. 295.

Rarer instances of elisions in dactylic feet occurring in the poems are :

1. *3rd syll. of 1st ft.*   *De Cons.* 57 'fore ut'; *Ph.* 405 'dum Nepa et.' (The harshness of the former example is somewhat mitigated by the natural connexion existing between the two words.)
2. *3rd syll. of 2nd ft.*   *Ph.* F. v. 1 'altera apud': the only instance.
3. *2nd syll. of 3rd ft.*   *Ph.* F.v . 2 'esse Helice'; *Ph.* 11, 287, 354, 417, 479.
4. *2nd syll. of 4th ft.*   *Ph.* 55.
5. *1st syll. of 5th ft.*   *Ph.* F. x. 1 ; *Ph.* 8 (' namque est ') 311, 340.
6. *2nd syll. of 5th ft.*   *Ph.* 372—probably in imitation of the early poets. (*N.B.* the periphrasis ' vis aquilai ' and archaic gen.)
7. *3rd syll. of 5th ft.*   *Ph.* F. xxv. ; *Ph.* 179, 348, 431—all elisions of ' e.'
8. *1st syll. of 6th ft.*   *Ph.* 32 : the only instance and probably in imitation of the early school. Cf. too Lucret. i. 1054 ' sine ullis ' ; *Georg.* iii. 274 ; *Aen.* ii. 544.

Rarer instances in spondaic feet are :

1. *2nd syll. of 2nd ft.*   *De Cons.* 82 ; *Ph.* 12, 78 ; *Il.* vi. 2; *Misc. Vv.* x. 1.
2. *2nd syll. of 3rd ft.*   *Ph.* F. xxvi. 1 ; xxvii. 1 ; *Ph.* 82, 254, 395, 401, 449, 450, 481 ; *Il.* vi. 2.

In dealing with elision Cicero was influenced, as was natural, by the subject-matter. Hence the use of elision n the *Aratea* is proportionately less than in the other poems on account of the tranquillity of their theme. But when Cicero finds it necessary to arrest the attention or to convey some vivid piece of imagery, he accomplishes this by deft elisions, as, for example, when he describes the gleaming eagle, " At propter se Aquila ardenti cum corpore portat " (*Ph.* 87), or the dark Argo " Atque usque a prora ad celsum sine lumine malum " (*ib.* 135), or the Zodiac " Signifero ex orbi sex signorum ordine fultum " (*ib.* 340), or the Crown " Partem etiam supera atque alia de parte repulsa est " (*ib.* 354).

The smoothness of the *Prognostica*—there being only

four elisions in all—is at once apparent. This is partly due to Cicero's immaturity, partly to the subject-matter. But that he could, and did, use elision successfully in his early work, cf. *Il. F.* i. verses 6, 10, 25, *ib.* vii. 4 ; *Ody.* i. 3 ; *Mar.* 7 and 8 (two verses finely descriptive of the bird struggling with the snake and then hurrying off in flight). In the *De Cons.* verses 5, 21, 53, 54, 62, 79 are noteworthy. Sometimes an especially harsh elision is admitted as in *Il. F.* vii. 4 'firmo animo,' the 'ō' before the 'ă' in the thesis of the foot being particularly unpleasant. This has no parallel elsewhere in the poems. There is no doubt that many of these harsh elisions are deliberate archaisms, due to the poet's affectionate regard for Ennius and the earlier school. In this he was not alone, as readers of Lucretius and Virgil will readily admit.

THE FIFTH AND SIXTH FEET

Abnormal endings usually avoided by the Augustans were :

(*a*) A spondaic 5th foot.
(*b*) Quadrisyllabic or pentesyllabic endings.
(*c*) A final monosyllable.
(*d*) The 5th thesis composed of a pyrrhic.

(*a*) The Homeric hexameter averaged one spondaic verse in eighteen. In Latin this spondaic fifth was much less popular. Ennius and Lucretius used it without definite purpose, the former showing 9 in 523 verses, the latter 32 in 7415. Horace has only one example, *Ep.* ii. 3. 467, in all the *Satires* and *Epistles* ; Tibullus and the ps-Sulpicia none. Catullus and the ' neoteroi,' on the other hand, under Alexandrine influence, used this ornament frequently. Of the 391 verses (excluding the refrain) of the *P. & T.* 27 are spondaic, 8 being composed of Greek words ; the *Ciris* has 13, 8 being Greek. But this device became less and less popular in the later poets.

Lucan's *Pharsalia* has but 14 examples, Silius writes 6, Val. Flaccus 1, Statius 7 (all in the *Thebaid*).

Cicero rightly disliked the spondaic fifth, and only one legitimate example is found in the poems, namely, *Ph.* 3, which Virgil probably copied in *Aen.* iii. 517. An imitation also occurs in the *Ciris*, 535, " Scorpius alternis clarum fugat Oriona." (That Cicero ever wrote ' Ŏăriōnis,' as has been suggested, is unlikely, seeing that Quint. ix. 4. 65 speaks of the form as a quadrisyllable.) The second example, the notorious verse " Flavit ab Epiro lenissimus Onchesmites," was composed by Cicero and sent to Atticus with the sarcastic remark quoted in the note on this verse. Its object was to poke fun at the ' neoteroi,' the new school of poets who were subject to Greek influence, like Catullus and his followers. In both verses Cicero followed the normal usage of keeping the fourth foot dactylic and of not allowing the fifth to end with a word. Both examples arise from Greek words.

(*b*) Quadrisyllabic endings were employed in Greek words or to produce some particular effect (i.e. *Aen.* xi. 667). Their comparative rarity is possibly due to the fact that the same rhythm can be obtained by a trisyllable followed by a monosyllabic enclitic, e.g. ' animumque,' or by a trisyllable preceded by a monosyllable, e.g. ' ad amores.' The poems show only two examples (other than *Ph.* 3), both in the *Ph.*, " spatio a Capricorno " (311) and " magna Aquilai " (372). It will be seen that both endings are formed from Latin words, the latter being archaic and reminiscent of Ennius.

Pentesyllabic endings were admitted as proper names or as especially descriptive words (i.e. *Aen.* xi. 614). Frequent in early verse, they fell into disuse in the classical period. Quintilian (ix. 4. 65) spoke of this ending as ' praemolle.' Lucretius used it in imitation of Ennius, Book i of the *De Rerum Natura* containing no less than sixty examples. The *Ph.* contains six of these pentesyllabic endings : there are none in the other poems.

> F. xiii. " caput Anguitenentis."
> F. xxxii. 1. " stellarum Cassiepia."
> Verse 23 " intendit Cassiepiae."
> Verse 35 " Celaeno Taygeteque."
> Verse 293 " simul Anguitenentis."
> Verse 388 " iam posteriores."

Here it is to be noticed that three of the endings are composed of Latin, three of Greek words. The *P. & T.* has three pentesyllabic endings, 115, 153, 206, all being Latin words : there are twenty-six quadrisyllabic, seventeen being Latin. The *Ciris* provides two examples of pentesyllabic ending, 326, 472, both being Greek : there are eleven quadrisyllabic, eight being Greek.

(*c*) Monosyllabic endings may be of two kinds, those (1) preceded by another monosyllable, or those (2) preceded by a word of two or more syllables. It is clear from the small number of monosyllabic endings in Cicero that he did not favour this abnormality and that he used it only in imitation of Ennius. All the examples occur in the *Ph.* with the exception of *Misc. Vv.* viii, which was almost certainly intentionally archaic.

> (1) F. vii. 4 " usus in hac est."
>   Verse 153 " quam iacit ex se."
>   Verse 431 " corpore prae se."
> (2) F. xxx. 2 " dexterque simul pes."
>   Verse 57 " visit equi vis."
>   Verse 64 " curriculo nox."
>   Verse 189 " curriculo nox."
>   Verse 264 " curriculum sol."
>   Verse 477 " signipotens nox."

Not one of the three Ciceronian endings falling under (1) above observes the rule usually obeyed by other poets, namely, that there should be a pause before the two monosyllables and no pause at the end of the verse (cf. *Aen.* v. 624; *Georg.* ii. 49). A true monosyllabic ending—div. 2 above—is uncommon in other poets. Virgil has in all some forty instances, Ovid eleven. The objection to it seems to have been that it prevented coincidence of word accent and verse ictus which was desirable in the last two feet of a line. When it was used, its purpose was to arrest attention (like any other metrical irregularity) or, as in the case of Cicero, by way of compliment to imitate some predecessor. But at the same time it is clear that this monosyllabic ending was regarded as ornamental when used with definite purpose. Quintilian commenting on the ' exiguus mus ' of Virgil (*Georg.* i. 181) says : " Clausula ipsa unius syllabae non usitata addidit gratiam " (viii. 3. 20). The *Ciris* shows three examples, 137 (2), 264 (1), 520 (2).

P. & T. has one, 316 (2). The numbers in brackets refer to the two kinds of monosyllabic endings discussed above.

(*d*) A pyrrhic in the second half of the fifth foot is archaic in origin. In his use of it, Virgil seems to have wished to retain, so far as possible, the coincidence between word accent and verse ictus by regarding the three following conditions :

> (*a*) The pyrrhic is preceded by a monosyllable which is itself preceded by a pause—thus emphasising the dactylic nature of the ending.
> (*b*) The verse is generally a ' run-on ' verse.
> (*c*) The monosyllable is closely connected with what follows. This obviates the harsh break after the fifth arsis which would otherwise arise. (A fifth foot pause weakens the force of the disyllabic ending.)

Cicero's verses which follow the Virgilian form are underlined. There is only one example, *Ody.* ii. 1, other than those in the *Ph.* Ff. xvi. 2 ; xxiii. 1 ;

xxiv. *Ph.* 2 8 32 89 105 121 (5th foot pause) 130 158 173 187 (5th foot pause) 254 258 276 309 325 343 376 413 456 462 470 478.

Ciris : 12 15 44 98 (5th foot pause) 134 328 (5th foot pause) 359.   *P. & T.* : 23 59 305 316.

In the *Aratea* the structure of the fifth foot is often monotonous.   There are no less than 263 verses in which it is composed of one word :

" Aestifer est pandens ferventia/sidera/Cancer."

In the *De Cons.* out of 87 verses only 22 take this form, showing that the poet realised this harshness in his later work.   The enclitic -que was found useful in mitigating this unpleasant rhythm and is employed 22 times in the fifth foot in the *De Cons.*, as compared with 16 instances in the 581 verses of the *Aratea*.   The second method of breaking up the structure of the fifth foot was the use of a pyrrhic which, as has been seen above, is employed 25 times in the *Ph.*, although in the later work it was entirely abandoned.   Herein Cicero differs much from Lucretius, who sought to impart a much more archaic touch to his work by a conscious imitation of Ennius.   That Cicero's sensitive taste was such as to enable him to point the way for his great successor and the Augustan school is particularly evinced in his treatment of the last two feet, as exemplified in the *De Cons.*

MISCELLANEOUS POINTS.   RHYTHM

When Cicero undertook to Latinise the Greek dactylic hexameter, he stressed the contrast between his own and the Greek language with too great emphasis.   This is evidenced, in his early work, by the excess of spondees over dactyls—which excess decreases as he himself advances in technique, so that finally the dactyl becomes more prominent.   That he used rhythm to some purpose can be seen by the tentative list of verse references appended to the section on the composition of the first four feet. The structure of a verse is almost invariably . . . adj/ . . . noun, and such verses as

"Horrificos metuens rostri tremebundus acuti" (*Ph.* 122),

where this arrangement is reversed, are very rare. (Cf. *ib.* 159 ; *De Cons.* 13, 71.) Sometimes the adjective comes first, the noun last, as

" aeternumque volens mundi pernoscere motum " (*Ph.* 224).

(Cf. *ib.* 225, 303, 320, 433 ; *Il.* i. 27 ; *De Cons.* 34), but whatever variations occur in word order, the principle of allowing adjective to precede noun is exhibited more than 70 times in the *Aratea* alone. This tends to stress the solidity and compactness of the verse.

So-called ' golden lines ' (two adjectives at the beginning followed by a verb and ended by two nouns) are as rare in Cicero as in Virgil. " Tum fixum tremulo quatietur frigore corpus " (*Ph.* 68). Cf. too *ib.* 111 and, for somewhat similar arrangement, 64, 189. Occasionally one finds parallelism, such as " Consimili specie stellas parilique nitore," *ib.* 165 (cf. 115, 165, 333 ; *De Cons.* 18, 56), or the opposite, " Hunc sura laeva Perseus humeroque sinistro," *ib.* 256 (cf. 88, 471 ; *De Cons.* 74), or chiasmus, " luce serenanti vitalia lumina liquit ? " *De Cons.* 24 (cf. *ib.* 73, *Mar.* ii. 1, and *Il.* i. 8).

An unhappy rhythm used to excess in the *Ph.*, due partly to Cicero's inexperience, partly to the exigencies of the subject-matter, is the monotonous cadence of the fourth and fifth feet which is produced by a combination of adjective, noun, and medial preposition, as

" In caelum victor magno sub culmine portat " (*Ph.* 26).

There are more than forty instances of this. Cf. in the first two hundred verses 27, 28, 47, 81, 87, 95, 107, 132, 164, 180. In the other poems this rhythm is comparatively rare, whilst in the *De Cons.* all four examples are broken up by elision, 13, 61, 75, 80, and in two cases by an extra word :

> " Albano in monte."
> " celsa est in sede."
> " primo iam a flore."
> " prima a parte."

Pauses are employed for the most part with skill and an obvious understanding of their value.   Cf. *Ph.* 157–8 :

" atque Gubernaclum stellae quas contegit omnes
  formidans acrem morsum, Lepus : his neque nomen . . ."

The light pause after 'morsum' and the heavy after 'Lepus' are skilfully inserted.   Cf. too *ib.* 372–4, 470 ; *Il.* i. 3 (where the pause after 'scire' is very effective before the indirect question which follows) and 14.   On the other hand, such felicity is not habitual : awkward pauses in conjunction with a repeated 2½ caesura sound a discordant note, as, for example, *Ph.* 170–3 :

> " At prope conspicies, expertes nominis omnes,
>   inter Pistricem et Piscem, quem diximus, Austri
>   stellas, sub pedibus stratas radiantis Aquari."

Cf. too the heavy rhythm in the pairs of verses, 329 and 330 ; 442 and 443 ; 452 and 453.   Rarely does the fifth foot fail to maintain coincidence of word accent and verse ictus, as it does in :

" Sed tantum supera terras semper tenet ille " (*Ph.* 309).

Cicero anticipates the Virgilian use of five-word verses to obtain a grave and dignified effect.   He shows considerable skill and taste in not employing the device too frequently, cf. *Ph.* 137, 138, 148, 163, 178, 225, 291, 306 (and chiasmus), 318, 328, 426, 431, 436 ; *Prog.* i. 2 ; *Il.* i. 11, 23 ; *De Cons.* 22, 38, 63, 74.   Each of these verses seems to be deliberately so written.

ALLITERATION. RHYME. HOMOEOTELEUTA

Under this heading we must consider also onomatopoeic words and verses as being connected with alliteration which Virgil and the Augustans regarded as something of an antiquarian ornament. This explains Lucretius's predilection for it, a predilection which was shared to the full by Cicero. In the poems we find a number of examples, many with some definite purpose, as, for instance,

"Haec dextram Cephei dextro pede pellere palmam
    gestit" (*Ph.* 52),

but a great many more which appear to be fortuitous. Sometimes a verse has degenerated into mere jingle, as in

"Sed tamen anni iam labuntur tempore toto" (*ib.* 69),

and sometimes Cicero's partiality for alliteration has led him to insert in his translation some phrase not represented in the original: cf. *Ph.* F. xxxii. 8 and verse 218. Scores of examples of two- and three-word phrases occur in the poems, such as: 'caeca caligine,' 'minitanti murmure,' 'lustravit luce lacunas,' 'scopulorum saepes,' 'mirabile monstrum,' 'sanctusque Senatus.' Onomatopoeia is used fairly frequently, but the subject-matter of the *Aratea* naturally tends to restrict the poet in his use of this figure. Some noticeable examples, however, can be found:

Of the wind, 'b' and 'u': *Ph.* 67, 100 and 101, 195.
  (Cf. too 141, 206, 253, 261, 280)
Of water, 'u' and 'm': *ib.* 71

Further instances in the *Prognostica* are noted in the commentary.

Of a snake's hissing, 's': *Marius* ii. 1–3.

Rhyme is unusually frequent in Cicero. It is found not only at the ends of two or more consecutive verses, but also between the middle and end of a verse. Examples of final rhyme in the *Aratea* number 19, in the *De Cons.* 7, in the Homeric translations 3, and in the *Marius* 1.[1] Examples of medial and final rhyme, such as :

" Et magis horrisonis Aquilonis tangitur alis " (*Ph.* 13),

occur also in verses 199, 200, 209, 248, 323, 361, 391, 429.

The suggestion has been put forward that these many instances of rhyme are too numerous to be accidental or purposeless, and that Cicero was ' preparing Latin poetry for the time when rhyme was to be one of its characteristics ' (Peck, *Amer. Philol. Assoc.*, 1897, vol. 28). A closer examination of the passages quoted above will show the cause of this rhyming to be due merely to the structure of the verse. This is almost invariably, as we saw above, . . . adj/ . . . noun. When these chance to have identical case endings, rhyme ensues. Furthermore, as we also noticed in dealing with the question of final pauses, the didactic nature of the subject-matter coupled with Cicero's own inexperience of verse writing led to ' one-line ' verses. This frequently results in rhyme, each hexameter being ended by a verb, noun, or other suitably heavy word. Even in the *De Cons.* a medial and final rhyme is not unusual, cf. 2, 26, 35, 43, 63, 72. That Cicero entertained any idea of this becoming part of verse technique seems very unlikely.

Homoeoteleuta (words ending in similar syllables) is more noticeable in the early, than in the late, work.

---

[1] Final rhyme :

> *Ph.* 10, 11 ; 45, 46 ; 65, 66 ; 100, 101 ; 147, 148 ; 171, 172 ; 193, 194 ; 242, 243 ; 252, 253 ; 279, 280 ; 300, 301 ; 315, 316 ; 339, 340 ; 359, 360 ; 381, 382 ; 459, 460.
> *F.* xv. 3, 4 ; *F.* xxvi. 1, 2.
> *Prog. F.* i. 1, 2.
> *De Cons.* 12, 13 ; 14, 15 ; 50, 51, 52 ; 53, 54 ; 56, 57 ; 60, 61, 62, 63, 64 ; 69, 70.
> *Il.* i. 5, 6 ; 8, 9 ; 27, 28.
> *Marius* 3, 4.

Two short syllables, or a short and a long, are often found in juxtaposition : *Ph.* F. ix. 3 'fervidă lumină'; *Ph.* 76 'iam propĕ praecipitantĕ licebit viserĕ noctē'; 465 'Lepus abditus'; *De Cons.* 63 'sceptră columnā'; 74 'pectorĭs artīs,' are amongst some of the many examples. Similar long vowel terminations occur most commonly when the former is in the arsis, the latter in the thesis, of a foot, *Ph.* F. xix. 'tenui contenti,' *Ph.* 305 'caelo divino,' 370 'terris vis.' Cf. too *ib.* 171, 184 (96). This arrangement is not invariable, as is seen from 63, 153, 187, 313.

It is interesting to note that later Cicero seems to have taken more care to prevent the occurrence of these similar endings in close proximity :

(1) By interposing a verse ending, *Il.* i. 11 and 12 ; *De Cons.* 11 and 12.
(2) By inserting a pause and punctuation, *Il.* i. 14, 28.
(3) By using enclitic -que, *De Cons.* 6.
(4) By abnormal order, *ib.* 9. (Cf. too *Ph.* 94, 159, 308, 412.)
(5) By elision, *Il.* i. 18 ; vii. 4. *De Cons.* 1, 11, 51, 53, 73, 82. (Cf. too *Ph.* F. xvi. 2 ; xxvi. 3 ; *Ph.* 22, 135, 154, 276, 407.)

It should also be remembered that some phrases, such as 'populus sanctusque Senatus' (*De Cons.* 57), are in all probability reminiscences of Ennius.

Synizesis and Hiatus

The poems contain few instances of metrical irregularities. In *Ph.* F. xv. 2 'eius' is presumably a monosyllable ; 'eodem' occurs as a disyllable in *Ph.* 229 ; *Mar.* 4 shows 'semianimum' treated, as is usual, as a quadrisyllable. There is only one case of semi-hiatus, *Ph.* F. xxiv., "Hoc motu radiantis E/tēsĭă/(e) in vădă/ Ponti," and no case of hiatus. Semi-hiatus has been

defined as " the elision of one short vowel and the reten-
tion of the preceding vowel." Cf. *Aen.* iii. 211, " Insulae
Ionio in magno quas dira Celaeno." It is rare, and
occurs mostly with Greek words, being admitted as a
conscious imitation of Greek. Cicero's own opinion on
this is quoted in the note *ad loc.*, cf. too n. *De Cons.* 73.
The poems offer no example of a short vowel being
lengthened, either under influence of its original quantity
or through the ictus of the verse : syllables containing
a short vowel followed by a mute (or f) + l or r, are con-
sistently treated as short, except ' mediŏcre ' (*Ph.* 51)
and ' ācredula ' (*Prog.* vi. 2). ' Deum,' ' divum ' take
the place of the longer forms, but ' Graiorum ' appears
in the *De Cons.* as well as ' Graium ' in the *Ph.* The
contracted form in ' ēre ' for the 3rd pl. perf. ind. is used
eight times, six examples appearing in the *De Cons.*
(cf. *Or.* 157 : " nec vero reprehenderim ' scripsēre alii
rem ' : ' scripserunt ' esse verius sentio, sed consuetudini
auribus indulgenti libenter obsequor "). Many times is
' sŭpĕrā ' used for ' sŭprā ' in the *Aratea*, and of this
Priscian xiv. 6. 52 says : " ' supera ' antiqui frequenter
protulerunt et maxime Cicero in poematibus." Final
' o ' is regarded as long, but we have ' duŏ ' (*Ph.* 175) and
' egŏ ' (*ib.* 234). Syncopated forms are found such as
' vincla ' (*ib.* 150), ' gubernaclum ' (*ib.* 137, 157), ' oracla '
(*De Cons.* 28), and verbs like ' nosse,' ' violasse ' *passim.*
' Cavĕ ' appears once (*Ph.* 62), ' vēmens ' for more usual
' vĕhĕmens' (*Ph.* 53) ; uncommon forms are ' porgens '[1]
(for ' porrigens ' *ib.* 211), ' subrigit ' (for ' surgit,' *Mar.*
ii. 3).

SUPPRESSION OF FINAL ' s '

The suppression of final ' s ' after a short vowel and
before a word beginning with a consonant occurs seven

---

[1] Imitated from Ennius, cf. Serv. *Aen.* i. 26 : the form occurs again
in *Aen.* viii. 274 : " et pocula porgite dextris."

(eight, if Orelli's emendation be included) times : three times in the first foot, *Ph.* F. viii. 2 'torvu' Draco serpit'; *ib.* F. xxiii. 3 'magnu' Leo'; *Ph.* 263 'magnu' Leo'; four times in the fifth, *ib.* 25 'elapsu' repente'; 82 'lustratu' nitore'; 97 'Aquiloni' locatae'; 335 'mortalibu' cedit' (Or. corr. for MS. 'edit'); once in the second, 121 'Orioni' iacet.' The suppression of 's' in the second foot is rare, but is paralleled by Lucret. i. 159. The fact that most of the cases occur in the fifth foot is probably due to Cicero's insistence on a dactyl in this position in order to avoid a spondaic verse. The figure was, of course, an archaism, and both Cicero and Lucretius use it deliberately : it is noticeable that the former employed it only in his early work. *The Orator* 161—written in 46 B.C.—has the following comment : "quin etiam quod iam subrusticum videtur, olim autem politius. . . . Ita non erat ea offensio in versibus quam nunc fugiunt poetae novi." (Cf. too Quint. ix. 4. 38.)

§ THE TEXT

FOR the greater part of the present edition I have used, without deviation, the latest edition of *Fragmenta Poetarum Latinorum*, ed. by W. Morel, Teubner, 1927. This is a revised version of Baehrens's edition of 1886. But it does not include the text of the *Phaenomena*, the *Prognostica*, the dramatic fragments from the Greek tragedians, or some of the *Miscellaneous Verses*.

For textual purposes the *Phaenomena* must be considered in two divisions—the fragments and the continuous poem. Almost all the fragments are included in Book ii of the *De Nat. Deorum*. For these I have availed myself of J. B. Mayor's edition (1891), and, wherever a reading occurs of importance from the point of view of the original Greek or of the different opinions of various editors, I have printed the variants. The MSS. to which I have referred are as follows :

A. Cod. Leid. (Vossianus), No. 84, 11th cent.
B. Cod. Leid. (Vossianus), No. 86, 12th cent.
C. Cod. Leid. (Vossianus), No. 118, 12th cent.
E. Cod. Erlangensis, No. 38, 15th cent.
P. Cod. Palatinus, No. 1519, a defective but early MS.
V. Cod. Vindobonensis, No. 189, 10th cent.

The following abbreviations are employed :

Asc.	.	.	. Editio Ascensiana, Paris, 1511
Or.	.	.	. The revised Orelli ed., 1861
Ba.	.	.	. Stereotype ed. of Baiter, 1864
Mu.	.	.	. Ed. of C. F. W. Müller, 1878

Reference is also made to three further MSS. printed by Mayor at the end of his edition, which were collated by Swainson :

L. Harleian 4662, latter part of 15th cent.
O. Additional MSS. 19586, end of 14th cent.
R. The Roman ed., 1471. Two copies exist in the British Museum, one (720. 1. 6) defective, the other (C. 1 c. 11) complete.

For additional information concerning these MSS., see Mayor, Intro., p. liv, sect. 5, 1891.

Since no modern edition of the continuous poem exists, and no new MSS. have come to light during the last fifty years, so far as I have been able to ascertain, I have been obliged to base my text on Baehrens's edition of 1886. This relies upon two MSS., and the following remarks concerning them are translated from Baehrens's Latin preface.

H. Cod. Harl., 647, 9th cent.

This is a good MS., illustrated with the constellations. Ottley dealt with it (pp. 145 *et sqq.*, vol. xxvi. *Archaeologia Brit.*), ascribing it to the second or third century, but authorities are agreed that it cannot possibly be earlier than the ninth century. The Ciceronian verses (bearing in the margin the title " Inc. Ciceronis de Astronomica ") suffered the hand of a corrector in the tenth century (H2) ; he emended correctly some errors of the archetype and first hand (H1), but not infrequently introduced errors into the text. This MS. was collated by Baehrens himself in 1875.

D. Cod. Dresdensis 183, 10*th cent.* (see B. Bunte, *Hygini Astronomica*, Pref., pp. 11 *et sqq.*)

Fol. 94*a*–97*b* bears the title " Incipiunt versus Ciceronis de signis." To each part of the poem titles such as 'De Andromeda,' 'De Piscibus,' etc., were prefixed. Baehrens claimed to be the first to use this good MS., which he collated in 1876. Its value lies in the fact that it often shows what H (with which it descends from the same archetype) had from the first hand.

Some occasional help is also derived from the MSS. of the *De Nat. Deor.*, in which a few verses of the continuous poem are quoted.

The *De Div.* contains twenty-three of the extant verses of the *Prognostica*, and has recently been edited by A. S. Pease (Univ. of Illinois, 1920–23). In his edition he has used the text of Müller (Teubner, Leipzig, 1878, and later impressions), and in his prefatory note says : " In the brief critical apparatus here printed, only those passages are treated in which readings are adopted either unsupported by any MSS. constituting the C group . . . or differing from the text of Müller. The apparatus is based upon that of Christ (1861), supplemented by those of Moser (1828), Orelli (1828), Baiter (1864), and Müller (1905), by the work of Deiter, 'De Ciceronis cod. Leid., No. 118 denuo collato' (1882), and the photographic facsimiles of codices H and A published by Plasberg in 1912 and 1915 respectively."

For the translations from Aeschylus, Sophocles, and for some of those from Euripides I have used the critical edition of the *Tusc. Disp.*, by T. W. Dougan (Camb. Univ. Press, 1905).

§ THE POEMS

DE CONSULATU

Book ii

Principio aetherio flammatus Iuppiter igni
vertitur et totum conlustrat lumine mundum
menteque divina caelum terrasque petessit,
quae penitus sensus hominum vitasque retentat
aetheris aeterni saepta atque inclusa cavernis.   5
Et, si stellarum motus cursusque vagantes
nosse velis, quae sint signorum in sede locatae,
quae verbo et falsis Graiorum vocibus errant,
re vera certo lapsu spatioque feruntur,
omnia iam cernes divina mente notata.   10
Nam primum astrorum volucres te consule motus
concursusque graves stellarum ardore micantes
tu quoque, cum tumulos Albano in monte nivales
lustrasti et laeto mactasti lacte Latinas,
vidisti et claro tremulos ardore cometas,   15
multaque misceri nocturna strage putasti,
quod ferme dirum in tempus cecidere Latinae,
cum claram speciem concreto lumine luna
abdidit et subito stellanti nocte perempta est.
Quid vero Phoebi fax, tristis nuntia belli,   20
quae magnum ad columen flammato ardore volabat,
praecipites caeli partes obitusque petessens ?
Aut cum terribili perculsus fulmine civis
luce serenanti vitalia lumina liquit ?
Aut cum se gravido tremefecit corpore tellus ?   25
Iam vero variae nocturno tempore visae
terribiles formae bellum motusque monebant
multaque per terras vates oracla furenti

pectore fundebant tristes minitantia casus,
atque ea quae lapsu tandem cecidere vetusto,   30
haec fore perpetuis signis clarisque frequentans
ipse deum genitor caelo terrisque canebat.
Nunc ea Torquato quae quondam et consule Cotta
Lydius ediderat Tyrrhenae gentis haruspex
omnia fixa tuus glomerans determinat annus.   35
Nam pater altitonans stellanti nixus Olympo
ipse suos quondam tumulos ac templa petivit
et Capitolinis iniecit sedibus ignes.
Tum species ex aere vetus venerataque Nattae
concidit elapsaeque vetusto numine leges   40
et divom simulacra peremit fulminis ardor.
Hic silvestris erat Romani nominis altrix,
Martia, quae parvos Marvortis semine natos
uberibus gravidis vitali rore rigabat ;
quae tum cum pueris flammato fulminis ictu   45
concidit atque avolsa pedum vestigia liquit.
Tum quis non artis scripta ac monumenta volutans
voces tristificas chartis promebat Etruscis ?
Omnes civilem generosa stirpe profectam
vitare ingentem cladem pestemque monebant,   50
tum legum exitium constanti voce ferebant.
Templa deumque adeo flammis urbemque iubebant
eripere et stragem horriblem caedemque vereri ;
atque haec fixa gravi fato ac fundata teneri,
ni prius excelsum ad columen formata decore   55
sancta Iovis species claros spectaret in ortus :
tum fore ut occultos populus sanctusque senatus
cernere conatus posset, si solis ad ortum
conversa inde patrum sedes populique videret.
Haec tardata diu species multumque morata   60
consule te tandem celsa est in sede locata,
atque una fixi ac signati temporis hora
Iuppiter excelsa clarabat sceptra columna
et clades patriae flamma ferroque parata
vocibus Allobrogum patribus populoque patebat.   65

Rite igitur veteres, quorum monumenta tenetis,
qui populos urbesque modo ac virtute regebant,
rite etiam vestri, quorum pietasque fidesque
praestitit et longe vicit sapientia cunctos,
praecipue coluere vigenti numine divos.   70
Haec adeo penitus cura videre sagaci
otia qui studiis laeti tenuere decoris
inque Academia umbrifera nitidoque Lyceo
fuderunt claras fecundi pectoris artes.
E quibus ereptum primo iam a flore iuventae   75
te patria in media virtutum mole locavit.
Tu, tamen, anxiferas curas requiete relaxans,
quod patriae vacat, id studiis nobisque sacrasti.
                                   De Div. i. 11. 17.

atque animo pendens nocturna eventa timebat.
                 Non. Marcell. p. 204 ; M. Linds. p. 300.

Book III

Interea cursus, quos prima a parte iuventae
quosque adeo consul virtute animoque petisti,
hos retine atque auge famam laudesque bonorum.
                                   Ep. ad Att. ii. 3. 4.

DE CONSULATU

Fragments of Uncertain Location

quorum luxuries fortunas, censa peredit
                 Non. Marcell. p. 202 ; M. Linds. p. 298.
nam quasi vos sibi dedecori genuere parentes
                           Probus iv. p. 248, K.
Cedant arma togae, concedat laurea linguae
                                   De Off. i. 22. 77.
O fortunatam natam me consule Romam.
                           Ps-Sall. *in Cic.* iii. 5.
in montes patrios et ad incunabula nostra.
                                   Ep. ad Att. ii. 15. 3.

DE TEMPORIBUS MEIS

See introductory essay, p. 16.

MARIUS

I

Nuntia fulva Iovis, miranda visa figura.

De Legg. i. 1. 2.

II

Hic Iovis altisoni subito pinnata satelles
arboris e trunco, serpentis saucia morsu,
subrigit ipsa feris transfigens unguibus anguem
semianimum et varia graviter cervice micantem.
Quem se intorquentem lanians rostroque cruentans   5
iam satiata animos, iam duros ulta dolores
abicit ecflantem et laceratum adfligit in unda
seque obitu a solis nitidos convertit ad ortus.
Hanc ubi praepetibus pinnis lapsuque volantem
conspexit Marius, divini numinis augur,   10
faustaque signa suae laudis reditusque notavit,
partibus intonuit caeli pater ipse sinistris.
Sic aquilae clarum firmavit Iuppiter omen.

De Div. i. 47. 106.

OF UNCERTAIN LOCATION

Tunc se fluctigero tradit mandatque paroni.

Isid. Orig. xix. 1. 20.
(Cf. Plut. Mar. 35. 9 ; 37. 3 ; 40. 1.)

For titles of work no longer extant, see p. 25.

PHAENOMENA

F. 1.   Ab Iove Musarum primordia.

De Legg. ii. 3.

F. II. Quem neque tempestas perimet neque longa
        vetustas
     interimet, stinguens praeclara insignia caeli.
                              Prisc. x. 2. 11.

F. III. Cetera labuntur celeri caelestia motu
     cum caeloque simul noctesque diesque feruntur.
                              De Nat. Deor. ii. 41.

F. IV. Extremusque adeo duplici de cardine vertex
     dicitur esse Polus.
                                        Ib.

F. V. Ex his altera apud Graios Cynosura vocatur,
     altera dicitur esse Helice :
                                        Ib.

F. VI. Quas nostri septem soliti vocitare Triones.
                                        Ib.

F. VII. Hac fidunt duce nocturna Phoenices in alto :
     sed prior illa magis stellis distincta refulget,
     et late prima confestim a nocte videtur.
     Haec vero parva est : sed nautis usus in hac est :
     nam cursu interiore brevi convertitur orbe.
                    Ib. and *Academ. Prior.* ii. 20.

F. VIII. Has inter, veluti rapido cum gurgite flumen,
     torvu' Draco serpit subter superaque revolvens
     sese conficiensque sinus e corpore flexos.
          De Nat. Deor. ii. 42 and Prisc. xiv. 6. 52.

F. IX. Huic non una modo caput ornans stella relucet,
     verum tempora sunt duplici fulgore notata,
     e trucibusque oculis duo fervida lumina flagrant,
     atque uno mentum radianti sidere lucet.
     Obstipum caput a tereti cervice reflexum
     obtutum in cauda maioris figere dicas.
                              De Nat. Deor. ii. 42.

F. v. Ex his B.E. ; Ex iis A.C.V.
F. viii. Flexo Grot.
   F. ix. a tereti MSS. *generally* ; e tereti R. ; at tereti Madv., Or.,
Ba., Mu. ; et tereti Lamb., Allen.

F. X. Hoc caput hic paullum sese summo aequore
     condit
ortus ubi atque obitus partim admiscentur in
     unam.

Ib. and Hygin., *P.A.*, iv. 3.

F. XI. Attingens defessa velut maerentis imago
     vertitur.

De Nat. Deor. ii. 42.

F. XII. Engonasin vocitant, genibus quia nixa feratur.
Hic illa eximio posita est fulgore Corona.

Ib.

F. XIII. (Propter caput Anguitenentis)
quem claro perhibent Ophiuchum nomine
     Graii.

Ib.

F. XIV. Huic supera duplices humeros adfixa videtur
stella, micans tali specie talique nitore.

Prisc. xiv. 6. 52.

F. XV. Hic pressu duplici palmarum continet Anguem
atque eius ipse manet religatus corpore torto ;
namque virum medium serpens sub pectora
     cingit.
Ille tamen nitens graviter vestigia ponit
atque oculos urget pedibus pectusque Nepai.

De Nat. Deor. ii. 42.

F. XVI. Arctophylax vulgo qui dicitur esse Boötes
quod quasi temoni adiunctam prae se quatit
     Arcton.

Ib. and Prisc. xiv. 6. 63.

F. x. summo aequore condit Dav.; subitoque recondit MSS.
generally ; subito aequore condit Or., Ba., Mu., *after* Grot. Partim . . .
in unam Klotz ; partim . . . in una MSS. *generally*.
  F. xvi. temoni Madv. *and editors* ; temone MSS.

F. XVII.
Subter praecordia fixa videtur
stella micans radiis, Arcturus nomine claro.
De Nat. Deor. ii. 42.

F. XVIII. Spicum illustre tenens splendenti corpore
Virgo.
Ib.

F. XIX. Malebant tenui contenti vivere cultu.
Lact. *Inst.* v. 5.

F. XX. Ferrea tum vero proles exorta repente est,
ausaque funestum prima est fabricarier ensem
et gustare manu vinctum domitumque iuven-
cum.
De Nat. Deor. ii. 63.

F. XXI. Et Iovis in regno caelique in parte resedit.
Lact. *Inst.* v. 5.

F. XXII. Tertia sub cauda ad genus ipsum lumina pandit.
Prisc. vi. 4. 19.

F. XXIII. Et natos Geminos invises sub caput Arcti.
Subiectus mediae est Cancer, pedibusque
tenetur
magnu' Leo tremulam quatiens e corpore
flammam.
De Nat. Deor. ii. 43.

F. XXIV. Hoc motu radiantis Etesiae in vada Ponti.
Orator 45.

F. XXV. Navibus absumptis fluitantia quaerere aplustra.
Prisc. vii. 15. 74.

F. xviii. spicum illustre ferens insigni corpore Virgo, Serv., *ad Georg.*,
i. iii.

F. xx. vinctum (B.E.) A. ; *corr. from* ' victum.'

F. xxiii. mediae est *editors after* Grot.; media est (= mediaest)
MSS.

F. XXVI.   Sub laeva Geminorum obductus parte feretur.
Adversum caput huic Helice truculenta tuetur
At Capra laevum humerum clara obtinet.

De Nat. Deor. ii. 43.

F. XXVII.   Verum haec est magno atque illustri praedita
signo ;
contra Haedi exiguum iaciunt mortalibus
ignem.

Ib.

F. XXVIII.   Corniger est valido connixus corpore Taurus.

Ib.

F. XXIX.   Has Graeci stellas Hyadas vocitare suërunt.

Ib.

F. XXX.   Tam Tauri laevum cornu dexterque simul pes.
Probus (*De ult. syll.* p. 223. 29. K.)

F. XXXI.   Namque ipse ad tergum Cynosurae vertitur
Arcti.

De Nat. Deor. ii. 43.

F. XXXII.   Obscura specie stellarum Cassiepia :
hanc autem illustri versatur corpore propter
Andromeda aufugiens aspectum maesta par-
entis.
Huic Equus ille iubam quatiens fulgore
micanti
summum contingit caput alvo, stellaque iun-
gens
una tenet duplices communi lumine formas,
aeternum ex astris cupiens connectere nodum.
Exin contortis Aries cum cornibus haeret.

Ib.

F. xxvi. Helice, Elicae MSS. *generally* ;   Helicae *editors after*
Grot. ; Hellices Allen.
F. xxxi. ipse Dav., Hein., Or., Ba. ; ipsum MSS. *generally.*
F. xxxii. Andromeda aufugiens V. (*by corr. in* A.B.) ; Andromeda
haud fugiens C.T. ; Andromeda haut fugiens E. ; Andromeda fugiens
Asconius.

E quibus hunc subter possis cognoscere fultum.
Nam caeli mediam partem terit, ut prius illae
Chelae : tum pectus quoque cernitur Orionis.
Et prope conspicies parvum sub pectore claro
Andromedae signum, Deltoton dicere Graii   5
quod soliti, simili quia forma littera claret :
huic spatio ductum simili latus exstat utrumque ;
at non tertia pars lateris—namque est minor illis—
sed stellis longe densis praeclara relucet.
    Inferior paullo est Aries et flamen ad Austri   10
inclinatior, atque etiam vehementius illi
Pisces, quorum alter paullo praelabitur ante
et magis horrisonis Aquilonis tangitur alis,
at quae horum e caudis duplices velut esse catenae
dicuntur, sua diversae per lumina serpunt,   15
atque una tandem in stella communiter haerent,
quam veteres soliti caelestem dicere Nodum.
Andromedae laevo ex humero, si quaerere perges,
appositum poteris supera cognoscere Piscem.
    E pedibus natum summo Iove Persea vises,   20
quos humeris retinet defixo corpore Perseus,
quem summa ab regione Aquilonis flamina pulsant.
Hic dextram ad sedes intendit Cassiepiae,
diversosque pedes, vinctos talaribus aptis,
pulverulentus uti de terra elapsu' repente   25
in caelum victor magno sub culmine portat.
    At propter laevum genus omni ex parte locatas

  1. hunc Grot. ; hinc D.H.
  2. nam Grot. ; iam D. ; ima caeli H 2.
  3. quoque Grot. ; quod D.H. ; qua Baeh.
  4. claro *vulgo* ; clarae D.H.
  8. namque est minor H 2 ; nam non minor D ; nam onminor H 1.
  13. horrisonis Grot. *and* Morel. *supported by* H. Horriferis . . . auris,
Cic., *De Nat. Deor.*, ii. 43.
  14. at quae *vulgo*.
  16. tandem *edd.* ; tamen D.H.
  22. quem Cic., *De Nat. Deor.*, ii. 44 ; quam D. ; quom H. ; qua Baeh.
  27. omni ex parte Prisc. ; omnis parte D.H.

parvas Vergilias tenui cum luce videbis.
Hae septem vulgo perhibentur more vetusto
stellae, cernuntur vero sex undique parvae.   30
At non interiisse putari convenit unam :
sed frustra temere a vulgo ratione sine ulla
septem dicier, ut veteres statuere poetae,
aeterno cunctas sane qui nomine dignant,
Alcyone Meropeque, Celaeno Taygeteque,   35
Electra Steropeque, simul sanctissima Maia.
Hae tenues parvo labentes lumine lucent :
at magnum nomen signi clarumque vocatur,
propterea quod et aestatis primordia clarat
et post, hiberni praepandens temporis ortus,   40
admonet ut mandent mortales semina terris.
Inde Fides posita et leviter convexa videtur
Mercurius parvus manibus quam dicitur olim
in cunis fabricatus in alta sede locasse :
haec genus ad laevum Nixi delapsa resedit,   45
atque inter flexum genus et caput Alitis haesit.

   Namque est ales avis, lato sub tegmine caeli
quae volat et serpens geminis secat aëra pennis.

   Altera pars huic obscura est et luminis expers ;
altera nec parvis nec claris lucibus ardet,   50
sed mediocre iacit quatiens e corpore lumen.
Haec dextram Cephei dextro pede pellere palmam
gestit : iam vero clinata est ungula vemens
fortis Equi propter pinnati corporis alam.

   Ipse autem labens utrisque Equus ille tenetur   55
Piscibus ; huic cervix dextra mulcetur Aquari.
Serius haec obitus terrai visit equi vis,
quam gelidum valido de pectore frigus anhelans

34. sane H 2 ; sano D.H. ; dignant D.H. ; signant H 2.
42. posita et leviter convexa Baeh. ; leviter posita et convexa D.H. ;
conversa Bouh.
44. in cunis Grot., Grut. ; infirmis H *and* Baeh.
47. namque MSS., inde Cic., *De Nat. Deor.*, ii. 44.
55. utrisque *edd.* ; multis D. ; mutis Turneb.
58. quam MSS. ; tum Cic., *De Nat. Deor.*, ii. 44.

corpore semifero magno Capricornus in orbe ;
quem cum perpetuo vestivit lumine Titan,   60
brumali flectens contorquet tempore currum.
Hoc cave te ponto studeas committere mense :
nam non longinquum spatium labere diurnum :
non hiberna cito volvetur curriculo nox :
humida non sese vestris Aurora querelis   65
ocius ostendet, clari praenuntia Solis :
at validis aequor pulsabit viribus Auster :
tum fixum tremulo quatietur frigore corpus.
Sed tamen anni iam labuntur tempore toto,
nec cui signorum cedunt neque flamina vitant,   70
nec metuunt canos minitanti murmure fluctus.
    Atque etiam supero navi pelagoque vagato
mense, Sagittipotens Solis cum sustinet orbem,
nam iam tum nimis exiguo lux tempore praesto est.
Hoc signum veniens poterunt praenoscere nautae :   75
iam prope praecipitante licebit visere nocte,
ut sese ostendens emergit Scorpios alto,
posteriore trahens flexum vi corporis Arcum.
Iam supera cernes Arcti caput esse minoris
et magis erectum ad summum versarier orbem.   80
Tum sese Orion toto iam corpore condit
extrema prope nocte et Cepheus conditur ante
lumborum tenus a palma depulsus ad umbras.
    Hic, missore vacans, fulgens iacet una Sagitta,
quam propter nitens pinna convolvitur Ales :   85
haec clinata magis paullo est Aquilonis ad auras.
At propter se Aquila ardenti cum corpore portat,
(igniferum mulcens tremebundis aethera pinnis,)

72. vagato D.H. ; vagatur H 2 ; vacato Patric.
74. tum nimis Lamb. ; tum minus D.H. ; cum minus H 2.
77. ostendens emergit Cic., *De Nat. Deor.*, ii. 44 ; ostendens ostendat
(-dat ? D.) D.H. ; emergens ostendit Asc. *and some edd.*
82. ante *vulgo* ; alto Grot.
83. a palma Morel ; a prima D.H.
84. hic H. ; hinc D. ; missore vacans Morel. ; misso revocans D.
85. pinna H. ; penna D.

non nimis ingenti cum corpore, sed grave maestis
ostendit nautis perturbans aequora signum.   90
　　Tum magni curvus Capricorni corpora propter
Delphinus iacet, haud nimio lustratu' nitore,
praeter quadruplices stellas in fronte locatas,
quas intervallum binas disterminat unum.
Cetera pars late tenui cum lumine serpit.   95
Illae, quae fulgent luces ex ore corusco,
sunt inter partes gelidas Aquiloni' locatae,
atque inter spatium et laeti vestigia Solis.
At pars inferior Delphini fusa videtur
inter Solis iter, simul inter flamina venti,   100
viribus erumpit qua summi spiritus Austri.
　　Exinde Orion, obliquo corpore nitens,
inferiora tenet truculenti corpora Tauri :
quem qui suspiciens in caelum nocte serena
late dispersum non viderit, haud ita vero   105
cetera se speret cognoscere signa potesse.
　　Namque pedes subter rutilo cum lumine claret
fervidus ille Canis stellarum luce refulgens.
Hunc tegit obscurus subter praecordia venter :
nec toto spirans rabido de corpore flammam   110
aestiferos validis erumpit flatibus ignes :
totus ab ore micans iacitur mortalibus ardor.
Hic ubi se pariter cum Sole in lumina caeli
extulit, haud patitur foliorum tegmine frustra
suspensos animos arbusta ornata tenere.   115
Nam quorum stirpes tellus amplexa prehendit,
haec augens anima vitali flamine mulcet :
at quorum nequeunt radices findere terras,
denudat foliis ramos et cortice truncos.
　　Hunc propter subterque pedes, quos diximus ante, 120
Orioni' iacet levipes Lepus.　Hic fugit, ictus
horrificos metuens rostri tremebundus acuti.

　　109. venter Turneb. *and* Grot. ;　vesper D.H.
　　110. nec *vulgo* ;　at vero toto D. ;　et vero toto H.
　　121. Orionis D.H.

Nam Canis infesto sequitur vestigia cursu,
praecipitantem agitans, oriens iam denique paullo,
curriculum nunquam defesso corpore sedans.   125
    At Canis ad caudam serpens prolabitur Argo
conversam prae se portans cum lumine puppim :
non aliae naves ut in alto ponere proras
ante solent rostro Neptunia prata secantes,
sed conversa retro caeli se per loca portat :   130
sicut cum coeptant tutos contingere portus,
obvertunt navem magno cum pondere nautae,
aversamque trahunt optata ad litora puppim.
Sic conversa vetus super aethera labitur Argo,
atque usque a prora ad celsum sine lumine malum   135
a malo ad puppim cum lumine clara videtur :
inde gubernaclum, disperso lumine fulgens,
clari posteriora Canis vestigia tangit.
    Exin semotam procul in tutoque locatam
Andromedam tamen explorans fera quaerere Pistrix 140
pergit, et usque sitam validas Aquilonis ad auras
caerula vestigat finita in partibus Austri.
Hanc Aries tegit et squamoso corpore Pisces,
Fluminis inlustri tangentem pectore ripas.
    Namque etiam Eridanum cernes in parte locatum 145
caeli, funestum magnis cum viribus amnem,
quem lacrimis maestae Phaëthontis saepe sorores
sparserunt, letum maerenti voce canentes.
Hunc Orionis sub laeva cernere planta
serpentem poteris proceraque vincla videbis,   150
quae retinent Pisces, caudarum a parte locata
Flumine mixta retro ad Pistricis terga reverti.
Haec una stella nectuntur quam iacit ex se

127. conversam Hyginus ; convexam D.H.
133. adversamque MSS. ; aversamque *coni.* Grot.
136. cum lumine clara Grot. ; clara cum luce D.H.
138. tangit Hyginus ; condit D. ; candet H.
144. inlustri Cic., *De Nat. Deor.*, ii. 44 ; illustri D.H 2 ; lustri
H 1 ; inlustris *coni.* Orelli ; pectore Hein., Allen, Baeh. ; corpore D.H.

Pistricis spina evalida cum luce refulgens.
   Exinde exiguae tenui cum lumine multae 155
inter Pistricem fusae sparsaeque videntur
atque Gubernaclum stellae, quas contegit omnes,
formidans acrem morsum, Lepus : his neque nomen
nec formam veteres certam statuisse videntur.
Nam quas sideribus claris natura polivit 160
et vario pinxit distinguens lumine formas,
has ille astrorum custos ratione notavit
signaque signavit caelestia nomine vero :
has autem, quae sunt parvo sub lumine fusae,
consimili specie stellas parilique nitore, 165
non potuit nobis nota clarare figura.
   Exinde, australem soliti quem dicere Piscem,
volvitur inferior Capricorno versus ad Austrum,
Pistricem observans, procul illis Piscibus haerens.
At prope conspicies, expertes nominis omnes, 170
inter Pistricem et Piscem, quem diximus, Austri
stellas, sub pedibus stratas radiantis Aquari.
   Propter Aquarius obscurum dextra rigat amnem
exiguo qui stellarum candore nitescit.
E multis tamen his duo late lumina fulgent : 175
unum sub magnis pedibus cernetur Aquari.
Quod superest, gelido delapsum flumine fontis,
spiniferam subter caudam Pistricis adhaesit :
hae tenues stellae perhibentur nomine Aquai ;
hic aliae volitant parvo cum lumine clarae, 180
atque priora pedum subeunt vestigia magni
Arcitenentis et obscurae sine nomine cedunt.
   Inde Nepae cernes propter fulgentis acumen

154. spinae valida D.H.; *corr.* Grot.
160. quas ('s' *corr. ex* 'e ?') H.; neque D.
162. has ('s' *in ras.*) H 2.
163. signavit ('s' *in ras.*) H 2 ; dignavit D.
167. dicere H.; discere D.
176. magni Aldus.
179. Aquai Morel.; Aquarii D.; Aquari H.

Aram, quam flatu permulcet spiritus Austri,
exiguo superum quae lumina tempore tranat :   185
nam procul Arcturo est adversa parte locata.
Arcturo magnum spatium supera dedit, orbem
Iuppiter huic parvum inferiori in parte locavit.
Haec tamen aeterno invisens loca curriculo nox,
signa dedit nautis, cuncti quae noscere possent,   190
commiserans hominum metuendos undique casus.
Nam cum fulgentem cernes sine nubibus atris
Aram, sub media caeli regione locatam,
a summa parte obscura caligine tectam,
tum validis fugito devitans viribus Austrum :   195
quem si prospiciens vitaveris, omnia caute
armamenta locans, tuto labere per undas,
sin gravis inciderit vehementi flamine ventus,
perfringit celsos defixo robore malos :
ut res nulla feras possit mulcere procellas,   200
ni parte ex Aquilonis opacam pellere nubem
coeperit et subitis auris diduxerit Ara.
Sin humeros medio in caelo Centaurus habebit,
ipseque caerulea contectus nube feretur,
atque Aram tenui caligans vestiet umbra,   205
ad signorum obitum vis est metuenda Favoni.
Ille autem Centaurus in alta sede locatus,
qua sese clarum conlucens Scorpios infert,
hunc subter, partem praeportans ipse virilem,
cedit, equi partes properans subiungere Chelis.   210
Hic dextram porgens, Quadrupes qua vasta tenetur,
quam nemo certo donavit nomine Graium,
tendit et illustrem truculentus caedit ad Aram.
  Hic sese infernis de partibus erigit Hydra,

185. lumine tempora D.H. ; lumina tempore *corr.* Turneb.
187. spatium supera Grot. ; spatium supero H. ; spatiumq super D. ;
spatio supera Lamb. ; orbem D. ; orbe═H.
209. hunc Orelli ; haec D. ; ═a═c H.
210. subiungere Cic., *De Nat. Deor.*, ii. 44 ; Grot. ; properat con-
iungere D.H.
213. caedit B.C.V., *De Nat. Deor.*, ii. 44 ; cedit D.H.

praecipiti lapsu flexo cum corpore serpens.   215
Haec, caput atque oculos torquens ad terga Nepai,
convexoque sinu subiens inferna Leonis,
Centaurum leni contingit lubrica cauda :
in medioque sinu fulgens Cratera relucet.
Extremam nitens plumato corpore Corvus   220
rostro tundit, et hic Geminis est ille sub ipsis
Ante-Canis, Graio Procyon qui nomine fertur.
   Haec sunt quae visens nocturno tempore signa
aeternumque volens mundi pernoscere motum,
legitimo cernes caelum lustrantia cursu.   225
Nam quae per bis sex signorum labier orbem
quinque solent stellae simili ratione notari
non possunt : quia quae faciunt vestigia cursu,
non eodem semper spatio protrita feruntur.
Sic malunt errare vagae per nubila caeli,   230
atque suos vario motu metirier orbes.
Hae faciunt magnos longinqui temporis annos,
cum redeunt ad idem caeli sub tegmine signum :
quarum ego nunc nequeo tortos evolvere cursus :
verum haec quae semper certo volvuntur in orbe   235
fixa, simul magnos edemus gentibus orbes.
   Quattuor, aeterno lustrantes lumine mundum,
orbes stelligeri portantes signa feruntur,
amplexi terras caeli sub tegmine fulti.
E quibus annorum volitantia lumina nosces,   240
quae densis distincta licebit cernere signis.
Tum magnos orbes magno cum lumine latos,
vinctos inter se et nodis caelestibus aptos,
atque pari spatio duo cernes esse duobus.
At si nocturno convisens tempore caelum   245
cum neque caligans detersit sidera nubes,

222. Ante-canis Lamb., Orelli ; Ante-canem MSS. *and* Baeh.
229. feruntur *vulgo* ; teruntur D.H.
232. hae H. ; haec D.
234. tortos H. ; ot ' tuos (= tortuos ?) D. ; totos *vulgo*.
242. tum D.H. ; tam Orelli.

nec pleno stellas superavit lumine Luna,
vidisti magnum candentem serpere circum ;
Lacteus hic nimio fulgens candore notatur.
Is non perpetuum detexens conficit orbem :   250

    .   .   .   .   .

sed spatio multum superis praestare duobus
dicitur et late caeli lustrare cavernas.
   Quorum alter tangens Aquilonis vertitur auras,
ora petens Geminorum illustria : tum genus ardens
in sese retinens Aurigae portat utrumque.   255
Hunc sura laeva Perseus humeroque sinistro
tangit : at Andromeda hic dextra de parte tenetur ;
imponitque pedes duplices Equus ; et simul ales
ponit avis caput et clinato corpore tergum :
Anguitenens humeris connititur ; illa recedens   260
Austrum consequitur devitans corpore Virgo.
At vero totum spatium convestiet orbis
magnu' Leo et claro conlucens lumine Cancer,
in quo consistens convertit curriculum Sol
aestivus, medio distinguens corpore cursus.   265
Hic totus medius circo disiungitur : iste
pectoribus validis atque alvo possidet orbem.
Hunc octo in partes divisum noscere circum
si potes, invenies supero convertier orbe
quinque pari spatio, partes tres esse relictas,   270
tempore nocturno quas vis inferna frequentat.

    .   .   .   .   .

Alter ab infernis Austri convertitur auris.
(Arcitenens humeris connititur ille recedens)   272a
Distribuens medium subter secat hic Capricornum,
atque pedes gelidum rivum fundentis Aquari,
caeruleamque ferae caudam Pistricis, et illum   275
fulgentem Leporem, inde pedes Canis, et simul amplam
Argolicam retinet claro cum lumine Navem :
tergaque Centauri atque Nepai portat acumen :

  265. aestivus H. ; aestivos D.
  272a. Cf. 260. *The verse is found in* D.H.

inde Sagittari defixum possidet arcum.
Hunc a clarisonis auris Aquilonis ad Austrum   280
cedens, postremum tangit rota fervida Solis ;
exinde in superas brumali tempore flexens
se recipit sedes : huic orbi quinque tributae
nocturnae partes, supera tres luce dicantur.

    Hosce inter mediam partem retinere videtur   285
tantus, quantus erit conlucens Lacteus orbis.
In quo auctumnali atque iterum Sol lumine verno
exaequat spatium lucis cum tempore noctis.
Hunc retinens Aries sublucet corpore totus,
atque genu flexo Taurus connititur ingens :   290
Orion claro contingens pectore fertur :
Hydra tenet flexu : Cratera et Corvus adhaeret :
et paucae e Chelis stellae : simul Anguitenentis
sunt genua et summi Iovis Ales nuntius instat :
propter Equus capite et cervicum lumine tangit.   295
    Hosce aequo spatio devinctos sustinet axis,
per medios summo caeli de vertice tranans.
Ille autem claro quartus cum lumine circus
partibus extremis extremos continet orbes,
et simul a medio media de parte secatur,   300
atque obliquus in his nitens cum lumine fertur :
ut nemo cui sancta manu doctissima Pallas
sollertem ipsa dedit fabricae rationibus artem,
tam tornare cate contortos possiet orbes,
quam sunt in caelo divino numine flexi,   305
terram cingentes, ornantes lumine mundum,
culmine transverso retinentes sidera fulta.
Quattuor hi motu cuncti volvuntur eodem.
Sed tantum supera terras semper tenet ille
curriculum, oblique inflexus tribus orbibus unus,   310
quanto est divisus Cancer spatio a Capricorno ;
at subter terras spatium par esse necesse est :

   291. pectore Morel. ; corpore D.H.
   292. Cratera et Turneb., *app.* Grot. ; Crateram D.H.
   304. possiet *vulgo* ; possidet D. ; posceret H.

et quantos radios iacimus de lumine nostro,
quis hunc convexum caeli contingimus orbem,
sex tantae poterunt sub eum succedere partes,   315
bina pari spatio caelestia signa tenentes.
Zodiacum hunc Graeci vocitant, nostrique Latini
orbem signiferum perhibebunt nomine vero :
nam gerit hic volvens bis sex ardentia signa.
Aestifer est pandens ferventia sidera Cancer.   320
Hunc subter fulgens cedit vis torva Leonis,
quem rutilo sequitur conlucens corpore Virgo.
Exin proiectae claro cum lumine Chelae :
ipsaque consequitur lucens vis magna Nepai,
inde Sagittipotens dextra flexum tenet arcum :   325
post hunc ore fero Capricornus vadere pergit :
humidus inde loci conlucet Aquarius orbe.
Exin squamiferi serpentes ludere Pisces :
quis comes est Aries, obscuro lumine labens,
inflexoque genu proiecto corpore Taurus,   330
et Gemini, clarum iactantes lucibus ignem.
Haec Sol aeterno convestit lumine lustrans,
annua conficiens vertenti tempora cursu.
Hic quantum terris convexus pellitur orbis,
tantumdem ille patens supera mortalibus exit.   335
Sex omni semper cedunt labentia nocte,
tot caelum rursus fugientia signa revisunt.
Hoc spatium tranans caecis nox conficit umbris,
quod supera terras prima de nocte relictum
signifero ex orbi sex signorum ordine fultum.   340
    Quod si Solis aves certos cognoscere cursus,
ortus signorum nocturno tempore vises :
nam semper signum exoriens Titan trahit unum.

327. orbe *vulgo* ; orbem D.H.
328. squamiferi D.H.
333. vertenti Grot. ; vertentia D.H.
335. tantumdem ille patens *vulgo* ;   tantumdem pandens D.H. ;
tantum se pandens Baeh. ; exit *vulgo* ; edit D.H. ; mortalibu' cedit Or.
340. orbi sex H. ; orbis sex D. ; orbist et Grot.

Sin autem officiens signis mons obstruet altus,
aut adiment lucem caeca caligine nubes :   345
certas ipse notas caeli de tegmine sumens,
ortus atque obitus omnes cognoscere possis.
Quae simul existant, cernes ; quae tempore eodem
praecipitent obitum, nocturno tempore nosces.

    Nam simul ut supero se totum lumine Cancer   350
extulit, extemplo cedit delapsa Corona,
et loca convisit cauda tenus infera Piscis.
Dimidiam retinet stellis distincta Corona
partem etiam supera, atque alia de parte repulsa est :
quam tamen insequitur Piscis, nec totus ad umbras   355
tractus sed supero contectus corpore cedit.
Atque humeros usque a genibus clarumque recondit
Anguitenens validis magnum a cervicibus Anguem.
Iam vero Arctophylax non aequa parte secatur,
nam brevior clara caeli de parte videtur,   360
amplior infernas depulsus possidet umbras.
Quattuor hic obiens secum deducere signa
signifero solet ex orbi : tum serius ille,
cum supera sese satiavit luce, recedit,
post mediam labens claro cum corpore noctem.   365
Haec obscura tenens convestit sidera tellus ;
at parte ex alia claris cum lucibus errat
Orion, humeris et lato pectore fulgens,
et dextra retinens non cassum luminis ensem.

    Sed cum de terris vis est patefacta Leonis,   370
omnia quae Cancer praeclaro detulit ortu,
cedunt obscurata, simul vis magna Aquilai
pellitur, ac flexo considens corpore Nixus
iam supero ferme depulsus lumine cedit :
sed laevum genus atque illustrem linquit in altum   375
plantam. Tum contra exoritur clarum caput Hydrae
et Lepus et Procyon qui sese fervidus infert
Ante-Canem : inde Canis vestigia prima videntur.

355. quam H (*apographa*) ; cum D.
372. simul vis magna Aquilai Turneb ; simul vis maior Aquari *vulgo*.

Non pauca e caelo depellens signa, repente
exoritur pandens illustria lumina Virgo.   380
Cedit clara Fides Cyllenia, mergitur unda
Delphinus, simul obtegitur depulsa Sagitta,
atque Avis ad summam caudam primasque recedit
pinnas et magnus pariter delabitur Amnis.
Hic Equus a capite et longa cervice latescit :   385
longius exoritur iam claro corpore serpens
Crateraque tenus lucet mortalibus Hydra.
Inde pedes Canis ostendit iam posteriores,
et post ipse trahit claro cum lumine Puppim ;
insequitur labens per caeli lumina Navis,   390
et cum iam toto processit corpore Virgo,
haec medium ostendit radiato stipite malum.

At cum procedunt obscuro corpore Chelae,
exsistit pariter larga cum luce Boötes,
cuius in adversum est Arcturus corpore fixus,   395
totaque iam supera fulgens prolabitur Argo :
Hydraque quod late caelo dispersa tenetur,
nondum tota patet, nam caudam contegit umbra.
Iam dextrum genus et decoratam lumine suram
erigit ille vacans vulgato nomine Nixus ;   400
quem nocte exstinctum atque exortum vidimus una,
persaepe ut parvum tranans geminaverit orbem.
Hic genus et suram cum Chelis erigit alte :
ipse autem praeceps obscura nocte tenetur,
dum Nepa et Arcitenens invisant lumina caeli :   405
nam secum medium pandet Nepa, tollere vero
in caelum totum exoriens conabitur Arcus.
Hic tribus elatus cum signis corpore toto
lucet ; at exoritur media de parte Corona,
caudaque Centauri extremo candore refulget.   410
Hic se iam totum caecas Equus abdit in umbras,
quem rutila fulgens pluma praetervolat Ales.
Occidit Andromedae clarum caput et fera Pistrix

394. exsistit H 2 ; existet D.H 1.
395. adversum *vulgo* ; adverso H. ; adversa D.

labitur, horribiles epulas funesta requirens.
Hanc contra Cepheus non cessat tendere palmas :   415
illa usque ad spinam mergens se caerula condit.
At Cepheus caput atque humeros palmasque reclinat.
    Cum vero vis est vehemens exorta Nepai,
late fusa volat .   .   .   .
    .   .   .   .   haec per terras fama vagatur :   420
ut quondam Orion manibus violasse Dianam
dicitur, excelsis errans in collibus amens,
quos tenet Aegaeo defixa in gurgite Chius,
Bacchica quam viridi convestit tegmine vitis.
Ille feras vecors amenti corde necabat,   425
Oenopionis avens epulas ornare nitentes.
At vero pedibus subito percussa Dianae,
insula discessit disiectaque saxa revellens
perculit et caecas lustravit luce lacunas :
e quibus ingenti exsistit cum corpore prae se   430
Scorpios infestus praeportans flebile acumen.
Hic valido cupide venantem perculit ictu,
mortiferum in venas figens per vulnera virus :
ille gravi moriens constravit corpore terram.
Quare cum magnis sese Nepa lucibus effert,   435
Orion fugiens commendat corpora terris.
Tum vero fugit Andromeda et Neptunia Pistrix
tota latet : cedit converso corpore Cepheus,
extremas medio contingens corpore terras.
Hic caput et superas potis est demergere partes :   440
infera lumborum nunquam convestiet umbra.
Nam retinent Arctoe, lustrantes lumine suras.
Labitur illa simul, gnatam lacrimosa requirens,
Cassiepia neque ex caelo depulsa decore
fertur : nam verso contingens vertice primum   445
terras, post humeris eversa sede refertur.
Hanc illi tribuunt poenam Nereïdes almae,
cum quibus, ut perhibent, ausa est contendere forma.

423. Chius Grot.; Echinus Ald.; Echineis *vulgo*.
424. Bacchica Lamb.; brachia D.H.; quam D.H 1; quae H 2.

Haec obit inclinata : et pars exorta Coronae est
altera cum caudaque omnis iam panditur Hydra.   450
At caput et totum sese Centaurus opacis
eripit e tenebris, linquens vestigia parva
antepedum contecta, simul cum lumine pandit
ipse feram dextra retinet . . . .
. . . . Prolabitur inde   455
Anguitenens capite et manibus : profert simul Anguis
iam caput et summum flexo de corpore lumen.
   Hic ille exoritur converso corpore Nixus,
alvum, crura, humeros simul et praecordia lustrans,
et dextra radios laeto cum lumine iactans.   460
Inde Sagittipotens superas cum visere luces
institit, emergit Nixi caput et simul effert
sese clara Fides et promit pectore Cepheus.
Fervidus ille Canis toto cum corpore cedit :
abditur Orion : obit et Lepus abditus umbra ;   465
inferiora cadunt Aurigae lumina lapsu.
Crus dextrumque pedem linquens obit infera Perseus
in loca, tum cedens a puppi linquitur Argo.
Inde obiens Capricornus ab alto lumine pellit
Aurigam instantemque Capram, parvos simul Haedos, 470
et magnam antiquo depellit nomine Navem.
Obruitur Procyon ; emergunt alite lapsu
e terris Volucres ; exsistit clara Sagitta.
Sed cum se medium caeli in regione locavit
magnus Aquarius et vestivit lumine terras,   475
tum pedibus simul et supera cervice iubata
cedit Equus fugiens : at contra signipotens nox
cauda Centaurum retinens, ad se rapit ipsa :
nec potis est caput atque humeros obducere latos :
at vero serpentis Hydrae caligine caeca   480
cervicem atque oculorum ardentia lumina vestit :
hanc autem totam properant depellere Pisces.

462. emergit *vulgo* ; et mergit H.D.
465. obiit simul abditus umbra est H.

PROGNOSTICA

F. I.   Ut cum luna means Hyperionis officit orbi,
stinguuntur radii caeca caligine tecti.

Prisc. x. 2. 11.

F. II.   Ast autem tenui quae candet lumine Phatne.

Ib. xvi. 2. 16 ; xviii. 21. 172.

F. III.   Atque etiam ventos praemonstrat saepe futuros
inflatum mare, cum subito penitusque tumescit,
saxaque cana salis niveo spumata liquore
tristificas certant Neptuno reddere voces,
aut densus stridor cum celso e vertice montis
ortus adaugescit scopulorum saepe repulsus.

De Div. i. 7. 13.

F. IV.   Cana fulix itidem fugiens e gurgite ponti
nuntiat horribiles clamans instare procellas,
haud modicos tremulo fundens e gutture cantus.

Ib. i. 8. 14.

F. V.   Vos quoque signa videtis, aquai dulcis alumnae,
cum clamore paratis inanes fundere voces
absurdoque sono fontes et stagna cietis.

Ib. i. 9. 15.

F. VI.   Saepe etiam pertriste canit de pectore carmen
et matutinis acredula vocibus instat,
vocibus instat et assiduas iacit ore querellas,
cum primum gelidos rores aurora remittit ;
fuscaque nonnunquam cursans per litora cornix
demersit caput et fluctum cervice recepit.

Ib. i. 8. 14.

F. VII.   Mollipedesque boves spectantes lumina caeli
naribus umiferum duxere ex aëre succum.

Ib. i. 9. 15.

F. VIII. Iam vero semper viridis semperque gravata
Lentiscus triplici solita grandescere fetu
ter fruges fundens tria tempora monstrat arandi.
Ib.
Pliny *N.H.* xviii. 25. 61.

F. IX. Caprigeni pecoris custos de gurgite vasto.
Prisc. vi. 1. 3.

HOMERIC TRANSLATIONS

THE ILIAD

I

Ferte, viri, et duros animo tolerate labores,
auguris ut nostri Calchantis fata queamus
scire, ratosne habeant an vanos pectoris orsus.
Namque omnes memori portentum mente retentant,
qui non funestis liquerunt lumina fatis.   5
Argolicis primum ut vestita est classibus Aulis,
quae Priamo cladem et Troiae pestemque ferebant,
nos circum latices gelidos fumantibus aris
aurigeris divom placantes numina tauris
sub platano umbrifera, fons unde emanat aquai,   10
vidimus inmani specie tortuque draconem
terribilem, Iovis ut pulsu penetraret ab ara ;
qui platani in ramo foliorum tegmine saeptos
corripuit pullos ; quos cum consumeret octo,
nona super tremulo genetrix clangore volabat,   15
cui ferus inmani laniavit viscera morsu.
Hunc ubi tam teneros volucres matremque peremit,
qui luci ediderat genitor Saturnius idem
abdidit et duro formavit tegmine saxi.
Nos autem timidi stantes mirabile monstrum   20
vidimus in mediis divom versarier aris.
Tum Calchas haec est fidenti voce locutus :
' Quidnam torpentes subito obstipuistis, Achivi ?
Nobis haec portenta deum dedit ipse creator

99

tarda et sera nimis, sed fama ac laude perenni. 25
Nam quot aves taetro mactatas dente videtis,
tot nos ad Troiam belli exanclabimus annos,
quae decumo cadet et poena satiabit Achivos.'
Édidit haec Calchas ; quae iam matura videtis.
De Div. ii. 30. 63.
Iliad ii. 299–330.

II

Qui miser in campis maerens errabat Aleïs,
ipse suum cor edens, hominum vestigia vitans.
Tusc. Disp. iii. 26. 63.
Iliad vi. 201–2.

III

' Hic situs est vitae iam pridem lumina linquens
qui quondam Hectoreo perculsus concidit ense.'
Fabitur haec aliquis, mea semper gloria vivet.
De Gloria 2 (ap. Gell. xv. 6).
Iliad vii. 89–91.

IV

Prospera Iuppiter his dextris fulgoribus edit.
De Div. ii. 39. 82.
Iliad ix. 236.

V

Tertia te Phthiae tempestas laeta locabit.
De Div. i. 25. 52.
Iliad ix. 363.

VI

Corque meum penitus turgescit tristibus iris,
cum decore atque omni me orbatum laude recordor.
Tusc. Disp. iii. 9. 18.
Iliad ix. 646–8.

100

VII

Namque nimis multos atque omni luce cadentes
cernimus, ut nemo possit maerore vacare.
Quo magis est aequum tumulis mandare peremptos
firmo animo et luctum lacrimis finire diurnis.

Tusc. Disp. iii. 27. 65.
Iliad xix. 226–9.

THE ODYSSEY

I

O decus Argolicum, quin puppim flectis, Ulixes,
auribus ut nostros possis agnoscere cantus ?
Nam nemo haec unquam est transvectus caerula cursu,
quin prius adstiterit vocum dulcedine captus,
post variis avido satiatus pectore musis   5
doctior ad patrias lapsus pervenerit oras.
Nos grave certamen belli clademque tenemus,
Graecia quam Troiae divino numine vexit,
omniaque e latis rerum vestigia terris.

De Fin. v. 18. 49.
Odyssey xii. 184–91.

II

Tales sunt hominum mentes, quali pater ipse
Iuppiter auctiferas lustravit lumine terras.

Aug. *De Civ. Dei* 5. 8.
Odyssey xviii. 136–7.

MISCELLANEOUS VERSES

I.   ALCYONES.
. . . hunc genuit claris delapsus ab astris
praevius Aurorae, solis noctisque satelles.

Nonius, p. 65 ; M. Linds. p. 90.

101

II.   LIMON.
     Tu quoque, qui solus lecto sermone, Terenti,
     conversum expressumque Latina voce Menan-
       drum
     in medium nobis sedatis motibus effers,
     quiddam come loquens atque omnia dulcia
       dicens.

                    Suet. *in vita Ter.* 5.

III.   THALIA MAESTA (?).
     Iam mare Tyrrhenum longe penitusque pal-
       umbes
     . . . reliquit.

                    Serv. *ad Eclog.* i. 58.

IV.   ELEGIAC COUPLETS.
     (*a*) Fundum Vettus vocat quem possit mittere
        funda :
        ni tamen exciderit, qua cava funda patet.
           Quint. *Inst. Orat.* viii. 6. 73.

     Extractam puteo situlam cum ponit in horto,
     ulterius standi non habet ille locum.
          Charis iv. p. 246 (ed. Putschius).
          Diomed. ii. p. 457.

     (*b*) Mors mea ne careat lacrimis : linquamus
        amicis
        maerorem ut celebrent funera cum gemitu.
          Tusc. Disp. i. 49. 117.

     (*c*) Dic, hospes, Spartae nos te hic vidisse
        iacentes,
        dum sanctis patriae legibus obsequimur.
          Ib. i. 42. 101.

V.   Ignaris homines in vita mentibus errant :
     Euthynous potitur fatorum numine leto.
     Sic fuit utilius finiri ipsique tibique.
          Ib. i. 48. 115.

VI. Consiliis nostris laus est attonsa Laconum.
Ib. v. 17. 49.

VII. Quod fore paratum est, id summum exsuperat
Iovem.
De Div. ii. 10. 25.

VIII. Croesus Halyn penetrans magnam pervertet opum
vim.
Ib. ii. 56. 115.

IX. Terrigenam, herbigradam, domiportam, sanguine,
cassam.
Ib. ii. 64. 133.

X. Haec habeo, quae edi quaeque exsaturata libido
hausit, at illa iacent multa et praeclara relicta.
Tusc. Disp. v. 35. 101.

XI. Flavit ab Epiro lenissimus Onchesmites.
Ep. ad Att. vii. 2. 1.

VERSES OF DOUBTFUL AUTHENTICITY

I. Emori nolo, sed me esse mortuum nihil aestimo.
Tusc. Disp. i. 8. 15.

II. Ego providebo rem istam et albae virgines.
De Div. i. 37. 81.

III. Bene qui coniciet, vatem hunc perhibebo optimum.
Ib. ii. 5. 12.

IV. Vitam regit Fortuna, non Sapientia.
Tusc. Disp. v. 9. 25.

V. Quam quisque norit artem, in hac se exerceat.
Ib. i. 18. 41.

VI. Vigilantem habemus consulem Caninium :
in consulatu somnum non vidit suo.
Macr. ii. 3. 6.
(*Vide* Burmann, *Lat. Anth.* i. p. 307 ; ii. Ep. 128.)

TRANSLATIONS OF AESCHYLUS AND SOPHOCLES

AESCHYLUS

F. I.   *Oc.* Atqui, Prometheu, te hoc tenere existimo,
              mederi posse rationem iracundiae.
          Pr. Si quidem qui tempestivam medicinam
              admovens,
                 non ad gravescens vulnus illidat manus.

Tusc. Disp. iii. 31. 76.
Aesch. *Prom. Des.* 378 *et sqq.*

F. II.   Titanum suboles, socia nostri sanguinis,
           generata caelo, aspicite religatum asperis,
           vinctumque saxis, navem ut horrisono freto
           noctem paventes timidi adnectunt navitae.
           Saturnius me sic infixit Iuppiter,   5
           Iovisque numen Mulciberi adscivit manus.
           Hos ille cuneos fabricata crudeli inserens,
           perrupit artus : qua miser sollertia
           transverberatus castrum hoc Furiarum incolo.
           Iam tertio me quoque funesto die,   10
           tristi advolatu, aduncis lacerans unguibus
           Iovis satelles pastu dilaniat fero.
           Tum iecore opimo farta et satiata adfatim,
           clangorem fundit vastum et, sublime avolans,
           pinnata cauda nostrum adulat sanguinem.   15
           Cum vero adesum inflatu renovatumst iecur,
           tum rursus taetros avida se ad pastus refert.
           Sic hanc custodem maesti cruciatus alo,
           quae me perenni vivum foedat miseria.
           Namque, ut videtis, vinclis constrictus Iovis,   20
           arcere nequeo diram volucrem a pectore.
           Sic me ipse viduus pestes excipio anxias,
           amore mortis terminum anquirens mali.
           Sed longe a leto numine aspellor Iovis :
           atque haec vetusta, saeclis glomerata horridis,   25

104

luctifica clades nostro infixa est corpori :
e quo liquatae solis ardore excidunt
guttae, quae saxa adsidue instillant Caucasi.
Tusc. Disp. ii. 10. 23.

SOPHOCLES

F. III.   O multa dictu gravia, perpessu aspera,
quae corpore exanclata atque animo pertuli !
Nec mihi Iunonis terror implacabilis,
nec tantum invexit tristis Eurystheus mali,
quantum una vecors Oenei partu edita :   5
haec me irretivit veste furiali inscium
quae latere inhaerens morsu lacerat viscera,
urgensque graviter pulmonum haurit spiritus.
Iam decolorem sanguinem omnem exsorbuit :
sic corpus clade horribili absumptum extabuit. 10
Ipse illigatus peste interimor textili.
Hos non hostilis dextra, non terra edita
moles Gigantum, non biformato impetu
Centaurus ictus corpori inflixit meo,
non Graia vis, non barbara ulla immanitas,   15
non saeva terris gens religata ultimis,
quas peragrans undique omnem ecferitatem
   expuli ;
sed femineae vir, femineae interimor manu.
O nate, vere hoc nomen usurpa patri
ne me occidentem matris superet caritas.   20
Huc adripe ad me manibus abstractam piis.
Iam cernam mene an illam potiorem putes.
Perge, aude, nate, illacrima patris pestibus :
miserere : gentes nostras flebunt miserias.
Heu ! virginalem me ore ploratum edere,   25
quem vidit nemo ulli ingemiscentem malo !
Sic feminata virtus adflicta occidit ?
Accede, nate, adsiste ; miserandum aspice,
evisceratum corpus lacerati patris,
videte cuncti   30

. . . . Tuque caelestum sator,
iace, obsecro, in me vim coruscam fulminis.
Nunc, nunc dolorum anxiferi torquent vertices ;
nunc serpit ardor.   O ante victrices manus,
o pectora, o terga, o lacertorum tori !   35
Vestrone pressu quondam Nemeaeus leo
frendens efflavit graviter extremum halitum ?
Haec dextra Lernam taetram, mactata excetra,
pacavit ?   Haec bicorporem adflixit manum ?
Erymanthiam haec vastificam abiecit beluam ? 40
Haec e Tartarea tenebrica abstractum plaga
tricipitem eduxit Hydra generatum canem ?
Haec interemit tortu multiplicabili
Draconem, auriferam obtutu observantem
  arborem ?
Multa alia victrix nostra lustravit manus   45
nec quisquam e nostris spolia cepit laudibus.

Tusc. Disp. ii. 8. 20.
Soph. *Trachiniae* 1046 *et sqq.*

TRANSLATIONS OF EURIPIDES

F. I.   Neque nam terribilis ulla fando oratio est,
nec sors nec ira caelitum invectum malum
quod non natura humana patiendo ecferat.

Tusc. Disp. iv. 29. 63.
Eur. *Orestes* 1 *et sqq.*

F. II.   Nam si violandum est ius, regnandi gratia
violandum est : aliis rebus pietatem colas.

De Off. iii. 21. 82.
Eur. *Phœn.* 524–5.

F. III.   Nam nos decebat coetus celebrantes domum
lugere, ubi esset aliquis in lucem editus,
humanae vitae varia reputantes mala :

at qui labores morte finisset graves,
hunc omni amicos laude et laetitia exsequi.
                              Tusc. Disp. i. 48. 115.
                              Eur. Fr. *Cresphontes.*
                              (*Dindorf*, Fr. 452.)

F. IV.   Iuravi lingua, mentem iniuratam gero.
                              De Off. iii. 29. 108.
                              Eur. *Hippol.* 612.

F. V.   Mortalis nemo est quem non attingit dolor
         morbusque : multis sunt humandi liberi,
         rursus creandi : morsque est finita omnibus :
         quae generi humano angorem nequicquam ad-
            ferunt.
         Reddenda terrae est terra : tum vita omnibus
         metenda, ut fruges. Sic iubet Necessitas.
                              Tusc. Disp. iii. 25. 59.
                              Eur. Fr. *Hypsipyle.*

F. VI.   Nam qui haec audita a docto meminissem viro,
          futuras mecum commentabar miserias :
          aut mortem acerbam aut exsili maestam fugam,
          aut semper aliquam molem meditabar mali :
          ut, si qua invecta diritas casu foret,
          ne me imparatum cura laceraret repens.
                              Ib. iii. 14. 29.
                              Eur. Fr. *Theseus*

F. VII.   Si mihi nunc tristis primum illuxisset dies,
           nec tam aerumnoso navigassem salo,
           esset dolendi causa : ut iniecto equulei
           freno repente tractu exagitantur novo,
           sed iam subactus miseriis obtorpui.
                              Ib. iii. 28. 67.
         Galenus, *De dogm. Hippocr. et Platon.* iv. 7, vol. 5,
                              p. 418, ed. Kühn.

F. VIII.   Vides sublime fusum, immoderatum aethera,
qui terram tenero circumiectu amplectitur ?
Hunc summum habeto Divum : hunc perhibeto
Iovem.

De Nat. Deor. ii. 25. 65.
Eur. Fr. 836 (*Incert. Fab. Trag.* p. 825).

F. IX.   Suavis laborum est praeteritorum memoria.

De Fin. ii. 32. 105.
Eur. Fr. *Andromeda* (?).

§ THE COMMENTARY

DE CONSULATU

1–5.　" Lit by celestial fire, long years ago,
　　　　Jove on his course illumined all the world,
　　　　pervading earth and sky with holy mind
　　　　pent and confined in heaven's infinite wastes
　　　　wherein man's life and understanding lives."

1. *Principio.* Cf. Lucret. i. 271, 503; ii. 589, 1030, 1048, and Virg. *Georg.* ii. 9; iv. 8; *Aen.* iii. 381; vi. 724. The speaker throughout Book ii is the Muse Urania, an appropriate choice, inasmuch as most of the phenomena here described are astronomical. Book iii is given to Calliope, the Muse of epic poetry (see intro.).

aetherio . . . igni. Cf. Lucret. ii. 1098, 'ignibus aetheriis.'

flammatus Iuppiter. ' Flammatus ' is a favourite word of Cicero's. In this poem it occurs again in verses 21, 45. Cf. Lucret. ii. 672; Virg. *Aen.* i. 50; iii. 330. These first ten verses give the traditional Stoic account of the beginning of the world. Cf. *De Nat. Deor.* i. 37; ii. 23–8, 57–8; iii. 35. Virg. *Aen.* vi. 724 *et sqq.*

2. *conlustrat . . . mundum.* Cf. *Ph.* 332: " Haec Sol aeterno convestit lumine lustrans "; Virg. *Aen.* iv. 6: " Postera Phoebea lustrabat lampade terras." Pease (ed. *De Div.*) notes that in the *Ph.* ' lumine ' occurs in the 5th foot of the verse 47 times.

3. *petessit.* Cf. verse 22 below; also Lucret. iii. 648; v. 810. Festus (266 L), who writes ' petissit,' says that the form was frequentative.

5. *aetheris aeterni.* Note alliterations in this poem in

verses 7, 14, 18, 19, 24, 26, 27, 33, 39, 44, 45, 54, 57, 58, 60, 64, 65, 77. Jingles, formed by the repetition of similar syllables in close proximity, can be found (in addition to 'aetheris aeterni') in verses 10 ('omnia iam'), 12 ('stellarum ardore'), 14 ('mactasti lacte'). Cf., too, from amongst scores of examples in Cicero's poems: " O fortunatam natam me consule Romam."

inclusa cavernis. Cf. *Ph.* 252 : "caeli lustrare cavernas."

> 6–10. " And if to scan the movements of the stars
> upon their wandering courses be thy wish,
> to see which constellation harbours each—
> though Greeks in error claim they roam at will
> whereas spaced out they take an ordered course—
> not one thou'lt see which does not now appear
> by godlike inspiration clearly marked."

7. *signorum . . . locatae.* Cf. *Ph.* 317–19 :

" Zodiacum hunc Graeci vocitant, nostrique Latini orbem signiferum perhibebunt nomine vero : nam gerit hic volvens bis sex ardentia signa."

(Although the translation above and the quotation are in accordance with the usual interpretation of this passage, it is more probable that ' stellarum ' here means planets. (1) This sense gives more point to the clause " quae . . . locatae," having regard to the fact that the planets, in their orbits, move from one group of stars to another. (2) Cf. *De Nat. Deor.* ii. 20, where the planets are being discussed and note similarities of expression : " Maxime vero sunt admirabiles motus earum quinque stellarum, quae falso vocantur errantes. Nihil enim errat, quod in omni aeternitate conservat progressus et regressus reliquosque motus constantes et ratos." (3) In verse 11 ' astrorum ' = constellations, in contrast to ' stellarum ' in verse 6 and in verse 12.   (For the meaning of verse 12 cf. *Ph.* 233, remembering that this passage of omens is exaggerated.)

Against this interpretation is Cicero's own account of the planets in *Ph.* 226–34, where he appears to contradict the sense of verse 9 here.   But verse 9 is clearly inserted to suit the whole passage, which describes the ordered government of the universe.   Cf., too, " Nihil enim errat," etc., with *Ph.* 230 :

" Sic malunt (*sc.* planets) errare vagae per nubila caeli."

11–19.   " For first, when consul, thine it was to view
    the constellations speeding on their way,
    the ominous conjuncture of bright stars
    and many a sparkling comet's brilliant glare,
    what time thou did'st behold on Alba's hill
    her snow-capped mounds and graced the
       Latin rites
    with joyous stream of milk.   Thou did'st
      believe
    the turmoil of the night brought wild con-
      fusion ;
    since with that fateful time the Latin feast
    did almost coincide, when veiled the Moon
    her face, shining with massed array of
      splendour,
    and suddenly upon that star-decked night
    was all extinguished."

11. *Nam primum.* Cf. *In Cat.* iii. 18 *et sqq.* Sall. *Cat.* xxx. 2.   Cicero himself was not greatly perturbed by these omens. Cf. *De Div.* ii. 45–8. They have their use, however, for an author wishing to secure dramatic effect.   Considerable additional point would be imparted to ' astrorum volucres . . . motus ' by translating as " falling," or " shooting " stars.   The Latin could bear this meaning, although no exact parallels are available.

12. *ardore micantes.* ' Ardore ' is here used of light

rather than heat, although 'micare' is not necessarily connected with light (cf. verse 15). On 'micantes' Morel gives the following note: " micanti Anon. Philol. Anz., 1887, p. 399; micantis (-es). Cf. *Ph.* 112 micans . . . ardor." Neither reading affects the sense of the passage, and that in the text is perhaps preferable as being somewhat less obvious than 'micanti,' and as providing the common Ciceronian arrangement of a present participle in agreement with an already qualified noun.

13. *tu quoque.* In verse 11 note 'te consule'; the use of an ablative and a nominative referring to the same person (that person being the subject) is fairly common. The sense is emphasised by the addition of the ablative. Cf. " Profecto in aedes meas me absente neminem volo intromitti " (Pl. *Aul.* 98); " Me duce, ad hunc voti finem, me milite, veni " (Ovid *Am.* ii. 12. 13). Cf., too, Ovid *Fasti.* ii. 139; Lucret. vi. 142.

14. *laeto.* " Joyous " in the translation; but the word contains the idea of 'abundant.' Cf. *Georg.* iii. 310.

14. *mactasti.* Servius (*Aen.* ix. 641) says : " macte magis aucte, affecte gloria. Et est sermo tractus a sacris : quotiens enim aut tus aut vinum super victimam fundebatur, dicebant 'mactus est taurus vino vel ture,' hoc est cumulata est hostia et magis aucta." For the normal use of this word, cf. *In Vat.* vi. 14, " puerorum extis deos manes mactare," where the gods are object, the offerings ablative. Note the extension here whereby it takes the name of the festival as object.

14. *Latinas.* This rite, of great antiquity, had as its object the worship of Iuppiter Latiaris. This took place on the modern Monte Cavo, the highest peak (3,100 ft.) of the Alban hills. It was held at different times in each year, lasted usually for three or four days, and its most important result was the formation of a bond of union amongst the scattered tribes of Latium. Cf. Dion. Hal., *Ant. Rom.* iv. 154; Cic. *Pro Mil.* 31. 85. (Further in-

formation concerning this festival in Weiner, *De Feriis Latinis*, 1888.) This particular occasion must have coincided with the winter months—'tumulos . . . nivales'—possibly November. With this account of omens should be compared Lucret. i. 523 ; Ovid *Met.* xv. 782 ; Virg. *Georg.* i. 464.

15. *cometas.* Pease (*op. cit.*) in a long note would identify these astronomical phenomena with the ' aurora polaris.' As reasons he cites : (1) the use of the plural ' cometas,' which might well describe the rays of an aurora ; (2) the appropriateness of the words ' claro tremulos ardore ' ; (3) the fact of the winter season, when the aurora is more frequent ; (4) the verse " multaque . . . strage," as being more suitable when applied to the northern lights than to the Catilinarian conspiracy.

18. *lumine luna.* Cf. *Ph.* 247.

19. *abdidit.* This eclipse is said to have occurred on May 3rd, 63 (Guizel Spezieller, *Kanon der Sonnen und Mondfinsternisse*, 1899). It therefore could not have coincided with this festival, which Cicero has shown by the insertion of ' ferme ' in verse 17.

Cicero himself was doubtless acquainted with the physical causes of an eclipse. Cf. *De Nat. Deor.* ii. 103 ; *De Rep.* i. 23–5.

20–32.   " What thoughts were thine when Phoebus'
      fiery disc,
    stern messenger of war, scaled heaven's
      heights,
    sought heaven's slope, then downwards sank
      to rest ?
    Or when a Roman struck by ruthless bolt
    forsook the realms of light, though fair the
      day,
    or when again the teeming earth did quake ?
    Many a dread shape now appeared by night
    which war and revolution prophesied :

> many a rune foretelling dire mishap
> Seers inspired proclaimed throughout the
>   land.
> Repeatedly by bright and constant signs
> did Jove himself predict to earth and sky
> that all would one day chance which now at
>   length
> the course of rolling years hath brought to
>   pass."

20. *Phoebi fax*. Pease (*op. cit.*) suggests that these words did not refer to the sun, but to general meteoric phenomena. Cf. Pliny *N.H.* ii. 96.

23. *perculsus fulmine*. Pliny *N.H.* ii. 137, says : " In Catilinianis prodigiis Pompeiano ex municipio M. Herrenius decurio, sereno die fulmine ictus est." This was considered an evil omen. Cf. Livy x. 31. 8 ; xxii. 36. 8. ; xxv. 7. 7 ; Dion. Hal. v. 46.

27. *terribiles formae*. Ghosts. Plut. *Cic.* 14 mentions φάσματα at this time. Cf. Dio. Cass. xxxvii. 25. 2.

30. *Atque ea*. . . . It has been suggested by Pease that Cicero was here referring to the year 87, for he considers ' vetusto ' inappropriate to describe events only two years previous to 63 (the consulship of Torquatus and Cotta having occurred in 65). His interpretation assumes that these verses relate to what follows in verse 33. We know that portents did take place before the civil wars of Marius and Sulla from *De Nat. Deor.* ii. 14, and Pliny *N.H.* ii. 92. In this way ' cecidere ' will translate ' failed,' ' fore,' ' recur.' But is this elaborate explanation really necessary ? These three verses can be indefinite as to time, forming merely a convenient break between two passages describing omens, and inserted probably to heighten the dramatic effect. For ' cecidere,' in this same sense of ' happening,' cf. verse 17 above.

33–41. " Each word the Lydian seer of Tuscan race
          had spake three years before was ratified,
          gathered within the limits of thy year.
          For Jove himself with thunder from on
             high,
          leaning from starred Olympus, once took
             aim
          at mounds and temples sacred to himself,
          and fired his shrine upon the Capitol.
          Then Natta's brazen statue was o'erthrown
          (of ancient date and noble cast it was),
          and from Jove's hallowed care the laws
             escaped,
          whilst forms of gods his blazing bolt
             destroyed."

33. *Nunc ea.* . . . Cf. *In Cat.* iii. 19 : " Nam pro-
fecto memoria tenetis Cotta et Torquato consulibus com-
plures in Capitolio res de caelo esse percussas, cum et
simulacra deorum depulsa sunt et statuae veterum homi-
num deiectae et legum aera liquefacta. . . ." Cf. Dio.
Cass. xxxvii. 9. 1–2.

34. *Lydius.* Nothing is known about this particular
' haruspex.' Probably the word is used in a general sense,
the Etruscans, as is well known, being famous for their
powers of divination. Some support is lent, by the use
of this word, to the supposed Lydian origin of the
Etruscans. Herod. i. 94 relates the story of the early
settlers leaving the kingdom of Atys and, under his son
Tyrsenus, setting out to found a new race. The Etrus-
cans are frequently called Lydians in literature, and
' Lydian ' is used for ' Etruscan.' Cf. *Aen.* ii. 781–2 ;
Catull. xxxi. 13.

35. *glomerans.* Cf. Cic. trans. Aesch. *Prom.*, verses
25–6 :

    " atque haec vetusta, saeclis glomerata horridis,
      luctifica clades nostro infixa est corpori."

36. *Nam pater . . . ignes.* Lactantius, *Inst.* iii. 17. 14, quotes these lines with a different version for the second :

> " Nam . . . Olympo
> ipse suas arces atque incluta templa petivit
> et . . . ignes " (aedibus, Codd. B.R.)

altitonans. Ennius, *Ann.* 541, uses this word to render ὑψιβρεμέτης. Cicero here copies him in applying it to Jupiter.

37. *tumulos.* The plural presumably refers to the two summits of the Capitoline hill.

39. *Nattae.* Cf. *In Cat.* iii. 19 : " cum et simulacra deorum immortalium depulsa sunt, et statuae *veterum hominum* deiectae, et legum aera liquefacta." Nothing is known of this Natta, although Pais (*Storia di Roma* i. 2, 1899, p. 665, note 1) offers various suggestions as to whom this statue may have represented (Pease, note *ad loc.*).

42–51.   " Here stood the woodland nurse of Roman name,
> the wolf of Mars who suckled his twin babes
> with life-giving milk, drained from swollen breasts.
> She and her sons, struck by the flaming bolt,
> lay shattered there, with imprint only left
> where foot was torn away. Who then thought not
> on records and writings wise of Tuscan race,
> and from their rolls unearthed dread oracles ?
> Bitter the baneful scourge they bade be shunned,
> sprung from citizen stock of high repute.
> The death of every law their constant theme."

42–46. *Hic silvestris . . . liquit.* The original statue was probably early fifth-century work. Strong thought that this wolf might represent " the ancient art of statuary native to Italy." Ducati (*L'Arte Classica*, 1920) revived the theory that the wolf might have been the offering dedicated to the Capitoline Jupiter after the expulsion of the Tarquins. Livy x. 23, says that in 295 the aediles Gnaeus and Quintus Ogulnius " ad ficum Ruminalem simulacra infantium conditorum urbis sub uberibus lupae posuerunt." These words imply that the figures of the twins were added to an already existing monument, in which case the historical significance of the statue is destroyed. In the *Catalogue of the Palazzo dei Conservatori* (British Sch. at Rome, Oxford, 1926, pp. 56–8), occurs the passage : " A group of the wolf and twins on the Capitol was struck by lightning in 65— Cicero's words clearly mean that the figure was torn from its base, leaving the feet only attached, and from Cicero's allusion in *In Cat.* iii. 19, it may be inferred that the group in question was not restored. Cf. *De Div.* ii. 20. 45 ; Dio. Cass. xxxvii. 9."

(This suggests that the existing statue is not the one referred to in this passage in *De Cons.* The traces of damage by fire, observable on the hind legs, are not necessarily attributable to lightning. In the Middle Ages the figure was placed in front of the Lateran Palace, and after finding various resting-places, was finally removed in 1921 to its present position in the Sala dei Fasti Consolari. It has been described by Byron, *Childe Harold*, iv. 88, 89. An illustration can be seen in the *Catalogue of Ancient Sculptures of Rome*, ed. H. Stuart Jones, 1926, plate 17.)

43. *Mavortis.* Only twice used by Cicero to elucidate a supposed etymology—*De Nat. Deor.* ii. 67 ; iii. 62. It is in origin a cult name. *Insc. Lat. Dessau,* 3144, 3142, and cf. Livy, xxii. 1. 11. These five verses supply clear evidence of Cicero's poetical ability. Virgil may have

borne them in mind when writing *Aen.* viii. 630–34.   I do not agree with the explanation of Cicero's words given above with reference to the line " . . . avolsa pedum vestigia liquit."   Taking ' avolsa ' as a transferred epithet with ' pedum,' I incline to the interpretation presented in the translation.

For the same phrase cf. Lucret. iii. 389 : " pedum vestigia quaeque."

45. *fulminis ictu.*   A favourite ending in Lucretius.   Cf. iii. 488 : " ut fulminis ictu " ; v. 400 : " repenti fulminis ictu " ; vi. 386 : " de caelo fulminis ictus " ; *ib.* 406 : " caveamus fulmine ictum."   Cf., too, *Ph.* 432 and *Aen.* viii. 419 : " validi incudibus ictus " ;   also Lucret. vi. 311 : " vehementi perculit ictu."

49. *generosa stirpe.*   The MSS. here read ' generosam,' corrected by editors to ' generosa.'   The reference is either to Catiline (" nobili genere natus," Sall. *Cat.* v. 1), or to the whole patriciate as being responsible for the conspiracy.   Cf. Lucret. iv. 1222 : " ab stirpe profecta."

50. *vitare ingentem,* B 2 ; vir, A. V. ; viri, H. ; vire, B. ; volvier, Baehrens.

51. *tum legum,* Baehrens ; voltum legum, MSS.

52–65.   " Warning they gave to rescue from the flames
the city and the temples of her gods,
and to fear destructive ruin's deadly train.
These the decrees relentless fate enjoined
unless Jove's form, divinely fair, should first
on lofty pillar face the radiant east :
then should the state and holy Senate share
the power to penetrate these secret plots,
if, turned toward the rising of the Sun,
Jove gaze on rich and poor man's home alike.
Slowly the form took shape, though long
    delayed,
but in thy year at last it stood aloft.

> When came the appointed hour decreed by
>   time,
> Jove clothed with light his sceptre, throned
>   on high,
> and foreign lips to one and all revealed
> that train of ruin for thy country laid
> by fire and sword."

50–54. It will be noticed that of these five verses the first three, and the last two, rhyme. Cf., too, verses 60, 61 below. Cicero had no compunction in employing rhyme between the first and second half of a verse. In this poem alone cf. verses 2, 26, 35, 43, 63, 72. His final rhymes probably arose from the fact that his hexameters are often each a single thought, separated from each other by a pause and sense. A verse will therefore tend to be concluded by a verb. Of the 78 verses of Book ii of this poem, 22 end with a finite verb and 12 with a participle in the nominative or accusative case.

52. *deumque.* For the misplaced -que, cf. Munro, on Lucret. ii. 1050.

55. *ni prius . . . in ortus.* The erection of a marble statue was ordered in the consulship of Torquatus and Cotta : this was to support a new statue of Jupiter. The work was not completed until 63. Cf. *In Cat.* iii. 20 : " Idemque iusserunt simulacrum Iovis facere maius et in excelso conlocare et contra atque antea fuerat ad orientem convertere : ac se sperare dixerunt si illud signum quod videtis solis ortum et forum curiamque conspiceret fore ut ea consilia quae clam essent inita contra salutem urbis atque imperi inlustrarentur ut a Senatu populoque Romano perspici possent." Cf. also Dio. Cass. xxxvii. 9. 2 ; *De Div.* ii. 20 ; Arnob. vii. 38. 40.

57. *sanctusque senatus.* Ennius *Ann.* 238 : " foro lato sanctoque senatu." Virg. *Aen.* i. 426 : " iura magistratusque legunt sanctumque senatum."

60. *tardata diu.* Cf. *De Div.* ii. 46–7 ; *In Cat.* iii.

20 and 21 ; Dio. Cass. xxxvii. 34. 3-4 ; Quint. v. 11. 42 : " Cicero . . . in contione contra Catilinam cum signum Iovis columnae impositum populo ostendit."

65. *Allobrogum.* Cf. *In Cat.* iii. *passim* ; Sall. *Cat.* 40-41.

The Allobroges, a powerful Gallic tribe, dwelt between the Rhône and the Isère (Isara), as far as the Lake of Geneva (L. Lemannus)—the modern Dauphiné and Savoy. They are first mentioned in Hannibal's invasion in 218 B.C.—Livy xxi. 31. Q. Fabius Maximus Allobrogicus conquered them in 121 B.C., but they were always turbulent, and disposed to rebellion.

patribus populoque. Cf. 59 above. Virg. *Aen.* viii. 679. " cum patribus populoque penatibus et magnis dis." Cf., too, *Aen.* ix. 192.

66-78. " The ancients, then, whose records ye observe,
who governed city states by wise restraint,
did well to worship with especial zeal
the gods' undying power : well, too, the men
of thine own age whose loyal devotion won
for them a foremost place, whose wisdom too
hath far transcended that of every man.
With careful thought they plumbed those hidden depths,
who passed a life of peace, delighting much
in noble studies, and did oft declaim
the brilliant logic of a fertile mind
in bright Lyceum and the shady Grove.
Recalled thence in the heyday of thy youth,
thy country hailed thee Honour's champion.
Yet thou didst lay all anxious care aside
who served the Muses and thy country's need."

70. *vigenti numine.* Cf. Lucret. i. 925 : " instinctus mente vigenti." Cf., too, verses 3 and 10 above, and Lucret. i. 1022 ; iii. 15 ; v. 420.

73. *inque . . . umbrifera.* The difficulty is one of quantity. By treating the phrase as Ăcădēmīā͡umbrĭfĕrā, we retain the Greek quantity of the penult. of ' Academia,' and lose the caesura ; by reading it as Ăcădēmĭă ūmbrĭfĕrā we introduce hiatus and shortening of the final vowel of ' Academia.' The former alternative is preferable, for two reasons. Cicero was averse to hiatus : there is only one example in all his verses—*Ph. F.* xxiv. ; cf. note and quotation on this F. A freedman of Cicero's, Laurea Tullius, described a Ciceronian villa in a verse (Pliny *N.H.* xxxi. 8) as follows : " atque Academiae celebratam nomine villam." A freedman would, in all probability, adopt his master's pronunciation in speaking of his master's estates.

umbrifera. Plut. *Sulla* 12, says of the general : καὶ τήν τε ᾽Ακαδήμειαν ἔκειρε δενδροφορωτάτην προαστείων οὖσαν.

This enclosure lay about three-quarters of a mile outside Athens : its olive-groves and plane-trees were famous, and had originally been planted by Cimon. " The Academy, hitherto a barren, dry, and dirty locality, he turned into a well-watered grove. He made shady walks to stroll down and open courses for racing " (Plut. *Cimon* 13). According to references made to the Academy in Hor. *Ep.* ii. 2. 45 ; *De Fin.* v. 1 ; Pliny *N.H.* xii. 9, the trees must have been replanted after Sulla's depredations.

For ' umbrifera ' cf. Hom. *F. Il.* i. 10 : " sub platano umbrifera " ; Virg. *Aen.* vi. 437 : " in nemus umbriferum."

Lyceo. *De Nat. Deor.* i. 59 ; *De Fin.* i. 16 ; *Brut.* 315, all serve to show that Cicero, when he visited Greece in the years 79–77, did not confine himself to the Academy and the Lyceum. He also heard Antiochus of the Old Academy, Phaedrus and Zeno (Pease, note *ad loc.*). The Lyceum was a public palaestra with covered walks on the south-east side of Athens, named after the temple of Apollo Λύκειος.

74. *fuderunt.* This use of the word derived from Ennius. Cf. *Ann.* 540 : " effudit voces proprio cum pectore." It was used extensively by the later poets. Cf. Lucret. i. 412 ; vi. 6. Cat. lxiv. 125, 202. Virg. *Aen.* v. 482 ; vii. 292 ; viii. 70 ; xi. 482. Cicero also uses it above in verse 29, and again in *Prog.* iv. 3 ; v. 2.

77. *anxiferas.* A word of Cicero's coinage, found only here and in *Tusc. Disp.* ii. 9. 21.

atque . . . timebat. Nonius quotes this verse to illustrate the varying gender of ' eventus.' He refers it to Book ii of this poem, and writes ' noctu.' Thus the verse is corrupt on metrical grounds. ' Nocturna,' Junius ; ' noctu. (tu),' Linds. ; ' (quae) n.e.t.' L. Müller.

A note in Schutz's edition (p. 681) says : " Pertinere videtur aut ad illam sollicitudinem cum vereretur Cicero ne a C. Cornelio et Cethego occideretur domi, simulantibus salutationem, aut cum detecta iam per Allobroges coniuratione et coniuratis plerisque comprehensis, secum agitaret quid iis facturus esset."

Trans. " And apprehensive feared what night would bring."

BOOK III

" This path from early youth to consulship
with brave determination hast thou trod.
' Forward ! ' Of worthy men thus strive to win
greater renown and praise."

Interea . . . bonorum. Cf. intro. and passage there quoted from *Ep. ad Att.* ii. 3, 4 ; cf. verse 75 in Bk. ii ; Virg. *Aen.* vii. 162 : " primaevo flore iuventus " ; Sen. *Phaedr.* 620 : " iuventae flore primaevo " ; Quint. *Decl.* ix. 9 ; Sil. Ital. xvi. 405.

bonorum. Two possible interpretations are to be considered : (1) objective gen.—" renown accorded you by worthy men " ; (2) subjective gen.—" renown accorded to worthy men."

FRAGMENTS OF UNCERTAIN LOCATION

quorum . . . peredit. Trans., " and spendthrift spent the all that fortune gave." Nonius, discussing the gender of ' census,' says : " Neutro Cicero in Consulatu suo ' quorum . . . peredit.' "

Nam . . . parentes. Trans., " Shame for themselves thy parents bore with thee." Cf. Morel, note Frag. *P.L.* p. 72 (1927).

Cedant . . . linguae. Trans. " Let war to peace, the crown to eloquence give pride of place."

This famous line is quoted in the *De Off.*, where Cicero tells his son Marcus that a wise legislator is of more value than a military leader. A Solon is of more account than a Themistocles. Cf. intro. and further references to this verse there quoted. Cicero especially disliked the significance attributed to it, viz. its vanity and its suggested disparagement of Pompey's military glory.

Ps-Sall. *in Cic.* iii. 5. 7 : " Etiamne aures nostras onerabis tuo odio ? Etiamne molestissimis verbis insectabere ? ' Cedant . . . linguae.' Quasi vero togatus et non armatus ea quae gloriaris confeceris." And again Ps-Cic. *in Sall.* ii. 7 : " An ego tunc falso scripsi ' cedant arma togae ' qui togatus armatos et pace bellum oppressi ? "

The best MSS. read ' laudi.' In Quint., however, we have ' linguae ' and γλώττῃ in Plutarch's paraphrase (*Dem. cum Cic.* 2). The elder Pliny, *N.H.* vii. 30 writes : " Salve primus omnium parens patriae appellate, primus in toga triumphum *linguaeque* lauream merite et facundiae Latinarumque litterarum parens." The Ps-Sall. quoted above also reads ' linguae.' As all old Latin poetry is wretchedly rich in alliteration, Cicero himself probably preferred " laurea laudi " to " laurea linguae," and Morel (*F.P.L.* p. 72) says : " Fort. offensionem in ' linguae ' ab inimicis motam ipse tacite corr. Tullius." ' Laudi,' Cic., *In Pis.* xxix. 72 ; *De Off.* (Codd. mel.).

Cassius probably had this verse in mind, for he wrote (*Ad Fam.* xii. 13. 1) : " Est enim tua toga omnium armis felicior." Cf., too, Quint. xi. 1. 24 (intro.), and Serv. *Aen.* i. 1.

O fortunatam . . . Romam. Trans. " O Rome the luck-borne, born in my year of grace ! " Diomedes i. p. 466 K., quotes this notorious verse, but does not mention Cicero by name. Ps-Sall. *in Cic.* iii. 5 : " Atque is cum eiusmodi sit tamen audet dicere ' O . . . Romam ' : te cos. fortunatam, Cicero ! Immo vero infelicem et miseram ! " Cf. intro. and Quint. ix. 4 ; xi. 1. Juvenal (quoted intro., p. 28) skilfully ridicules the verse by the jingle in " . . . Antoni gladios potuit contemnere *si sic. . . .*" (Cf. Pascal, *Athenaeum* iv. 309 ; Rolfe, *Class. Journ.* xiii. 688 ; Tatham, *Class. Review,* xxxix. 71.)

in montes . . . nostra. " Back to my native hills and homeland dear." *Ad Att.* ii. 15. 3 : " Ego vero ' in . . . nostra ' pergam." Some edd. have assigned this verse to the *Marius,* others to the *De Cons.* There is **no** definite evidence for Ciceronian authorship ; the only ancient reference to it is in the above letter, where it is quoted anonymously.

MARIUS

" Of beauteous form Jove's tawny eagle seen . . ."

Nuntia . . . figura. Atticus, Quintus, and Marcus Cicero meet at Arpinum. Whereupon Atticus remarks : " Lucus quidem ille et haec Arpinatium quercus agnoscitur saepe a me lectus in Mario." (Cf. intro. The use of ' saepe ' infers considerable familiarity with the work on the part of Atticus.) Quintus replies that it matters little whether the tree before them is the actual one " ex qua olim evolavit ' nuntia . . . figura ' " or not. " Here there will always be an oak tree called the Oak of Marius," he says, " even after lapse of time has destroyed the original tree." In fact, " this tree, as Scaevola says about my brother's poem ' Marius,' ' canescet saeclis innumerabilibus.' " A criticism which implies that this poem was regarded as more than an early attempt at versification.

1. *Hic Iovis.* This longer passage, quoted in the *De Div.*, occurs in a conversation between the two brothers on divination. Quintus continues : "Quid est illo auspicio divinius quod apud te in Mario est ? Ut utar potissimum te auctore : ' Hic . . . omen.' " There are two Homeric passages (*Il.* xii. 200–29 ; *Od.* xv. 161–78) upon the first of which this Fragment is based, as a brief analysis will show.

Iovis altisoni pinnata satelles. αἰετὸς ὑψιπέτης. (' altisoni ' is a trans. of ὑψηχής, *Il.* v. 772 ; xxiii. 27. Cf. Ennius *Ann.* 575).

 serpentis saucia morsu. ἀλγήσας ὀδύνῃσι.
 subrigit ipsa anguem. δράκοντα (φέρων).
 transfigens unguibus. (φέρων) ὀνύχεσσι.
 semianimum . . . micantem. ζωὸν ἔτ' ἀσπαίροντα· καὶ οὔ πω λήθετο χάρμης.

In verse 5 Cicero altered the story and, contrary to the original, the bird gains the victory. Cf. *Il.*, *loc. cit.*, 204–6 :

 κόψε γὰρ αὐτὸν ἔχοντα κατὰ στῆθος παρὰ δειρὴν
 ἰδνωθεὶς ὀπίσω· ὁ δ' ἀπὸ ἔθεν ἧκε χαμᾶζε
 ἀλγήσας ὀδύνῃσι, μέσῳ δ' ἐνὶ κάββαλ' ὁμίλῳ.

1–7. " Straightway the feathered bird of thundering Jove
  smarting with pain transfixed in talons cruel,
  upreared from off the trunk, the half-dead snake
  darting its baneful tongue from spotted neck.
  Her beak befouled and tore the twining coils.
  Now fury spent, now grievous pain avenged,
  she casts it down nor ceases to attack
  the bloody carcase throbbing in the pool."

1. *Iovis . . . satelles.* For the phrase cf. *De Div.* ii. 73, and see similarities in the translation from Aesch. *Prom. Solut.* : " Iam . . . adulat sanguinem."

3. *subrigit.* This form occurs only here in Cicero's poems. The onomatopoeic effect of the snake's hissing is clearly intended by the frequently repeated ' s ' in the three verses.

4. *semianimum . . . cervice micantem.* Ennius, *Ann.* 472–3 :

> " Oscitat in campis caput a cervice revolsum
> semianimesque micant oculi."

Virgil also imitated this in *Aen.* x. 396 :

" semianimesque micant digiti ferrumque retractant."

cervice. In Cicero's prose, always in the plural ; in his verse, usually in the singular. The singular is also found in ff. of Ennius (*vide supra*), Pacuvius, and Afranius. Hence Quintilian's statement that Hortensius was the first to use the word in the singular was incorrect— Quint. viii. 3. 35. (Cf. Varro, *De L.L.* x. 78 ; Serv. xi. 496 ; Isidore xi. 1. 61, who all make the same mistake.)

6. *satiata animos.* This appears to be the only instance of the use of the Greek accusative in the poems, i.e. the retained object after the middle participle.

7. *abicit ecflantem.* In the original, ἦχε χαμᾶζε provides the only parallel. One cannot help regretting the omission of μέσῳ . . . ὁμίλῳ in the Latin !

in unda. The translation above takes ' adfligo ' in the sense of to ' worry.' Cf. Caesar *B.C.* iii. 27, for similar meaning. Editors who translate the word in its more usual meaning compare for the ablative after a verb of motion *De Nat. Deor.* ii. 124 : " aves quae se in mari mergerent," and *Aen.* xii. 256 (quoted *infra*, verse 8).

8–13. " Then wings her way from west to radiant east.
Her Marius marked, as fleet of wing
aloft she soared, marked too with augur's skill
signs propitious for his triumph and return.
Rent was the sky with thunder on the left ;
thus Jove confirmed the eagle's portent
plain."

8. *Seque . . . ortus.* Cf. Hom. (*loc. cit.*), 207 : αὐτὸς δὲ κλάγξας πέτετο πνοιῆς ἀνέμοιο.

Here all resemblance ceases. In Homer Polydamas relates the story of the omen, and then counsels Hector against an immediate attack on the Greeks, for " thus would they leave many a hero slain on the field, even as the eagle was compelled to leave his prey before reaching home and his young ones."

The simile is also used in *Aen.* xi. 751–6. Tarchon has seized Venulus, and is holding him on his horse, whilst he seeks a suitable spot for dealing a fatal wound. Venulus struggles to ward off the blow :

" utque volans alte raptum cum fulva draconem
fert aquila implicuitque pedes atque unguibus haesit,
saucius at serpens sinuosa volumina versat
arrectisque horret squamis et sibilat ore,
arduus insurgens : illa haud minus urget obunco
luctantem rostro, simul aethera verberat alis."

The omen appears a second time in *Aen.* xii. 247. Juturna is encouraging the faint-hearted Rutulians. The passage is too long for quotation here, but some interesting comparisons can be made between this Virgilian description, Cicero's version, and the account in the *Odyssey*. Virgil turns first to Homer. Telemachus is about to leave Sparta when the omen occurs. An eagle appears, bearing a *goose* in its claws. Contrary to the two other passages, the onlookers *rejoiced*, for Helen interpreted the omen favourably for Odysseus. Virgil depicts an eagle pursuing a *swan*; the bird is forced to drop his prey and " flee far off into the clouds of heaven." Whereat the Latins hailed the omen with shouts of *joy*. Tolumnius says that Aeneas " will take to flight and o'er the deep sail far away."   So far, then, Virgil is using the substance of the *Odyssey*, but he had Cicero's poem in mind.

Cicero	*Virgil.*
Iovis . . . pinnata satelles.	Volans . . . fulvus Iovis ales.
feris transfigens unguibus.	Pedibus rapit improbus uncis.

Remembering that the bird is victorious in Cicero, but vanquished in Virgil, we get, *mutatis mutandis*, a further similarity in :

Iam satiata . . . dolores
    . . . adfligit in unda . . .

and

" vi victus et ipso
pondere defecit praedamque ex unguibus ales
proiecit fluvio. . . ."

9. *praepetibus pinnis*.   Festus, p. 205 M, says : " praepetes aves quidam dici aiunt quia secundum auspicium faciant praetervolantes, alii quod aut ea quae praepetamus indicent aut quod praetervolent . . . ceterum poetae promiscue omnes aves ita appellant." Cf., too, Gell. vii. 6. 3 ; Serv. *Ad Aen.* vi. 15, and *Aen.* iii. 361 : " praepetis omnia pinnae." On the former passage of Virgil cf. H. E. Butler on *Aen.* vi. 15, where the conclusion reached is that the word came to mean ' prosperous.' Whether the original signification was " seeking what is in front " or " seeking a suitable spot to settle on in preference to all others " cannot be decided.

10. *augur.* Cic. *Ad Brut.* i. 5. 3 : " Gaius autem Marius cum in Cappadocia esset, lege Domitia factus est augur."

11. *faustaque . . . notavit.* Marius was absent from Rome in the years 88–87. For his connexion with eagles there is the well-known story of his discovery, when a boy, of a nest of seven eaglets, later interpreted as referring to his seven consulships. Cf. App. *B.C.* i. 75 ; Plut. *Mar. 36.*

12. *partibus . . . sinistris.* Cf. *Aen.* ii. 693 : " intonuit laevum."

13. *firmavit.* Cf. Anchises' prayer in *Aen.* ii. 691 :

" da deinde augurium, pater, atque haec omnia firma."

OF UNCERTAIN LOCATION

Tunc . . . paroni. Isidore, *Orig.* xix. 1. 20, says : " Paro [a small, light ship] navigium piratarum aptum et ex his ita vocatum. Cicero ' Tunc . . . paroni.' " See references to Plutarch quoted in text.

fluctiger. Cf. note on F. iii. of *Prognostica.* This word is ἅπαξ λεγόμενον.

PHAENOMENA

F. I. The first 18 verses of Aratus form the invocation to Jupiter. From them our Ff. i. and ii. are taken.

Ab Iove . . . primordia. Ar. Ἐκ Διὸς ἀρχώμεσθα, τὸν οὐδέποτ' ἄνδρες ἐῶμεν ἄρρητον·

Cicero's rendering is far superior to that of Germanicus who writes :

" Ab Iove principium magno deduxit Aratus
    carminis at nobis, genitor, tu maximus auctor " ;

or to Avienus, who begins :

" Carminis incentor mihi Iuppiter ! auspice terras
    linquo Iove et celsam reserat dux Iuppiter aethram.
    Imus in astra Iovis monitu, Iovis omine caelum
    et Iovis imperio mortalibus aethera pando."

Cf., too, Virg. *E.* iii. 60 : " Ab Iove principium, Musae, Iovis omnia plena."

F. II. Having recounted the benefits conferred by Jupiter on farmers, Aratus assigns to him the origin of the stars.

Quem . . . caeli. Orelli includes these two verses, but Buhle and Morelius doubt their authenticity, and Grotius omits them. ' Quem . . . interimet ' has no parallel in Aratus, but for ' stinguens . . . caeli,' cf. Ar. 10–11 :

> αὐτὸς γὰρ τά γε σήματ' ἐν οὐρανῷ ἐστήριξεν,
> ἄστρα διακρίνας

Cf. *Aen.* v. 783 ; *stinguens* apparently for the more usual ' distinguens.'

F. III. At verse 19 Aratus, having completed the invocation, turns to the main subject. He mentions the movement of the stars, the fixed axis upholding the earth, and the revolution of the heavens around this.

Ar. 19–20 :

> οἱ μὲν ὁμῶς πολέες τε καὶ ἄλλυδις {ἄλλοι ἐόντες (vulgo)
> {ἄλλοι ἰόντες (schol.)
> οὐρανῷ ἕλκονται πάντ' ἤματα συνεχὲς αἰεί.

Cicero seems to have followed those grammarians who, as the scholiast says, preferred ἰόντες to the vulgo ἐόντες, on the assumption that stars create their own power of movement. Germanicus 19 has ' vaga.' Further, ἄλλοσε εἶναι would be a strange expression here.

In translating οἱ μέν by ' cetera,' Cicero is thinking of those stars already mentioned by Aratus in verses 10–13. The alliterative effect of the two verses appears to be somewhat pointless. It was probably unintentional.

noctesque diesque. Munro (*Cat.*, p. 153) notices the trochaic rhythm of this line. The phrase itself is probably a borrowing from Ennius. Cf. *Ann.* 334 : " Sollicitari te, Tite, sic noctesque diesque." It was employed fairly frequently by Lucretius and Virgil.

F. IV.   At either end of the axis are the poles.

Extremusque . . . polus.   " And just the tip from off (i.e. of) the double axle is called the pole " (Mayor). ' Duplici de cardine ' for ' duplicis cardinis.'   ' Cardo ' is the pivot on which anything swings (κραδαίνει).

Germ. 21–3 :

> " axis et immotus semper vestigia servat
> libratasque tenet terras et cardine firmo
> orbem agit."

Ar. 24 : καί μιν πειραίνουσι δύω πόλοι ἀμφοτέρωθεν.

polus.   A term borrowed from the Greek.   Varro (*ap.* Gell. iii. 10) uses it for the arctic and antarctic circles.

F. V.   Encircling the north pole are the two bears. Some editors place F. vi. before F. v., assuming that Cicero interpolated it here after verse 27 of the original : Τὸ δὴ καλέονται Ἅμαξαι.   I have printed them in the order in which they appear in the *De Nat. Deor.*   The connexion with ' ex his ' is made in the *De Nat. Deor.* from the preceding sentence :   " Hunc circum [*sc.* polus] ἄρκτοι duae feruntur, nunquam occidentes, ' Ex his . . .
. . . Helice,'
cuius quidem clarissimas stellas totis noctibus cernimus, ' quas. . . . Triones.' "

Cynosura.   The little bear ;   lit. " the dog's tail." The word was probably suggested by the circular sweep of three of the stars, and then applied to the whole constellation (Mayor).   Cf. *Acad.* ii. 66.

apud Graios.   An addition of Cicero's.   He seems to insert these explanatory phrases whenever he uses the Greek rather than the Latin name.   Cf. F. xiii. and verse 5 of the continuous poem.

altera dicitur.   Munro, in his introduction to Lucretius, says :   " We find in Lucretius hundreds of instances in which the first two feet are marked off from the rest of the verse . . . with two dactyls."

Helice. The Great Bear ; lit. " a winding." Presumably the name arose from the Great Bear's revolution round the pole. Both Germanicus, 31 *et sqq.*, and Avienus, 108 *et sqq.*, refer to the story of the young Jupiter being nurtured by Helice and Cynosura in Crete, and their ultimate reward of being placed in the sky as constellations. Each bear has seven principal stars, and forms a convenient starting-point from which to explore the heavens, as they are always visible in latitudes north of 40° N. Lat. The chief star in the Great Bear is Mizar (the middle star in the handle), and in the Little Bear, Polaris (the last star in the handle). Polaris is computed to be two hundred light-years distant from the earth.

F. VI. *Triones.* Mayor in a long note (*De Nat. Deor.*, p. 222) suggests several etymologies of the word. Cf. Varro, *L.L.* vii. 74 ; Isid. *Orig.* xii. 1. §30 Fr. 1. 66 Ribb. ; Max Müller, Lect. II, 364.

F. VII. The comparative value of the two bears as guides to mariners.

Hac fidunt duce. Difficulty has been felt over ' hac.' From the order of our verses this must refer to Helice, but in Aratus, 39 (Τῇ δ'ἄρα Φοίνικες πίσυνοι περόωσι θάλασσαν) τῇ δ'ἄρα refers to Cynosura, who guided the Phœnicians, whilst Helice was used by the Greeks.

Germ. 40 says :

> " Dat Graiis Helice cursus maioribus astris,
> Phoenicas Cynosura regit. Sed candida tota
> et liquido splendore Helice nitet ; haut prius ulla,
> cum sol oceano fulgentia condidit ora,
> stella micat caelo, septem quam Cresia flammis.
> Certior est Cynosura tamen sulcantibus aequor,
> quippe brevis totam fido se cardine vertit
> Sidoniamque ratem nunquam spectata fefellit."

Avienus 124–5 :

> " Namque Helice Graios, Tyrios Cynosura per altum
> parva regit."

Cf., too, *Acad.* ii. 20. 66 : " Ego vero (Lucullus) ipse et magnus quidem sum opinator (non enim sum sapiens) et meas cogitationes sic dirigo, non ad illam parvolam Cynosuram,

 qua fidunt duce nocturna Phoenices in alto,
ut ait Aratus, eoque directius gubernant quod eam tenent,

 quae cursu interiore brevi convertitur orbe,
sed ad Helicen et clarissimos septentriones."

This passage makes it clear to which of the stars ' hac ' refers. (Cf. ' Nam cursu ' in our verse, ' quae cursu,' and Aratus, μειοτέρη γάρ.) ' Hic,' then, is used for Cynosura throughout these verses, and a possible explanation is the loss of some verses of Cicero, in which Cynosura was mentioned after Helice. One should remember that F. v. as it at present stands may not represent Cicero's final version.

Phoenices. They realised the closer proximity of the Little Bear to the true north. The pole, of course, is not stationary, owing to the precessional movement of the earth's axis. Sir Robert Ball, in the *Story of the Heavens*, Cassell, 1905, p. 493, explains this movement with a diagram. The complete journey of the pole occupies about 25,867 years. Cf. Ovid *Tris.* iv. 3. 1–2 ; *Fasti* iii. 107 *et sqq.*

Sed prior illa. Helice.

F. VIII. This, and the four succeeding Fragments, are concerned with the story of Hercules, the dragon, and the golden apples in the garden of the Hesperides. Draco is seen best in July, his head lying to the north of Hercules, his body being represented by a long, straggling line of stars lying chiefly between his own head and the body of the Little Bear. Like the bears, Draco is a circumpolar constellation in our latitude. The most important star is Alpha, about 4,700 years ago the pole-star.

Rapido . . . flumen. Ar. 45 : οἴη ποταμοῖο ἀπορρώξ. Germ. 48 : " abrupti fluminis instar."

torvu' Draco. : μέγα θαῦμα Δράκων.
Virgil probably had Cicero's version in mind when he
wrote, *Geor.* i. 244 :

> " Maximus hic flexu sinuoso elabitur Anguis
> circum perque duas in morem fluminis Arctos."

Cf., too, Sen. *Thyestes* 869 and *Medea* 694.

cum gurgite. For this use of ' cum ' instead of the simple
ablative, cf. *infra*, 146, 215, and Lucret. i. 287 ; iv. 1126.

subter . . . flexos. An extension of Ar. 46–7 : περί
τ'ἀμφί τ'ἐαγὼς / μυρίος.

conficiens . . . flexos. Trans. " Writhing his body
into sinuous coils." Some editors have preferred ' flexo '
(following Grotius) to ' flexos,' on the ground that the
latter form used with ' sinus ' is redundant. To destroy
MS. authority for such a reason seems unjustifiable.
For this account of Draco, cf. Germ. 48–64 ; Av. 138–68.

F. IX. The description of Draco is continued.
Astronomically, Aratus here misleads Cicero. As men-
tioned above, Alpha is the only bright star in Draco, and
the statement " one would say that his head . . . is
fastening its gaze upon the tail of the Great Bear," is
incorrect. His head is actually facing the feet of Hercules
(Engonasin).

non . . . stella. The careful translation of the
original is worth notice. Ar. 54–5 : οὐ μὲν . . . οἱόθεν
οὐδ' οἷος . . . ἀστήρ. For the archaic quantity of
' mŏdō,' cf. Munro on Lucret. ii. 1135.

verum . . . flagrant. A bold and successful expansion
of Ar. 56 :

> ἀλλὰ δύο κροτάφοις, δύο δ' ὄμμασιν.

For the phrase ' fulgore notata,' cf. Lucret. v. 612, who
uses it in the same position in the verse.

Germ. 56 writes :

> " Ardent ingentes oculi, cava tempora claris
> ornantur flammis, mento sedet unicus ignis."

Atque . . . lucet. The sense of the original is not fully expressed ; Ar. 56–7 writes :

εἰς δ' ὑπένερθεν
ἐσχατιὴν ἐπέχει γένυος δεινοῖο πελώρου.

" One (star) clings beneath the verge of the dread monster's chin."

obstipum . . . dicas. ' Obstipum ' (Greek λοξόν) normally means ' bent forward.' Cf. Hor. *Sat.* ii. 5. 92 ; Pers. *Sat.* iii. 80. Suetonius (*Tib.* 68), however, uses it of Tiberius, who showed his pride by walking " cervice rigida et obstipa," which Mayor interprets as " bent back." He compares, too, Lucret. iv. 517 and Columella vii. 10, and suggests that here the word probably means ' slanted ' or ' thrown back.' Cf. Ennius, *Ann.* 283, 420. This is possibly so, but in either sense it makes the passage astronomically incorrect. Cf. intro. above.

a tereti . . . dicas. Ar. 58–9 :

νεύοντι δὲ πάμπαν ἔοικεν
ἄκρην εἰς Ἑλίκης οὐρήν·

For the phrase ' tereti cervice ' used in the same position in the verse, cf. *Aen.* viii. 633 ; Lucret. i. 35. That this phrase is a reminiscence of Ennius is shown by Servius's remark on *Aen.* viii. 631 *et sqq.* : " *Totus hic locus Ennianus est.*"

in cauda. Grotius proposed ' in caudam,' having regard to the original. This seems unnecessary. The Greek νεύω normally requires the accusative, but no harshness can be felt in using ' figere obtutum ' with the ablative. Cf. *Aen.* i. 482 :

" diva solo fixos oculos aversa tenebat " ;

and again, *Aen.* xii. 70 :

" illum turbat amor figitque in virgine vultus."

135

Germanicus and Avienus seem to have missed the force of νεύοντι : the former 59–60 : . . . "lucetque novissima cauda/extremumque Helices sidus micat," the latter 156 : "in nutum veluti curvata."

F. X.   These two verses concern the setting of Draco. Only in latitudes north of 40° is this constellation circumpolar, but even when viewed from farther south, its interval between rising and setting is naturally very short.

Hoc . . . condit.   The reading of Hyginus and the MSS. generally is in disagreement with the facts of the case. The Dragon's head sets gradually.   Therefore various conjectures have been made amongst which are the following :

Orelli, reasoning that the Dragon's head lies within the Arctic circle, and so touches the northern horizon, suggested " seroque,' for it sets *late* in comparison with the other stars, and is for *a short time* below the horizon (as it would be from Soli).

Grotius, in his emendation, used 'subito' as a participle. There is no other example of its use in this way, however, and his emendation is somewhat far from the original : Ar. 61–2 :

κείνη που κεφαλὴ τῇ νίσσεται ἦχί περ ἄκραι

μίσγονται δύσιές τε καὶ ἀντολαὶ ἀλλήλησιν.   [v. l. νήχεται]

But it is not at all sure whether this is the original as Cicero read it.   Germ. has 60–61 : "hac radiatur/ serpentis *decline* caput "; Av. 165 : "hac in parte sacri *procumbere* cernitur axis."   These two translations rather suggest (together with Cicero's) that the ancients read, not νίσσεται or νήχεται, but some such word as νεύεται.

The emendation of Davisius has the merit of making sense astronomically, whilst it does not unduly violate MS. tradition.

partim.   For this archaic accusative cf. Lucret. vi. 87–8 :

"unde volans ignis pervenerit aut in utram se
verterit hinc partim, . . ."

and *ib.* 384, where Munro quotes Livy xxvi. 46. 8 " partim copiarum ad tumulum mittit, partim ipse ad arcem ducit" (Mayor).

ortus . . . unam: see intro. to this Fragment. As a result of this short interval, " rising and setting blend."

Ff. XI and XII. These two Fragments refer to Engonasin. This constellation is now known under the more familiar name of Hercules. Amongst the Romans he was variously named Effigies, Imago, or (as Cicero) Nixus. Cf. Av. 631, Germ. 271. The position of Hercules is such that his head is toward the south (cf. 355–6 below), whilst his foot rests on the head of the Dragon. This is appropriately so, and gave rise to the identification of these two constellations, with the familiar story of the destruction of the Dragon which guarded the golden apples of the Hesperides by Hercules. In our latitude Hercules is best seen about 9 p.m. in the early part of July. (For the myth see Av. 169 *et sqq.*)

Attingens. Grotius emended (without MS. authority) to ' quod tangens,' apparently because ' attingens ' did not give the necessary meaning of ' bordering upon.' For this usual meaning of the word cf. Caesar *B.G.* i. 1 ; ii. 15 ; Cic. *Ad Fam.* xv. 4. He also objected that Cicero incorrectly translated the original, Ar. 63 :

μογέοντι κυλίνδεται ἀνδρὶ ἐοικός,

since μογεῖν in Greek is paralleled in Latin by ' laborare,' not ' maerere.' In any case, this is a difference of degree rather than of kind, since either word expresses the same meaning in general. The conjecture ' morientis imago ' (Bouhierus) agrees neither with the words nor with the sense of Aratus.

Hic . . . Corona. Ar. 71 : Αὐτοῦ κἀκεῖνος Στέφανος.

The Greek has nothing to correspond to ' eximio fulgore,' the ablative qualifying ' Corona.' This is the Corona Borealis, the beautiful circlet of stars to the east of Boötes, easily recognised by the nearly perfect semicircle which its six stars form. It is said to have been set in the heavens by Bacchus as a memorial of his love for Ariadne (Hygin. *P.A.* ii. 5). It is easily visible near Hercules in the early evening hours of June and July.

F. XIII. Ophiuchus, the Serpent Bearer, and Serpens, the Serpent, are to be seen in the summer months just south of Hercules. Legend has it that Ophiuchus, as an earthly physician, was so successful that he could raise the dead. Pluto, fearing lest his kingdom should be depopulated, persuaded Jupiter to remove Ophiuchus to the sky! The Serpent is the symbol of his master's powers. The two constellations are very much confused, and it is difficult to distinguish the two separate outlines with any certainty. Also called Anguitenens, Serpentarius.

Propter . . . Graii. Editors of the *De Nat. Deor.* print: "Atque haec quidem a tergo, propter caput autem Anguitenens, 'quem . . . Graii,'" thus making 'caput' the accusative governed by 'propter.' But by a slight rearrangement it is possible to keep the Latin nearer Ar. 74–5:

> Νώτῳ μὲν Στέφανος πελάει κεφαλῇ γε μὲν ἄκρῃ
> σκέπτεο πὰρ κεφαλὴν 'Οφιούχεον . . .

"The Crown lies near the back (of Engonasin), but see, near at hand by his head, the head of Ophiuchus." Some word parallel to σκέπτεο is missing in Cicero, but by taking the whole sentence in this way ('propter' being an adverb) we do not depart so far from the original. The whole verse, 'quem . . . Graii,' is an addition. Cf. F. v. note 'apud Graios.'

F. XIV. Editors, notably Baehrens, following Grotius, have printed these two verses in this place in the Fragments. They are made to represent (in the arrangement of Grotius) Ar. 77–8:

> Τοῖοί οἱ κεφαλῇ ὑποκείμενοι ἀγλαοὶ ὦμοι
> εἴδονται.

This is clearly wrong. Looking farther on in the Greek, we come to the account of Protrygeter, a star of the third magnitude in Virgo, mentioned immediately after the description of that constellation. The original verses 137 and 139 are :

Τῆς ὑπὲρ ἀμφοτέρων ὤμων εἰλίσσεται ἀστὴρ

. . . .

Τόσσος μὲν μεγέθει, τοίη δ'ἐγκείμενος αἴγλη,

Grotius, in his supplementary verses in this place, borrows from Cicero, and writes :

" Huic, humeros supera duplices, convertitur alam
     ad dextram Graio Protrygeter nomine dicta,
     stella micans tali specie talique nitore,"

The traditional order has been maintained for convenience, but it seems certain that this verse should be transposed and inserted after F. xxi., being, of course, referred to Protrygeter and not to Ophiuchus.

F. XV. This Fragment describes the hero gripping the Serpent with both hands, and is connected, in sense, with F. xiii.

Hic . . . anguem. An accurate extension of Ar. 82 : ἀμφότεραι (i.e. χέρες) δ' Ὄφιος πεπονήαται (' are busied with '). " Atque . . . torto " is not represented in the Greek. Translate, " He grips the Serpent and holds it firmly between his two hands, whilst it holds him fast bound within its sinuous coils."

eius. Monosyllabic. Mayor (ed. *ad loc.*) compares ' cuius,' Lucret. i. 149, " principium cuius hinc nobis exordia sumet."

Nepai. Festus (p. 164 M) says : " Nepa Afrorum lingua sidus quod cancer appellatur vel, ut quidam volunt, Scorpios." For the story of Orion and the Scorpion, cf. 425 *et sqq.* in the continuous poem.

F. XVI. Arctophylax (usually Arcturus) is here used for the whole constellation of Boötes. Cf. Hesiod, *Op.*

566, 610. The group is easily recognised in June by its pentagonal shape : the most southerly star of this pentagon is Epsilon Boötis, one of the finest double stars in the heavens. It contains the brightest star in the northern hemisphere, Arcturus. See F. xvii.

quod quasi . . . Arcton. This verse shows how carefully Cicero dealt with the original when no suitable word could be found to render the Greek into Latin. The former of these two verses is an exact translation. For the second cf. Ar. 93 : οὕνεχ' ἀμαξαίης ἐπαφώμενος εἴδεται Ἄρκτου. Cicero takes ἀμαξαίης as an adjective in agreement with Ἄρκτου, " the wain-like Bear," and so translates ' Arcton adiunctam temoni.'

quatit Arcton. Cf. *Georg.* iii. 132 : ' quatit equum ' used in the same sense.

F. XVII. Even though Arcturus has recently been estimated to be distant from the earth twenty-one light years, it is one of the nearest of the stars to us. Its brightness is forty times that of the sun : it is one of the most rapidly moving stars in the sky. During the last sixteen centuries it is calculated to have moved from its position at the beginning of that period by as much as the apparent width of the moon. Thus the point where Arcturus is to be seen to-day is not the same as it was in the time of Cicero.

Subter . . . claro. In the text of the *De Nat. Deor.* the connexion between this and the preceding Fragment is made by " Huic Boöti," and between this and the succeeding Fragment by "cui subiecta fertur" (MS.'cuius.'). The MS. reading possibly arose from dittography of the ' subiecta ' : some editors retain this, inserting ' pedibus,' and thus giving a closer rendering of Ar. 96 :

Ἀμφοτέροισι δὲ ποσσὶν ὑποσκέψαιο Βοώτεω
Παρθένον, ἥ ῥ' ἐν χερὶ φέρει σταχὺν αἰγλήεντα.

F. XVIII. This, together with the three following Fragments, refers to Virgo. The constellation lies south and south-west of Boötes, and is one of the signs of the Zodiac. Spica, the brightest star in Virgo, is bluish-white in colour, and of the first magnitude. Known, too, as Astraea (the star-maiden), she lived on earth during the Golden Age : as man's wickedness increased in the Age of Silver, she no longer consorted with mortals, and finally, with the coming of the Iron Age, she forsook the earth, and took her place amongst the stars. This is described in full by Aratus.

Spicum. Found in all three genders. Serv. (*loc. cit.*) quotes the verse to show the neuter use of the word, but with ' ferens insigni ' for ' tenens splendenti.' ' Splendenti corpore ' is not found in Aratus.

Virgo. Mayor remarks that Aratus is describing her in words borrowed from Hesiod's description of Justice (*Op.* 192, 257). Cf. *Georg.* ii. 474 :

> " extrema per illos
> Iustitia excedens terris vestigia fecit " ;

and Ovid *Metam.* i. 150 :

> " et Virgo caede madentes
> ultima caelestum terras Astraea reliquit."

F. XIX. The sense of this Fragment does not occur in Aratus. Our authority for including it here is Lactantius, who, after discussing the glories of the Golden Age, says : " Malebant . . . ut Cicero in suo ait Arato." Av. 316–17 :

> " Omnia sed cunctis nasci dabat aurea terris
> Iustitia et nullo discreverat aere regna."

Orelli would insert this Fragment after Ar. 110, αὕτως δ' ἔζωον, but Buhle (with more probability) after 112, where he suggests that one or even two verses may have been lost from the original.

F. XX. For concise and dramatic effect these three verses undoubtedly surpass the original, Ar. 129–32 :

ἀλλ’ ὅτε δὴ κἀκεῖνοι ἐτέθνασαν, οἱ δ’ ἐγένοντο,
χαλκείη γενεή, προτέρων ὀλοώτεροι ἄνδρες,
οἳ πρῶτοι κακόεργον ἐχαλκεύσαντο μάχαιραν
εἰνοδίην, πρῶτοι δὲ βοῶν ἐπάσαντ’ ἀροτήρων·

The weakness of οἱ δ’ ἐγένοντο is at once apparent when compared with ‘ exorta repente est,’ whilst the terse rendering of verse 2 is superior to οἳ πρῶτοι . . . εἰνοδίην. Cf. *Georg.* ii. 536 *et sqq.* :

“ et ante
impia quam caesis gens est epulata iuvencis,
aureus hanc vitam in terris Saturnus agebat ;
necdum etiam audierant inflari classica, necdum
impositos duris crepitare incudibus ensis.”

Cf., too, Ovid *Metam.* xv. 120 *et sqq.*, and Pope’s *Essay on Man* iii. 147 *et sqq.*

vinctum. Some editors have needlessly changed to ‘ victum,’ asserting that ‘ bos manu victus ’ would be the equivalent of the Greek χειροήθης. But Aratus 132 merely writes πρῶτοι δὲ βοῶν ἐπάσαντ’ ἀροτήρων, thus providing no clue to help us in our choice. It seems preferable to leave the MS. reading, and thus avoid sacrificing a poetical expression for a hackneyed phrase.

F. XXI. Schutz, in his edition, quotes from Lactantius (*loc. cit.*) as Cicero’s, the verses :

“ Deseruit propere terras iustissima Virgo
et Iovis in regno caelique in parte resedit.”

The former belongs to the *Ph.* of Germanicus, verse 137. Grotius would read ‘ recepta est ’ for ‘ resedit ’ in verse 2, but as Buhle points out : “ Haec lectio librarium christianum redolet ! ” ‘ Resedit ’ is nearer to Aratus’s νάσσατο.

F. XXII. Aratus next speaks of the star Protrygeter

or Vindemiator (Ovid *Fast.* iii. 395 *et sqq.*), and likens it to those stars which shine near the Great Bear. " Such stars are borne along, beautiful and great, one in front of her forefeet, one on her flank, and one beneath her hind knees " (Ar. 143-5).

genus. Used for the more common ' genu,' *metri gratia*, here and in 27, 45, 46, 254, 375, 399, 403 of the continuous poem. In every case, the insertion of ' s ' admits of a dactyl, preventing elision. This seems to be somewhat similar to the suppression of final ' s ' (see note p. 70), which was also brought about by the exigencies of scansion, i.e. to secure a greater number of dactylic feet and in imitation of the old school of poets.

The nom. ' genus ' is found in Lucil. in Non. 207, 28. I am indebted to Dr. C. M. Knight, of King's College, London, for the following remarks and references thereto. The confusion existing in Latin in the ' u ' stems is due to analogy, generally to analogy with the ' o ' stems. Thus we find : ' in sinistrum cornum ' (acc. sing.), Ter. *Eun.* 775 ; ' verum ' for ' veru,' Plaut. *Truc.* 628. This use of ' genus ' by Cicero must have been due originally to such analogy.

F. XXIII. On a March evening, directly south of the zenith, can be seen the Twins, Castor and Pollux. The former is a double star, and each of these two stars is, in turn, a double star. Therefore Castor is composed of four suns slowly revolving about a common centre of gravity. Pollux is the more southerly of the Twins, lying due north of Procyon (Ante-Canis). They are easily visible, forming a part of the ' arch ' of Orion. . . .

> " And starry Gemini hang like glorious crowns
> Over Orion's grave low down in the west."

The Crab is situated between the Twins and the Lion. Its stars are very faint, and include Praesepe, the Manger (cf. *Prog.* ii.). The Lion is identified by its sickle-shaped formation of stars, of which Regulus is the handle. All these constellations are near one another, and each is a sign of the Zodiac.

subiectus mediae, " beneath her [*sc.* Helice] waist."

pedibusque . . . flammam. Ar. 148 :

$$\pi\text{οσσὶ δ' ὀπισθοτέροισι Λέων ὕπο καλὰ φαείνε.}$$

This is one of the many passages where Cicero allowed himself to improve the original by a vigorous and poetical expansion. He seems to wish to make the stars alive, as it were, and so endows them with physical attributes. From amongst many examples of this may be cited verses 51 (the Swan), 110 (the Dog), 121 (the Hare). Cf., too, F. xxxii. 4, note *ad loc*.

quatiens. Used with reference to the twinkling of the star. The dactylic rhythm is as aptly used here, as in F. xxxii. 4, to represent the quick movement of the animal. The fourth spondee abruptly retards the verse, and emphasises the rhythm by contrast. One is reminded of the famous Virgilian verse : " Quadrupedante putrem sonitu quatit ungula campum."

F. XXIV. Having described the position of the Lion, Aratus continues : " There is the Sun's hottest summer path. Then in the tilled fields no ears of corn are seen, when first the Sun meets the Lion. Then the raging Etesian winds sweep the waters of the broad sea in massed array, and no longer then can oars be used for voyaging. Then better for me a vessel broad, with steersmen to hold the rudder into the wind."

Hoc motu . . . Ar. 152–3. The Etesian winds, beginning with the rising of Sirius, blow every year in the Mediterranean for approximately two months—Gell. ii. 22 ; *De Nat. Deor.* ii. 53. The nom. sing. 'Ætesias' is used by Pliny *N.H.* xviii. 34. Cf. Sen. *N.Q.* v. 10.

With the possible exception of verse 73 of the *De Consulatu*, this is the only instance of hiatus (strictly speaking semi-hiatus) in Cicero. He himself quotes the verse in *Or.* xlv. 152, with the significant remark : " Hoc idem nostri saepius non tulissent, quod Graeci laudare etiam solent." (See note *ad loc.* p. 69.)

F. XXV. This verse corresponds to nothing in Aratus. Grotius, therefore, appended it at the end of his edition, doubting whether it belonged to the poem. It might be part of an extension of Cicero's now lost, in which case it would not be out of place if inserted after Ar. 154, " and no longer then can oars be used for voyaging."

F. XXVI. Due north of Orion, and lying near the zenith in February, can be seen Auriga, the Charioteer, with Capella, the Goat, in his arms. Capella is one of the most brilliant stars of the northern hemisphere, being almost exactly equal in brightness to the two summer-month stars, Arcturus and Vega. Capella is distant from the earth about fifty light-years, and is computed to be more than two hundred times as bright as our own sun.

Auriga is identified with Erichthonius, the king of Athens, who was said to be the first to have used a chariot with four horses. Cf. *Georg.* iii. 114–15 :

" Primus Erichthonius currus et quattuor ausus
    iungere equos rapidusque rotis insistere victor."

obductus. Ar. 160. αὐτὸν μέν μιν ἅπαντα μέγαν Διδύμων ἐπὶ λαιὰ / κεκλιμένον δήεις·

Apparently here equivalent to ' obversus ' or ' obiectus.' The more usual sense would be ' veiled ' or ' covered,' but in this signification the word would be no translation of κεκλιμένον.

Helice. Trans. " whilst Helice's grim gaze is bent upon his head." There is a difficulty of reading here. Grotius (against MS. authority) emended to ' Helicae,' supporting the gen. by reference to the original, Ar. 161–2 :

Ἑλίκης δέ οἱ ἄκρα κάρηνα

ἀντία δινεύει.

He then took ' truculenta ' as an adverbial accusative. This awkward emendation further necessitates making 'adversum' a participle, so that 'adversum huic' = 'turned towards him' (i.e. the Charioteer), with the resultant harsh separation of these two words by 'caput.' With due regard for the frequency with which Cicero alters the phraseology of the original, there seems to be no real reason why he should not have done so here. In which case it seems more desirable to take 'Helice' as a nominative, with 'truculenta' in agreement. This necessitates 'adversum' becoming the adverb.

tuetur. Cf. original, δινεύει.

Capra. Or Capella, supposed to be the she-goat which nursed Jupiter on Mt. Ida. Cf. Hor. *Od.* iii. 7. 6; Ovid *Fast.* v. 113.

F. XXVII. The first verse of this Fragment refers to Capella, the second to the Kids. They form a group of three faint stars very close to the Goat. They are described by poets as 'the rainy ones,' because they rise in October. Cf. Hor. *Od.* iii. 1. 27; *Georg.* i. 205; *Aen.* ix. 668, and *Gk. Anth.* vii. 272:

φεῦγε θαλάσσῃ συμμίσγειν ἐρίφων, ναύτιλε, δυομένων.

Contra . . . ignem. Ar. 165–6:

οἱ δέ οἱ αὐτοῦ
λεπτὰ φαείνονται Ἔριφοι καρπὸν κάτα χειρός.

It will be seen that Cicero omits καρπὸν . . . χειρός, for which he substitutes 'mortalibus.'

F. XXVIII. The Bull, a zodiacal sign lying some way south of the zenith in the early evening hours of January, is easily recognised by the V-shaped group of stars called the Hyades. In this constellation of the Bull will also be found the famous Pleiades (cf. verse 27 *et sqq.* below).

connixus. Ar. 167 has πεπτηότα. There is some doubt as to the meaning of this word. He employs it five times in the *Ph.* 167, 318, 324, 353, 369. Mair (trans., p. 394 note) suggests that in some cases, e.g. 324, Aratus treated πεπτηώς as from πετάννυμι, in the sense of 'extended,' 'spread.' If the word be taken as coming from πτήσσω, it must mean 'crouching.' This latter meaning seems to have been that in which Cicero understood the word, being an extension of its more usual signification of 'leaning forward.' For this sense cf. *Aen.* ix. 410, and x. 127.

F. XXIX. Ovid (*Fast.* v. 163-4) tells of the rising of the Hyades in May, and says :

> " Ora micant Tauri septem radiantia flammis,
> Navita quas Hyadas Graius ab imbre vocat."

The name is also derived from ὕς, ' sus,' and they were also named Suculae for the same reason.

The verse is an explanatory one added by Cicero. For the rare form ' suërunt ' (not occurring elsewhere in the poems), cf. Lucret. iv. 369.

F. XXX. Aratus, in describing the position of the Hyades, says that they are scattered over the Bull's forehead : " One star occupies the tip of his left horn and the right foot of the Charioteer, who is close by."

In this Fragment, therefore, the words ' dexterque . . . pes' must be taken as referring to the Charioteer. Germ. 178-9 :

> " quae cornus flamma sinistri
> summa tenet, subit haec eadem vestigia dextra
> aurigae . . ."

Av. 437-8 :

> " una pedem aurigae dextrum cornumque sinistrum
> stella tenet pecoris."

F. XXXI. Now follows the story of Cepheus and his family. According to the legend, Cepheus, the king of Ethiopia, was the husband of Cassiepia. The queen dared to contend in a beauty contest with the sea-nymphs. As punishment a sea-monster was sent to ravage the coasts of the kingdom. To avert this calamity

the oracle ordered that their daughter, Andromeda,
should be chained to the rocks, and be devoured by this
monster. Perseus arrived on his winged horse, rescued
the maiden, and married her. Ultimately they were
transferred to the heavens : Cassiepia, with Cepheus,
was condemned to be swung continually round the north
pole that she might suffer for her pride. (Cf., too, Cic.
Tusc. Dis. v. 3. 8.)

Namque . . . Arcti. Is an exact translation of Ar.
182 : Αὐτὸς μὲν κατόπισθεν ἐὼν Κυνοσυρίδος Ἄρκτου.

Cynosurae. Presumably in apposition limiting ' Arcti,'
although Mayor suggests that it may be an adjective like
the ' cynosura ova ' of Pliny *N.H.* x. 167. Cf. Ovid
Trist. v. 3. 7 : ' stellis Cynosuridos Ursae.'

F. XXXII. This Fragment should, in accordance with
the original, be divided into four parts. The first verse
concerns Cassiepia, the second and third Andromeda,
the fourth to the seventh Pegasus, the eighth the Ram.
They are printed as one Fragment here in conformity
with the edition of Baehrens.

Obscura . . . Cassiepia. Cicero here translates the
sense of Ar. 188–9 :

> τοῦ δ᾽ ἄρα δαιμονίη προκυλίνδεται οὐ μάλα πολλὴ
> νυκτὶ φαεινομένη παμμήνιδι Κασσιεπεία.

Cassiepia is easily recognisable by the distinctive W-
shape of her stars. She and Cepheus lie in the path of
the Milky Way, which reaches its farthest northern point
in her. Both are circumpolar constellations.

Hanc autem illustri . . . Ar. 197–8 :

> Αὐτοῦ γὰρ κἀκεῖνο κυλίνδεται αἰνὸν ἄγαλμα
> Ἀνδρομέδης ὑπὸ μητρὶ κεκασμένον.

Cicero here translates freely, and there is a difficulty
of reading. One of the scholiasts on Aratus gives οἱονεί
κεχωρισμένον as an explanation of κεκασμένον (" arrayed ").
It is probable that he read κεχασμένον (" recoiling ")

from χάζομαι, which may, perhaps, be the origin of Cicero's ' aufugiens aspectum.' For the construction of ' aufugiens ' with an acc. cf. Prop. i. 9. 30, " assiduas aufuge blanditias " ; also Hygin. *Fab.* 258 : " quae sol aufugit." Mayor, in his edition, says that Lachmann on Lucret., p. 272, argues against the reading here, since the final ' a ' of Greek nouns is long and cannot be elided (*ib.*, p. 405). Muncker, however, instances ' Andromeda hic,' 257 below, ' Andromeda et ' 437, and the short ' a ' in ' hydra,' 292, 397.

maesta. This is not an adequate representation of αἰνὸν ἄγαλμα. It was probably suggested by the words of Aratus used just before of Cassiepia, ἀνιάζειν ἐπὶ παιδί.

Equus. The winged horse of Bellerophon. The remainder of this verse is added by Cicero. The original, 205–6 :

’Αλλ’ ἄρα οἱ καὶ κρατὶ πέλωρ ἐπελήλαται ῞Ιππος
γαστέρι νειαίρη.

Cf. note on F. xxiii. It is probable that Cicero derived his line from Ennius, who has (*Ann.* 517) " iubam quassat altam."

summum . . . alvo. Grotius emended ' summum,' which has full MS. authority, to ' summa ' on the ground that Aratus wrote γαστέρι νειαίρη. This seems unnecessary, as ' alvus ' can quite well represent the Greek. Cf., too, Av. 470–72 : " Andromedae capiti . . . suppingitur . . . alvus equi."

stellaque . . . nodum. Cf. Ar. 206 :

. . . ξυνὸς δ’ἐπιλάμπεται ἀστὴρ
τοῦ μὲν ἐπ’ ὀμφαλίῳ, τῆς δ’ἐσχατόωντι καρήνῳ.

Yet another instance of Cicero's skill as a translator and of his appreciation of pure ' poetry.' He adds the charming verse " aeternum . . . nodum."

The great square of Pegasus is very conspicuous. The star that marks its north-eastern corner is the head of

Andromeda who is resting on the shoulders of Pegasus. Thus the two constellations are closely connected. Andromeda and Pegasus are best seen in the early evening hours of November.

Exin . . . haeret. Aries, the Ram, is one of the zodiacal signs visible near the meridian on a December evening. It has no particularly bright stars in it. Legend makes it the ram which bore Phrixus and Helle A poetical touch is imparted to this otherwise prosaic line by the addition of 'contortis . . . cornibus ' ("with crinkled horns," Mayor). The original Ar. 225 has :

Αὐτοῦ καὶ Κριοῖο θοώταταί εἰσι κέλευθοι,

haeret. Greek ἐστήρικται (Ar. 230), regularly used of the fixed stars. Cf. *Ph.* 169.

1–3. Aratus has eight verses dealing with the Ram, of which the last line of F. xxxii. is the introduction. Aries is "weak and starless as on a moonlit night, but yet by the belt of Andromeda thou canst trace him out."

1. *hunc.* *sc.* the Ram ; *subter,* an adverb. Grotius's emendation for MS. ' hinc.'

2. Ar. 230–1 :

μεσσόθι δὲ τρίβει μέγαν οὐρανόν, ἦχί περ ἄκραι
Χηλαὶ καὶ ζώνη περιτέλλεται ᾽Ωρίωνος.

' Nam,' which is Grotius's emendation for ' iam,' suits μεσσόθι δὲ better. The MS. reading " ut prius illae/ Chelae cum pectus quod cernitur Orionis " is unintelligible. The emendations are those of Grotius.

Cicero here uses ' pectus ' for the more usual ' cingulum ' : cf. ζώνη. The sense of this difficult passage appears to be that the Claws revolve in the northern zone, rising first, whilst Orion follows the Ram. The Claws, now known as Libra, the Scales, at one time formed a part of Scorpion, its claws (cf. note verse 183). Hence the name. It lies to the north-west of Scorpion, is a sign of the Zodiac, and can be distinguished just to the south of Serpens and Ophiuchus on a July evening. For Orion cf. verse 102 below.

ut = ἦχι = ' where.'

3. A spondaic hexameter, due to the Greek word.

4–9. *Deltoton.* A small and insignificant constellation, now known as Triangulum, which can be found near Aries close to the meridian on a December evening.

dicere . . . claret. An addition of Cicero's to explain the Greek word. He likens the shape of the constellation to the capital letter Δ, and is careful to state that the name is Greek. Later, Av. 527–8 also said :

" Est etiam Graio quod semper nomine nostri
  Deltoton memorant."

7. *Huic . . . utrumque.* Trans. " two of its sides appear to be of equal length."

8. *namque . . . illis.* The MSS. D and H 1 are clearly in error ; H 2 corrects this, as printed in the text. Cf. Ar. 236 : ἡ δ'οὔτι τόση.

9. *sed . . . relucet.* This paraphrase is worthy of comparison with the original, to which it is superior. The spondaic rhythm seems to be used of set purpose to express the idea of clear radiance in infinite space. Similar is the effect obtained in verse 242. Ar. 236–7 :

μάλα δ'ἐστὶν ἑτοίμη
εὑρέσθαι· περὶ γὰρ πολέων εὐάστερός ἐστιν.

10–19. *The Fishes.* This constellation just south of Andromeda and Pegasus is the first sign of the Zodiac. The southern Fish appears extended in an east-to-west direction, the northern lies nearly north and south. The two touch at their south-eastern extremity.

There is no bright star in the constellation, and its chief importance lies in the fact that it contains the " equinoctial point," i.e. the point in the heavens where the Sun crosses the Equator on its journey northwards in the spring.

10. *flamen.* There is a MS. reading ' et flumen,' which is clearly a scribal error. A possible source of confusion may have been the river Eridanus—verse 145—which has no place in a discussion on the position of the Ram. For similar phrases cf. 22, 70, 198.

11. *vehementius.* Ar. 239-40 :

> οἱ δ'ἄρ' ἔτι προτέρω, ἔτι δ'ἐν προμολῇσι νότοιο,
> Ἰχθύες.

" Still farther in advance of the Ram and still in the vestibule of the South are the Fishes."

illi Pisces. ' Illi ' is not represented in Aratus. It here probably has the meaning of ' well-known.' Cf. 236, ' illae Chelae,' 289 ' Equus ille.' Hipp. i. 6. 8 remarks that only one of the Fishes is south of the Ram : the schol. on Aratus seems to think that he meant south of Deltoton.

12. *alter.* i.e. Piscis Borealis, the northern fish.

13. *et magis . . . alis.* The force of the wind is depicted by the dactylic nature of the verse. Cf. 141, 198. For ' horrisonis . . . alis,' cf. Aesch. F. ii. 3, and Lucret. v. 109, *Aen.* vi. 573, ix. 55. Lucretius imitates this method of describing the quarters of the heaven, cf. v. 689. The original has a slightly different metaphor, Ar. 241 :

> καὶ μᾶλλον βορέαο νέον κατιόντος ἀκούει.

14. *at quae.* Ald. has ' atque,' but this is felt to be harsh when compared with the second ' atque ' in verse 16 : ' quae ' is relative to ' catenae,' which it precedes. The sense of this and the next verse in Aratus is that two chains stretch out from their tails, which finally unite in the ' Knot of Tails.' Cf. Germ. 244-5 :

> " non illis liber cursus, sed vincula cauda
>   singula utrumque tenent uno coeuntia nodo,"

and Av. 552–4 :

> " sed tamen hi late stellis ex ordine fusis
> nectuntur caudas et lenta trahuntur utraque
> vincula. . . ."

17. *caelestem.* Ar. 245 : ὅν ῥά τε καὶ σύνδεσμον ὑπούραιον καλέουσιν. Cicero appears to have known another reading here not appearing in the extant MSS. of Aratus, for his ' caelestem . . . Nodum ' is the equivalent, not of σύνδεσμον ὑπούραιον, but of σύνδεσμον ὑπουράνιον. He was followed by Avienus, who writes, verse 556 :

" caelestem memorat quem sollers Graecia Nodum."

Cf. Enn. *Sat.* 70 : " soliti quod dicere Nodum."

18. *si quaerere perges.* Here Cicero omits the original phraseology and inserts this parenthesis of his own which causes further alteration in the next verse. The original 246–7 reads :

> Ἀνδρομέδης δέ τοι ὦμος ἀριστερὸς Ἰχθύος ἔστω
> σῆμα βορειοτέρου· μάλα γάρ νύ οἱ ἐγγύθεν ἐστίν.

Lucretius may have had this in mind in iv. 300, where he writes : " contra si tendere pergas."

19. *Piscem. sc.* Borealis.

20–26. *Perseus.* The reference to Andromeda naturally leads on to the introduction of Perseus, her deliverer. Just north of Taurus the constellation is easily discerned in January, being near the meridian in the early evening. Part of it borders the Milky Way, and legend relates that Perseus, in his anxiety to rescue Andromeda, stirred up a great dust (cf. verses 25, 26) which was afterwards represented by the innumerable small stars of the Milky Way at this point. Beta Persei is the well-known variable, Algol.

20–21. *E pedibus . . . Perseus.* Ar. 248–9 has :

> Ἀμφότεροι δὲ πόδες γαμβροῦ ἐπισημαίνοιεν
> Περσέος, οἵ ῥά οἱ αἰὲν ἐπωμάδιοι φορέονται,

Cicero's persistent realism—welcome in a poem of this nature—leads him to desert the phrasing of the original, and to insert such deft additions as ' natum summo Iove ' and ' defixo corpore.' *E pedibus. sc.* Andromedae.

22. *quem.* ' quam ' of D is clearly wrong here, the relative referring not to Andromeda, but to Perseus : ' quom ' H does not give the sense of Aratus, who starts a new sentence with αὐτὰρ ὅ γ'. Cicero omits the περιμήκετος ἄλλων (" a taller form than the others ") of Aratus.

23. *ad sedes . . . Cassiepiae.* Cicero prefers the use of the queen's name to the recondite allusion of Aratus, who calls her, 252, πενθερίου (δίφροιο) (" the mother of his bride "). The spondaic rhythm is certainly intentional here. Cf., too, verse 26 below.

24-6. *Diversosque . . . portat.* The interpretation of these verses is difficult. Ar. 252-3 writes :

τὰ δ'ἐν ποσὶν οἷα διώκων
ἴχνια μηκύνει κεκονιμένος ἐν Διὶ πατρί.

. . . " and, as if pursuing that which lies before his feet, he greatly strides, dust-stained, in the heaven of Zeus."

If Cicero was reading from a text similar to ours he misunderstood the first verse, he added ' de terra elapsu repente ' to the second, missed the force of ἴχνια μηκύνει, and extended ' in caelum ' by ' magno sub culmine.' Buhle (note *ad Ar. Ph.* 253. i. p. 406) and others seem to imagine that Cicero believed Aratus to be describing the actual rising of the constellation ; κεκονιμένος they understand in the sense of ' currens ' (see Lex. ἀποκονίσαι = to hurry) and take the Latin ' elapsus ' = ' ascendens.' This is all very far fetched and unnecessary. The Greek is perfectly clear. No astronomical signification is intended except is so far as Aratus represents the victorious warrior (cf. the story of Medusa) rising to the sky where, having already gained his place as a constellation, he continues to stride forward with mighty pace. The epithet ' dusty ' is to be taken literally as a poetical adorn-

ment, which both Cicero and Avienus realised. Cf. Av.
566–7 :

> " . . . ingentique dehinc vestigia passu
> pulverulenta quasi cano procul aere pandit."

diversos. This appears to mean ' in the opposite direction ' (i.e. from his right hand). Could it possibly = ' on both sides ' (of his body) ? Cf. ' diversae ' in verse 15 above.

talaribus aptis. " shod with sandals."

magno sub culmine. Archaic for ' magnum sub culmen.' Germ., who wrote, 253–4 :

> " . . . pedibus properare videtur
> et velle aligeris purum aethera tangere plantis "

doubtless had the version of Cicero before him, as is shown by his ' aligeris . . . plantis,' no suggestion of which appears in Aratus. That Avienus also used Cicero is probable from his employment of ' pulverulentus ' (note in similar position in the verse). Cf. note *Prog.* iii.

27–41. *The Pleiades.* Cf. intro. to F. xxviii. on the Bull, in which the Pleiades are situated. One of the most famous and beautiful constellations, the Pleiades, a short distance north-west of the Hyades, can be clearly distinguished in the evenings of the winter months. Six stars can be seen with the naked eye, the seventh being at the end of their tail-like formation and more difficult to find. Astronomers have discovered at least two hundred and fifty stars in this cluster, surrounded by a fiery, nebulous mist. Their distance from the earth is so prodigious that light from them is calculated to take three centuries to reach us, although travelling at the rate of 186,000 miles per second !

Tennyson, in *Locksley Hall*, describes them thus :

> " Many a night I saw the Pleiads, rising through the
>   mellow shade,
> Glitter like a swarm of fireflies tangled in a silver braid."

27. *genus.* Cf. note on F. xxii.

omni ex parte locatas. Ar. 254 ἤλιθα.

28. *parvas.* This takes the place of ὁ δ' οὐ μάλα πολλὸς ἁπάσας/χῶρος ἔχει, which Germ. 256 translates by "brevis et locus occupat omnes," and Avienus by "locus has habet artior omnes," 569.

28. *tenui cum luce.* For this use of ' cum ' cf. Lucret. iv. 1126.

29. *more vetusto.* Ar. 257 : ἑπτάποροι δὴ ταί γε μετ' ἀνθρώπους ὑδέονται. who thus expresses the same idea somewhat differently. Virgil later adopted this ending *Aen.* xi. 142, " de more vetusto."

32. Excessive repetition mars this verse, and, of course, Cicero, following Aratus, is incorrect in assuming that there were originally only six. Hipp. i. 6. 12 realised this, and stated that on a clear, moonless night seven stars could be seen.

34. A happy extension of Ar. 261 : . . . ἑπτὰ δ'ἐκεῖναι ἐπιρρήδην καλέονται. *Dignant,* the reading defended by Grotius, who says that it occurs in this active sense in Accius (quoted in Non. " exuvias dignavi Atalantae dare "). Cf. too *Aen.* iii. 475, " coniugio Anchise Veneris dignate superbo," where the passive use of ' digno ' warrants the use of the active verb also. For ' aeterno . . . nomine,' cf. *Aen.* vi. 235, *ib.* 381.

35-6. The final syllable of these names is long after the Greek form. Note ' Tāy̆gĕtēque.' Both Germ. 264-5 and Av. 573-5 mention that these were the daughters of Atlas, and the latter says that the missing Pleiad was variously supposed to be either Electra or Merope, 582-600.

sanctissima. Ar. πότνια ; Av. 581 ' famosa.'

37. For the phraseology, cf. Enn. *Ann.* 156, " . . . tum candida lumina lucent."

38. *at magnum . . . vocatur.* Ar. 264-5 :

ἀλλ' ὀνομασταὶ
ἦρι καὶ ἑσπέριαι, Ζεὺς δ' αἴτιος, εἰλίσσονται,

Whilst omitting the second of the above verses Cicero expands ἀλλ᾽ ὀνομασταί into a whole line.

39. *clarat.* Very rare in this transitive sense. Cicero uses it again in 166 and *De Cons.* 63. Cf. Lucret. iii. 36; Hor. *Od.* iv. 3. 4; Stat. *Th.* v. 286.

40. *hiberni . . . ortus.* Parallels for this and ' lumine verno' (287) are to be found in Lucret. v. 940 and 802.

41. *ut mandent . . . terris.* Ar. 267 says that Zeus bade them tell ἐπερχομένου τ᾽ ἀρότοιο, ' the coming of the ploughing-time.' This they do as they set in November. Cicero has transformed the original into a verse as charming as it is accurate. The rising of the Pleiades in May was also the sign of harvest-time. Cf. Theophrast. *De Sign.* i. 6: διχοτομεῖ δὲ τὸν μὲν ἐνιαυτὸν Πλειάς τε δυομένη καὶ ἀνατέλλουσα. Similar advice is given in *Georg.* i. 219–26.

42–6. *The Lyre.* A small but important constellation containing the beautiful star, Vega. This is a first-magnitude star, some forty light-years distant from the earth, not far from which can be seen, with a telescope, the noted Ring Nebula, which is a ring of luminous gas surrounding a central star. Our solar system is moving at more than a million miles a day in the direction of the Lyre, to a point south-west of Vega, which is known as The Apex of the Sun's Way. On an August evening the Lyre can be easily discerned in the southern sky, bordered on the east by the Swan and on the west by Hercules (Nixus).

42. *leviter.* The transposition of this word from ' posita ' to ' convexa ' is due to Baehrens, who rightly regarded ' leviter posita ' as a curious and unlikely expression ; presumably this would mean, " slightly sketched (or depicted)," as in Hor. *Od.* iv. 8. 8, where we have " ille . . . sollers hominem ponere." But ' leviter convexa ' as " slightly curved " is perfectly suitable. The conjecture of Bouhierus has but little to recommend it. It would appear to mean " turned aside (i.e. from the

Swan), slanting." He probably took this emendation from Manilius, who (*Astronomicon* i. 625) speaks of the Lyre as ' inversam,' apparently on no authority whatever and certainly incorrectly. No help is to be gained from Aratus ; both Germanicus and Avienus are silent on this one point, whilst Grotius's emendation ' convecta ' has little likelihood of being the true reading, although one cannot but admit that the Lyre *is* a small, massed constellation. Trans. " next the Lyre, slightly curved, is seen in its place."

42–4. *Inde . . . locasse.* Comparison of this passage with the original Ar. 268–71 reveals many omissions in the Latin. Nothing is said of the Lyre being formerly " the tiny Tortoise " (καὶ χέλυς, ἥτ' ὀλίγη), or of how " Hermes pierced it for strings " ('Ερμείης ἐτόρησε), or of how " he bade it be called the Lyre " (Λύρην δέ μιν εἶπε λέγεσθαι), or of how " he set it before the unknown Engonasin " (ἔθετο προπάροιθεν ἀπευθέος Εἰδώλοιο).

For the reputed invention of the Lyre, as a musical instrument, by Hermes, see *Hom. H. Hermes* 39 *et sqq.*

44. *in cunis.* Despite the reading of H, this is certainly to be preferred, having regard to the original παρὰ λίκνῳ of Ar. 268.

46. *atque.* Between this and the preceding verse Cicero has omitted Ar. 272–3 :

κεφαλή γε μὲν ἄκρη
ἀντιπέρην "Ορνιθος ἑλίσσεται·

Alitis. *sc.* Cygnus, the Swan.

47–54. *The Swan.* The principal stars in Cygnus form the Northern Cross, with the beautiful star Deneb at the top of the cross and Albireo, an orange and blue double star, at the foot. Albireo marks the head of the Swan, Deneb the tail.

47. *Namque.* The reading of our MSS. as opposed to that given in *De Nat. Deor.*, " inde," is due to the need for explaining ' Alitis ' in the preceding verse.

158

ales avis. The same phrase occurs in verse 258 without a Greek equivalent. In this passage we read in Ar. 275 αἰόλος ὄρνις. Translators of Aratus take the word in its late sense of " glittering," but if the Ciceronian ' ales ' is used as an epithet to ' avis,' which seems certain, one must conclude that he regarded αἰόλος in the Homeric sense, " nimble, fleet." Cf. Hom. *Il.* xix. 404 ; *ib.* xxii. 509. Neither Germanicus nor Avienus translates the word.

Cicero himself omits the second epithet of Aratus, who describes the bird as " wreathed in mist " (ἠερόεις), presumably with reference to the light of the Milky Way, part of which passes through the Swan.

48. *et serpens . . . pennis.* Ar. 278–9 writes :

αὐτὰρ ὅ γ' εὐδιόωντι ποτὴν ὄρνιθι ἐοικὼς
οὔριος εἰς ἑτέρην φέρεται . . .

" like a bird in joyous flight, with fair weather it glides to the west."

For the phraseology cf. verse 88, " tremebundis aethera pinnis," from which two passages it is clear that Avienus used Cicero's translation freely, for we find in verse 636 " secat aethera pinnis." Cf. too *Georg.* i. 406, 409.

49–50. *Altera pars . . . ardet.* These two verses markedly show Cicero's tendency to expand the original, which has :

τὰ δέ οἱ ἐπιτετρήχυνται
ἀστράσιν οὔτι λίην μεγάλοις, ἀτὰρ οὐ μὲν ἀφαυροῖς.

51. *sed . . . lumen.* An addition of Cicero's : the verse is not found in Aratus. Cf. *Ph.* F. xxiii. 3 (note) ; verses 52–4 also exemplify this partiality of Cicero's for animating astronomical groups.

The use of ' iacio ' in a similar signification is found in *Ph.* F. xxvii. 2 and 331 *infra.* Cf., too, Lucret. v. 576 ; vi. 389.

mediōcre.   Here the penultimate is regarded as long.
Cf. *Prog.* vi. 2, ' ācredula.'

52–3. *dextro pede pellere . . . gestit.*   Ar. 280 :

. . . ταρσοῖο τὰ δεξιὰ πείρατα τείνων.

τείνω, even in the sense of ' to exert oneself, struggle,'
cannot alone bear the meaning of ' pellere gestit.'   The
word ταρσός, in general any flat surface, can be used of a
wing or a foot.   Cicero incorrectly took it to be the
latter ; Aratus is right in saying ' wing,' but in any case
the description is hardly accurate, since the *left* wing of
the Swan points much more directly to Cepheus than the
right.   A further branch of this left wing also extends
towards Pegasus (cf. verses 53, 54).

clinata.   This very rare participle occurs here and in
verses 86, 259.   Cf. note *Prog.* F. iii. ' tristificas.'

ungula vemens fortis equi.   Ar. 281 : σκαρθμὸς . . .
Ἵππου.

alam.   sc. ' sinistram,' Ar. *ib.* λαιῇ δὲ πτέρυγι.

pinnati corporis.   An addition suitably realistic.

55–71. *Aquarius and Capricorn.*   (For Pegasus see
Ph. F. xxxii.)   Two zodiacal constellations visible low
down on the southern horizon on an October evening.
Neither is of particular interest, and the stars of each do
not contain amongst them any of first—or even second—
magnitude.   The water-jar carried by Aquarius is repre-
sented by a small Y of stars, from which flows a stream of
faint stars towards the south-east.   (See 173 *et sqq.*)

55. *utrisque.*   The ' multis ' of D is obviously impos-
sible on astronomical grounds.   Ar. 282 has δύ' Ἰχθύες.

56. *mulcetur.*   Ar. 284 writes τετάνυσθ', " is stretched."
Farther on in 173 Cicero talks of Aquarius's right hand
" scattering a faint stream of stars."   Hence his use of
' mulcetur ' here (in pursuance of his desire to animate
the constellations) suggests that Cicero had no clear
knowledge of the shapes of all the star-groups.

57–9. Serius . . . in orbe.   Ar. 284–6:

ὁ δ᾿ ὀπίστερος Αἰγοκερῆος
τέλλεται. αὐτὰρ ὅ γε πρότερος καὶ νειόθι μᾶλλον
κέκλιται Αἰγοκέρως, ἵνα τε τρέπετ᾿ ἠελίου ἴς.

There is considerable confusion here upon comparison with the original. First Cicero misunderstood the words ὁ δ᾿ . . . τέλλεται, for he refers them to Pegasus, although in the text of Aratus it is clear that they are used of Aquarius. Secondly, the verb "obitus terrai visit," signifying the setting of Aquarius, is not a possible translation of τέλλεται. But Germ. 286–7 expresses a similar idea :

"Quo prior Aegoceros semper properare videtur
    oceano mersus sopitas condere flammas."

This inclines one to believe that Cicero read ἕλκεται for τέλλεται in his copy of Aratus, and was afterwards followed by Germanicus. Thirdly, Cicero omits mention of Capricorn's position, which is "set in front and further down," and substitutes for it verses 58 and 59. Cf. verses 150 *et sqq.* for similar confusion.

equi vis. This periphrasis was commonly used by Ennius and his successors in imitation of the Greeks. Cicero affords the following examples : *Ph.* 78, 206, 271, 321, 324, 370, 372, 418 ; *Misc. Vv.* viii ; *Soph.* iii. 15, 31. Ennius has such endings as, "virum vis" (*Ann.* 276), "aquae vis" (*ib.* 379).

quam. As opposed to the ' tum ' of *De Nat. Deor.* is here necessary after ' serius ' in verse 57.

gelidum . . . frigus. The sun, of course, enters Capricorn at mid-winter, December 22nd. For similar phraseology, cf. Lucret. v. 641, "gelidis a frigoris umbris."

semifero. Objection has been raised against ' semifero ' on the ground that Capricorn is rather ' ferus.' That Capricorn is half goat, half fish easily explains the

word. Cf. Lucret. iv. 587, " semiferi capitis " ; *Aen.*
x. 212 " semifero sub pectore " for parallel phraseology.

orbe. sc. Zodiac.

60–61. *quem . . . currum.* Not occurring in Aratus
except for the reference to Capricorn being " where the
mighty sun turns." Translate :

> " The whole of whom in splendour Phoebus decks
> 'ere winter sees him turn again his car."

perpetuo. Usually understood as ' undying ' rays, but
surely more appropriate to refer it to the ' full ' stream
of light illuminating the whole constellation. For
' perpetuus ' in this sense cf. *Aen.* viii. 183.

flectens. Turning on his *rounded* course. From the
common use of the word in ' doubling ' a cape (*Ep. ad
Att.* v. 9) or rounding a point. Cf. *Georg.* iii. 359.

64. *Non . . . nox.* A neat paraphrase of Ar. 288–9 :

> οὔτε κεν ἠοῖ
> πολλὴν πειρήνειας, ἐπεὶ ταχινώταταί εἰσιν·

curriculo nox. See p. 62 (5th and 6th feet, § c.),
verses 189, 264, and *Aen.* viii. 407–8 :

> " Inde ubi prima quies medio iam noctis abactae
> curriculo expulerat somnum,"

66. *clari . . . Solis.* An addition : Cicero omits from
Ar. 292–3 :

> . . . ὁπότ' Αἰγοκερῆϊ
> συμφέρετ' ἠέλιος·

which is but a repetition of verse 60.

67. The alliteration on ' u ' is possibly onomatopoeic :
similar is verse 195. In the same way the sound of water
is imitated in verse 71 by ' m ' and ' u.'

69–71. *Sed tamen . . . fluctus.* Ar. 294–9 writes :
" *Not but that throughout the year's length the sea ever grows
dark beneath the keels,* and, like to diving seagulls, we often
sit, spying out the deep from our ship with faces turned

to the shore ; but ever farther back the shores are swept by the waves and only a thin plank staves off Death."

The sentence italicised is nearest to the Ciceronian version in feeling, but there is nothing in the Latin at all parallel to the Greek. With the sentiments expressed here by Cicero one is tempted to compare a similar passage in Horace :

> " Illi robur et aes triplex
> circa pectus erat, qui fragilem truci
> commisit pelago ratem
> primus, nec timuit praecipitem Africum
> decertantem Aquilonibus,
> nec tristes Hyades, nec rabiem Noti."
>
> (*Od.* i. 3. 9 *et sqq.*)

Difficulty is felt in verse 69 where the subject to ' labuntur ' must be supplied from the sense of the preceding verses by some word such as ' nautae ' or ' naves ' : ' anni ' then becomes genitive. Verses 70 and 71 preclude the possibility of taking it as nominative. Trans. " But yet at every season of the year sailors now pursue their course, submitting to no constellations, shunning no winds, undismayed by the threatening murmur of the foam-capped waves."

Both Germanicus (297 *et sqq.*) and Avienus (664 *et sqq.*) give versions of the passage in Aratus. This fact, together with the difficulty regarding the subject in verse 69, inclines one to suppose that some of Cicero's verses have been lost at this place.

72–83. *Sagittarius* (*The Archer*). Just east of Scorpio, this constellation is seen on an August evening, but so low down on the southern horizon that it is better viewed from the tropics than from the mid-latitudes of the northern hemispheres. One of the zodiacal groups, it contains no first-magnitude stars ; some astronomers have believed that here is the centre of the star system of which our solar system is but a minute part.

72. *vagato.* The reading of Patric. ' vacato,' which goes closely with ' navi pelagoque,' is too far from the original θαλάσσῃ πολλὰ πεπονθώς, and verse 74 is an awkward addition to verses 72, 73 : reading ' vagato ' we can make it depend in translation on verse 74.

supero . . . mense. i.e. superiori mense, November. Aratus ἐπὶ προτέρῳ.

73. *Sagittipotens.* Cf. note *Prog.* iii. ' tristificas.' The word was not adopted by succeeding poets : it is used by Cicero here and in verses 325 and 461 for the usual ' Sagittarius,' and may have been borrowed from some work by Ennius no longer extant.

74. *nam iam . . . est.* An addition of Cicero's. He omits Ar. 302 :

ἑσπέριος κατάγοιο, πεποιθὼς οὐκέτι νυκτί.

which Germanicus and Avienus both translate. Grotius ventured to insert a verse, " subducas fessam, veniet cum vespera, navim." The meaning of Cicero's verse appears to be that sailing is practised throughout the year—not only in December, but also in November, and even then there is insufficient daylight for much voyaging.

75–8. *Hoc signum . . . Arcum.* These four verses represent a paraphrased version of Ar. 303–7, but omit 305–6 :

ἤτοι γὰρ μέγα τόξον ἀνέλκεται ἐγγύθι κέντρου
Τοξευτής·

" For verily his great Bow does the Bowman draw close by the Scorpion's sting."

Mayor (ed. *De Nat. Deor.*) has a note on ' posteriore trahens . . . Arcum ' to the effect that Cicero mistook the force of Ar. 305, ἀνέλκεται ἐγγύθι κέντρου, where the verb = the Latin ' tendit ' and confounded it with ἕλκεται (Ar. 342) = the Latin ' trahitur.' This is incorrect, as Cicero in verses 77 and 78 is not translating

Ar. 305, but paraphrasing, as he so often does, verses 306–7 :

ὀλίγον δὲ παροίτερος ἵσταται αὐτοῦ
Σκορπίος ἀντέλλων, ὁ δ' ἀνέρχεται αὐτίκα μᾶλλον.

" and a little in front stands the Scorpion at his rising, but the Archer rises right after him."

77. *emergit.* The indicative in an oblique question is a colloquialism. Cf. *Ann.* 215 " audite ut *mitto* " ; Ter. *Hec.* iii. 5. 21 " si memorare velim quam fideli animo . . . *fui* " and a possible example in Virgil *Ecl.* iv. 52 " aspice venturo *laetantur* (the reading of R : ' laetentur ' vulgo) ut omnia saeclo ! "

Trans. " . . . to see how the Scorpion shows himself as he rises from the deep, drawing steadily behind him the Archer's crescent Bow."

80. *ad summum . . . orbem.* Ar. 308–9 :

. . . κεφαλὴ Κυνοσουρίδος ἀκρόθι νυκτὸς
ὕψι μάλα τροχάει,

Did Cicero read here ἀκρόθι κυκλοῦ ?

82. *ante.* In our northern latitudes Cepheus is, of course, one of the circumpolar constellations : in latitudes farther south his head sets *before* Orion. Cicero realising this adds ' ante ' ; Aratus makes the setting of the two constellations simultaneous. Aratus also remarks that Cepheus sets " from hand to waist." If Cicero literally translated the original, perhaps the conjecture of Morelius is preferable to the MS. ' a prima ' as being nearer the Greek. In either case the meaning is identical.

83. *lumborum tenus.* Peck (*Amer. Philol. Assoc.*, 1897, vol. 28) points out that in the *Aratea* Cicero uses ' tenus ' twice with the ablative and once, for the first time in extant literature, with the genitive. " It is an interesting coincidence," he continues, " that Cicero (' lumborum tenus '), Lucretius (' labrorum tenus ' i. 940) and Catullus (lxiv. 18 ' nutricum tenus ') each use ' tenus ' only once

with the genitive, the noun in the plural, denoting bodily organs, and placed at the beginning of the line."

84-101. *The Arrow (Sagitta), the Eagle (Aquila) and the Dolphin (Delphinus).* These three constellations lie close together almost due south of the Swan. It will be remembered (cf. note vv. 47-54) that Albireo marks "the foot of the cross": this points almost directly to the Arrow, the point of which is indicated by the easternmost star, the feather by two faint stars to the west. Slightly east of the Arrow is the charming little star-group known as the Dolphin. It is best seen through a telescope, as its five principal stars are only of the fourth magnitude. In this constellation is the most distant known object in the heavens, the globular star cluster (N.G.C. 7006), calculated to be 220,000 light-years from the earth! South of these two constellations is the Eagle which contains the beautiful first-magnitude star, Altair, distant from the earth about sixteen light-years.

84. *missore vacans.* The correction of Morelius. 'Missor' ἅπαξ λεγ. Ar. 312 αὐτὸς ἄτερ τόξου, "alone without a bow." Germ. 315 "incertum quo cornu missa." Av. 691 "inscia nam domini est."

85. *nītens pinna.* "hovers": Ar. 312 παραπέπταται. *Ales,* the Swan.

87. *ardenti . . . portat.* 'Propter' adverb; 'se' with 'portat.' Cf. Ar. 313 ἄηται, "tosses in storm."

88. There is no equivalent to this verse in Aratus. It may be an interpolation, and for this reason I have enclosed it in brackets.

89-90. *non nimis . . . signum.* Grotius believed either that one or two verses were missing here, or that Cicero did not clearly perceive the sense of the original. Ar. 314-15:

$$\chi\alpha\lambda\epsilon\pi\acute{o}\varsigma \ \gamma\epsilon \ \mu\epsilon\nu \ \dot{\epsilon}\xi \ \dot{\alpha}\lambda\grave{o}\varsigma \ \dot{\epsilon}\lambda\theta\epsilon\tilde{\iota}\nu$$
$$\nu\nu\kappa\tau\grave{o}\varsigma \ \dot{\alpha}\pi\epsilon\rho\chi\omega\mu\acute{\epsilon}\nu\eta\varsigma\cdot$$

"but cruel in its rising from the sea when the night is waning."

But Cicero's translation seems to be little more than one of his rather free paraphrases of the original, and there hardly seems to be sufficient justification for supposing the text to be incomplete.

91. *curvus.* Ar. 316 has οὐ μάλα πολλός, following which Heinsius wished to read ' parvus,' but Cicero merely inserts the traditional epithet of the Dolphin.

92. *haud . . . nitore.* Ar. 317 : μεσσόθεν ἠερόεις.

93. *fronte locatas.* Lucretius similarly ends verses 71 and 97 of Book iv, " fronte locata."

95. *Cetera . . . serpit.* A verse of Cicero's summarising the Dolphin, but wanting in Aratus.

96–101. *Illae . . . Austri.* This notorious passage is, perhaps, Cicero's most serious error in the poem, for here he entirely misunderstood the original. Ar. 319–21 wrote :

καὶ τὰ μὲν οὖν βορέω καὶ ἀλήσιος ἠελίοιο
μεσσηγὺς κέχυται· τὰ δὲ νειόθι τέλλεται ἄλλα
πολλὰ μεταξὺ νότοιο καὶ ἠελίοιο κελεύθου·

" Now these constellations lie between the North and the Sun's wandering path, but the others many in number rise beneath between the South and the Sun's course."

Aratus having discussed the northern constellations is now about to treat of those which lie south of the Ecliptic. But Cicero by τὰ μὲν οὖν understood the stars in the foremost part of the Dolphin (' luces ex ore corusco ') ; by τὰ δὲ νειόθι those in the lower part (' At pars . . . videtur '). The only transition, then, in Cicero between the northern and southern star-groups is the word ' exinde,' which takes the place of the three verses of Aratus quoted above. All the mistranslations of Cicero, where they occur, are due to his lack of familiarity with the constellations themselves rather than to a misunderstanding of the Greek.

simul inter . . . Austri. Cf. above μεταξὺ νότοιο. One cannot help feeling that verse 101 more than atones

167

for the wrong interpretation of Aratus, although it probably owes something to Ennius, who wrote,

> " Concurrunt veluti venti, cum spiritus Austri
> imbricitor aquiloque suo cum flamine contra
> indu mari magno fluctus extollere certant."
>
> *Ann.* 443 *et sqq.*

Cf. too verse 184 below.

Here ends the description of the constellations north of the Ecliptic : a discussion of those visible to the south of it extends from verse 102 to verse 222.

102–6 *Orion.*   107–19 *Sirius.*   120–25 *The Hare* (*Lepus*).   These three constellations form a part of the " Arch of Orion," the most magnificent sight in the heavens.   Between 8 and 9 p.m. in February Orion lies due south across the meridian.   He is to be seen facing the Bull (Aldebaran being the Bull's ' eye ').   Most of his stars are brilliant helium stars estimated to be over six hundred light-years from the earth.   Betelgeuze has recently had its diameter measured, the length being computed to be 275,000,000 miles, as compared with the diameter of our own sun, which is 864,000 miles ! Due south of Orion is the Hare, a faint group of third- and fourth-magnitude stars.   On the left-hand side of the ' Arch,' is visible Sirius, the brightest star in the sky, some eight and a half light-years distant from the earth. This is the principal star in Canis Major.   Farther north is Procyon, the beautiful first-magnitude star in Canis Minor.   It is visible in the eastern sky some time before Sirius appears ; hence its name.   It is ten light-years distant from us.   Castor and Pollux form, with some fainter stars, the ends of a square, the Gemini.   Capella is the brilliant star in Auriga, the Charioteer.

102. *Orion.*   Cf. verse 3 and verse 421 *et sqq.*

103. *inferiora . . . corpora.*   Ar. 322 Λοξὸς μὲν Ταύροιο τομῇ (" athwart the section (i.e. forequarters) of the Bull "). ' Truculenti ' is an addition of Cicero's which neither Germanicus nor Avienus adopted.

106. *quem qui . . . signa potesse.* Ar. 323–5 has :

μὴ κεῖνον ὅτις καθαρῇ ἐνὶ νυκτὶ
ὑψοῦ πεπτηῶτα παρέρχεται ἄλλα πεποίθοι
οὐρανὸν εἰσανιδὼν προφερέστερα θηήσασθαι.

" Let none who pass him spread out on high on a cloudless night imagine that, gazing on the heavens, one shall see other stars more fair."

The difference in meaning between the two versions is due to Cicero's translation of ἄλλα as if it were τἄλλα and of θηήσασθαι by ' cognoscere potesse.'

nocte serena. Cf. Enn. *Ann.* 396 : " Omnes occisi obcensique in nocte serena."

107. *pedes subter.* Ar. 327 : φαίνεται ἀμφοτέροισι Κύων ἐπὶ ποσσὶ βεβηκώς.

Aratus correctly refers this description to the feet of the Dog himself—not, as Cicero, to the feet of Orion. Av. 724–5 commits the same error ; astronomically (the Hare is placed beneath Orion's feet) both are wrong.

cum. This use of ' cum ' with a noun and an adjective, where in his prose Cicero would employ the simple modal ablative, is very common in the *Aratea* : it is an imitation of Ennius, and was later used by Lucretius.

108. *fervidus.* The ' Dog Days ' (supposed to extend from July 3 to August 11) marked the heat of summer : at this time the Sun rose with Sirius. Hesiod's advice to his country neighbours was good : " When Sirius parches head and knees, and the body is dried up by reason of heat, then sit in the shade and drink." Pope's reference in his translation of the *Iliad* recurs to mind :

" Terrific glory ! for his burning breath
Taints the red air with fever, plagues, and death."

109. *Hunc . . . venter.* Trans. " Below his chest his belly, enveloped in darkness, obscures the rest of his form."

venter. This is restored by Turneb. (and approved by Grotius) for MSS. ' vesper.' The error arose from the contraction ' ver '—falsely interpreted as ' vesper.' Ar. 328–9 :

$$\text{ἀλλὰ κατ' αὐτὴν}$$
$$\text{γαστέρα κυάνεος περιτέλλεται.}$$

110–12. *nec toto . . . ardor.* The first two of these verses are Cicero's expansion of verse 109 and do not occur in Aratus. The third is a condensed version of Ar. 329–31 :

$$\text{ἡ δέ οἱ ἄκρη}$$
$$\text{ἀστέρι βέβληται δεινὴ γένυς, ὅς ῥα μάλιστα}$$
$$\text{ὀξέα σειριάει·}$$

110. *nec.* Neither MS. reading can be defended here : cf. Ar. 328 ἀλλ' οὐ πάντα πεφασμένος·

111. *aestifer.* Cf. note *Prog.* iii. ' tristificas.' For the phraseology (320 ' Aestifer Cancer ') cf. Lucret. i. 663, " aestifer ignis uti lumen iacit."

112. *micans . . . ardor.* Cf. *De Cons.* 12, " Concursusque graves stellarum ardore micantes." In these three verses should be noted the vigorous power which animates this description of the Dog, the effect of phrases like ' spirans flammam,' ' rabido de corpore,' ' aestiferos ignes,' ' validis flatibus,' and the absence of any attempt at a literal translation. In Germanicus the account of Sirius is brief :

" ore vomit flammam, membris contemptior ignis " (334).

Avienus, in the course of a long passage, says :

" Sic flammigero distinguitur astro
aetheriae Canis ille plagae, cui plurimus ardor
aestuat in mento, multus rubor imbuit ora." (725–7.)

Between verses 112 and 113 is omitted Ar. 331–2 :

$$\text{καί μιν καλέουσ' ἄνθρωποι}$$
$$\text{Σείριον.}$$

113–119. *Hic ubi . . . truncos.* Ar. 332–5:

> οὐκέτι κεῖνον ἅμ’ ἠελίῳ ἀνιόντα
> φυταλιαὶ ψεύδονται ἀναλδέα φυλλιόωσαι.
> ῥεῖα γὰρ οὖν ἔκρινε διὰ στίχας ὀξὺς ἀΐξας,
> · καὶ τὰ μὲν ἔρρωσεν, τῶν δὲ φλόον ὤλεσε πάντα.

113. *in lumina caeli.* An addition : the rising occurred in July. Cf. note 108, and verse 405 for similar ending.

114. *extulit.* The perfect expressing indefinite frequency.

haud patitur . . . tenere. Trans. " he suffers not the trees, vainly decked with covering of green, to cling to a feeble life." It will be seen that Cicero expands verse 335 of the original into four, describing fully the τὰ μὲν and the τῶν δὲ of Aratus. A similar expansion occurs in verse 317 *et sqq.* The Latin contains no mention of verse 334.

Verses 116–19 are so carefully constructed as to suggest that Cicero's rhetorical training was influencing him in their composition : the two parallel sentences, each prefaced with a relative clause, rather suggest the orator. Cf., too, 69–71. At the same time the quality of their excellence is obvious, whilst one cannot help noticing the compact and admirable translation contained in 119. Ar. 336 and 337, " Of him too at his setting (i.e. at the end of November) are we aware, but the other stars of the Dog are set round with fainter light to mark his legs," is omitted from the Latin.

121. *levipes.* This charming epithet is inserted here by Cicero, as ' truculenti ' was in 103, and is clearly superior to the ' parvulus ' of Avienus. Germanicus uses ' auritus.'

ictus . . . acuti. An addition.

124. *oriens . . . paullo.* Ar. 341 : καὶ οἱ ἐπαντέλλει. A rather difficult phrase, presumably meaning " (the Dog) himself rising but little afterwards," in which ' denique ' is used for ' postea.' Grotius wrote " orien-

tem denique paullum," referring the words to the Hare. But there is no real objection to retaining the MS. reading.

125. *curriculum . . . sedans.* A considerably extended paraphrase of Ar. 340 : καί μιν κατιόντα διώκει. Cicero seems not to have read the usual δοκεύει here, but a variant διώκει.

126–38. *The ship Argo.* Somewhat east of Sirius and on the southern horizon in March can be seen the star representing the top of the mast. The constellation is the largest and most conspicuous in the southern skies and contains the blue-white star, Canopus, of greater brilliance than any other star save Sirius. The group is divided into Puppis, Carina, Vela. There is no prow.

126–7. *serpens prolabitur . . . conversam . . . puppim.* A rather clumsy rendering of Ar. 342–3 : ἕλκεται Ἀργώ πρυμνόθεν.

128–30. *non . . . portat.* A fairly faithful translation of Ar. 343–5.

Trans. "When on the sea, other ships are wont to cleave the plains of Neptune with their beaks, prow foremost, but she sails on through the spaces of the sky stern-first."

Of these three verses even Guendel (p. 64), stern as he is in his criticisms of the *Aratea,* says : "Cicero, versum 128 *et sqq.* cum elegantia quadam, raro quam in Arateis invenias, composuit. . . ." He instances the circumlocution 'caeli loca' and the fifth foot pyrrhic of verse 130 as imitations of the Ennian school and denies Cicero the credit of coining 'Neptunia prata,' mentioning that the periphrasis first occurs in Cat. lxiv. 2, and comparing *Aen.* viii. 695. But it is more than doubtful if Catullus was born at the time when the *Ph.* was written, as the earliest possible date of his birth was 87.

caeli . . . portat. Cf. Lucret. v. 694 " qui loca caeli/ notarunt."

131–3. *sicut . . . puppim.* This delightful simile is a

trans. of Ar. 345-7 : but verse 133 is a weak paraphrase of :

τὴν δ'αὐτίκα πᾶς ἀνακόπτει
νῆα, παλιρροθίη δὲ καθάπτεται ἠπείροιο.

aversam. The emendation of Grotius for MS. ' adversam,' which does not suit the context.

132. *obvertunt . . . nautae.* The spondaic rhythm, expressing difficulty, is noteworthy. Cf., too, 127 above.

135. *atque.* Before this verse Cicero omits from Ar. 349 : καὶ τὰ μὲν ἠερίη , " partly in mist."

137. *gubernaclum.* Ar. 351 talks of the rudder as κεχαλασμένον, " loosed." Cicero describes it as " disperso lumine fulgens."

138. *tangit.* This is the restoration of Grotius from Hyginus. ' Condit ' of D is astronomically incorrect, as the Argo does not obscure the hindmost tracks of the Dog. Not even the ' condunt ' of Turneb. is satisfactory, for this necessitates taking ' vestigia ' as the subject which implies that the Dog obscures the Argo. Both constellations, although very close to each other, are distinct. ' Tangit ' at least does not transgress astronomically, whilst it is reasonably near to the original. Ar. 351-2 :

καί οἱ πηδάλιον κεχαλασμένον ἐστήρικται
ποσσὶν ὑπ' οὐραίοισι Κυνὸς προπάροιθεν ἰόντος.

" Loosed is her Rudder and is set beneath the hind feet of the Dog, as he runs in front."

139-44. *Cetus. The Whale.* Unlike the Argo, this large constellation is visible in its entirety from northern latitudes. On a December evening it can be identified just south of Aries, extending westwards under Pisces, the Fishes. Its head is marked by a five-sided figure composed of faint stars. Cetus contains the star (Omicron Ceti) known as Mira : this rises from invisibility nearly to the brightness of a second-magnitude star once every eleven months, and its periodic change in brightness was first discovered by Fabricius in 1596.

140. *quaerere*. Infinitive of purpose after the early Latin usage. Cf. Ter. *Ph.* 102; Pl. *Ps.* 642; Lucret. iii. 895.

143. *squamoso*. This form is found in the MSS. of the *De Nat. Deor.* ii. 44, and is to be preferred to the 'squamosi' of the *Ph.* MSS.: Aratus, Germanicus, and Avienus all omit the epithet.

144. *inlustri*. The conjecture of Orelli—inlustris—is due to a wish to keep the Latin nearer to Aratus, who wrote: ποταμοῦ . . . ἀστερόεντος.

pectore. The MS. reading, 'corpore,' is clearly wrong here on astronomical grounds : it is only the upper part of the Whale which approaches Eridanus, as Hyginus saw (*Astron.* iii. 30), "Huius priorem partem corporis prope alluere flumen Eridanus videtur." Moreover, the repetition of 'corpore Pisces' and 'corpore ripas' would be harsh : the second 'corpore' was almost certainly due to the first. Aratus gives no help here. A similar confusion is apparent in verse 373, where H has 'corpore' and not, as wrongly stated by Ottley and Orelli, 'pectore.'

145–54. *Eridanus*. A constellation visible in January low down on the southern horizon. It starts close to Rigel in Orion (the bottom right-hand star of the four), winds westward for some considerable distance, then south, then east, and finally, curving south-west, disappears below the southern horizon and continues far into the southern hemisphere. Its brightest star, Achernar, is not visible from northern latitudes.

145. *Eridanum*. Ar. 360 : λείψανον Ἠριδανοῖο, πολυκλαύτου ποταμοῖο. "the poor remains of Eridanus, river of many tears." Cicero omits λείψανον, used by Aratus because Eridanus was supposed to have been partly burnt up when Phaëthon fell therein. The river has been identified with the Po. No reference is made to the Heliades (the sisters of Phaëthon who mourned him) by Aratus, except by the epithet πολυκλαύτου. We are indebted to Cicero for verses 147 and 148.

parte locatum. Cf. verses 151, 186, 188 and Lucret. iii. 98.

146. *magnis . . . amnem.* A similar ending is found in Lucret. i. 287, who has " validis cum viribus amnis."

148. *letum . . . canentes.* "lamenting his death in mournful numbers." The heavy rhythm of the verse is at once apparent. Cf. *Il.* i. 5 : " qui non funestis liquerunt lumina fatis."

149. *Hunc. sc.* Eridanum.

150. *vincla . . . Flumine mixta . . . reverti.* Ar. 363–5 :

> ἄμφω συμφορέονται ἀπ' οὐραίων κατιόντες.
> Κητείης δ' ὄπιθεν λοφίης ἐπιμὶξ φορέονται
> εἰς ἓν ἐλαυνόμενοι·

" . . . reach from their tails and join together, and behind the neck of Cetus they mingle their path and fare together."

Here Cicero mistook the original. Aratus mentions the Knot of Fishes *after* Eridanus, but Cicero describes the Chains which hold fast the Fishes as mingling with Eridanus. This is impossible, since the constellations of Pisces and Eridanus are separated by the Whale which runs in between them. Germ. 369–71 realised this and wrote :

> " Ambobus qui piscibus unus
> vincula conectit, nodus cristam super ipsam
> aequoreae pristis radiat."

Avienus, on the contrary, makes the same mistake as Cicero :

> " fusaque quae geminos adstringunt vincula pisces
> Eridani coeunt anfractibus, ut procul ille
> tenditur effusi vi gurgitis." (802–4.)

For a similar mistake on the part of Cicero cf. verse 57.

154. Similar endings are found in Cat. lxiv. 275, who

has " nantes cum luce " ; *Aen.* i. 588 " claraque in luce refulsit," *ib.* ii. 590 " per noctem in luce refulsit."

155–66. *The nameless stars.* Ar. 367–85 : " Other stars, mean in size and feeble in splendour, wheel between the Rudder of Argo and Cetus, and beneath the grey Hare's sides they are set without a name. For they are not set like the limbs of a fashioned figure, such as, many in number, fare in order along their constant paths, as the years are fulfilled—stars, which someone of the men that are no more noted and marked how to group in figures and call all by a single name. For it had passed his skill to know each single star or name them one by one. Many are they on every hand, and of many the magnitudes and colours are the same, while all go circling round. Wherefore he deemed fit to group the stars in companies, so that in order, set each by other, they might form figures. Hence the constellations got their names, and now no longer does any star rise a marvel from beneath the horizon. Now the other stars are grouped in clear figures and brightly shine, but those beneath the hunted Hare are all clad in mist and nameless in their course."

It is rare that Cicero departs much from the original in the number of his verses : the Latin is, for the most part, on the same scale of fulness as the Greek. But there are exceptional passages. Verse 116 and verse 317 *et sqq.* both show much expansion from the original ; much more rare are examples of condensation. The eighteen verses of Aratus translated above are rendered by Cicero in eleven, whilst verses 190 *et sqq.* and 245 *et sqq.* both introduce passages less full than the original. Cf. too, verse 266.

The first five verses of the Latin correspond fairly closely to the original, but Cicero aptly adds ' formidans acrem morsum,' referring, of course, to the Dog's pursuit of the Hare. Cf. 121 *et sqq.* Of the ' nameless ' stars between Cetus and the Argo Aratus was unable to mention Columba, the Dove, which was unknown as a constellation in his time.

162. *astrorum custos*. This use of 'custos' is in imitation of the Greek φυλάσσειν = the Latin 'observare.' The words are here equivalent to 'astrorum observator,' an astronomer, and are employed generically of the early school of astronomers. Cf. Ar. 373 τις ἀνδρῶν οὐκέτ᾽ ἐόντων.

167–72. *The Southern Fish (Piscis Australis) and, 173–82, the Stream of Water (Aqua).* (Cf. intro. 55–71.) From northern latitudes the southern Fish cannot be seen to advantage, nor is it very conspicuous to an observer farther south. It includes, however, the first-magnitude star, Formalhaut, probably one of the two stars mentioned in verse 175, the other being possibly Phoenix, named by Bayer in 1603 as one of the southern constellations. The northernmost star in this group is of second magnitude. The faint line of stars beneath Aquarius is supposed to represent the stream of water flowing from his hand.

167. *Piscem*. The attraction of 'Piscis' into its own clause and consequently into the case of the relative leads to grammatical confusion with 'observans,' which is nominative as if in agreement with 'Piscis' unattracted. It is doubtful if the use of 'australis' is earlier than Cicero.

169. *illis Piscibus*. The Northern Fishes (cf. verses 10–19) which are some way north-east of the southern Fish and separated from it by Aquarius.

173. *obscurum . . . amnem*. The Aratean Hydor, the Stream of Water.

174. *exiguo . . . nitescit*. Ar. 394 : χαροποὶ καὶ ἀναλδέες εἰλίσσονται.

Trans. " Nearby his right hand pours forth a faint stream of stars which shine with feeble glow."

175. *duo lumina*. See intro. above : Aratus adds of these two stars, 396, οὔτε τι πολλὸν ἀπήοροι, οὔτε μάλ᾽ ἐγγύς, a vague statement omitted by Cicero.

176. *unum.* Ar. 397 adds καλός τε μέγας τε.

177. *Quod superest.* The familiar form of transition used by Lucretius to excess : here employed with a definite purpose signifying " the other." Cf., too, a similar use of the phrase in *Aen.* ix. 157. The whole verse is a poetical addition of Cicero's not appearing in Aratus.

178. *spinifer.* Cf. note *Prog.* iii. ' tristificas.'

180–82. *hic aliae . . . nomine.* Ar. 399–401 :

ὀλίγοι γε μὲν ἄλλοι
νειόθι Τοξευτῆρος ὑπὸ προτέροισι πόδεσσιν
δινωτοὶ κύκλῳ περιηγέες εἱλίσσονται.

" But others low beneath the forefeet of the Archer (Centaur), turned in a circled ring, go wheeling round the sky."

aliae. The Corona Australis, so named by Ptolemy.

Arcitenentis. Not Sagittarius (cf. verse 73), but the southern constellation of Centaurus, sometimes identified with Cheiron.

182. *cedunt.* Grotius's emendation : other variants show ' condunt ' with ' obscure, obscurae.' The use of ' obscurus ' points to Cicero having read ἄγνωτοι for δινωτοί in Ar. 401. Cf. Germ. 391 " sine honore corona." In any case, κύκλῳ περιηγέες εἱλίσσονται does not appear in the Latin.

182–213. *The Altar (Ara) and the Centaur.* The Altar is a small constellation too far south to be visible from England. North-west of Ara is Centaurus and close beside him Lupus, the beast which legend says (cf. verses 211–13 below) that the Centaur is offering upon the Altar. The Centaur is one of the finest constellations in the southern hemisphere, and so extensive that a part can be seen from northern latitudes, far down on the southern horizon in midsummer. Slightly east are the northernmost stars in Lupus.

183. *Nepae.* The Scorpion, which is a sign of the

Zodiac, contains the beautiful, first-magnitude star Antares : of a deep reddish colour, it is, as its name proclaims, a rival of Mars, and is likely to be mistaken for the planet by one who is unacquainted with the constellations. Cf. note verse 2.

184. *quam . . . Austri.* Ar. 403 : ἄγχι νότοιο. Trans. " Caressed by the gentle breath of the southern wind."

185. *exiguo . . . tempore.* The use of the ablative of time ' within which ' in lieu of the accusative denoting duration of time. Roby quotes no instances earlier than Cicero. Cf. *De Div.* i. 19, " Negari non potest multis saeclis verax fuisse id oraculum." *De Off.* iii. 2, " Scriptum a discipulo eius Posidonio est, triginta annis vixisse Panaetium postea quam illos libros edidisset." Cf., too, Caes. i. 47 ; Livy xxi. 2.

186. *nam . . . locata.* Trans. " Being placed in the opposing hemisphere far from Arcturus."

The use of ' procul ' as a preposition is not common. Cf. Ovid *Pont.* i. 5. 73 ; Livy xxxviii. 16 ' mari ' ; Tac. *Hist.* iv. 22 ' haud procul castris.'

187–8. *Arcturo . . . locavit.* The use of ' Iuppiter . . . dedit . . . locavit ' is due to Cicero's fondness for personification where possible. By this feeling for romanticism he often effects an improvement upon the original. Ar. 406–7 : " High runs the path of Arcturus, but sooner passes the Altar to the western sea." ' Spatium supera ' is Grotius's emendation.

189. *aeterno . . . nox.* As in the preceding verses Cicero again improves the poetic imagery of Aratus who has, for these words, simply ἀρχαίη Νύξ (408).

190–91. *signa . . . casus.* As in verses 155–66, we see here much compression of Aratus. " (But that Altar even beyond aught else hath ancient Night), weeping the woe of men, set to be a mighty sign of storm at sea. For ships in trouble pain her heart, and other signs in other quarters she kindles in sorrow for mariners, storm-buffeted at sea " (409–12).

A little farther on Ar. 418–19 repeats himself : " For often Night herself reveals this sign, also, for the South Wind in her kindness to toiling sailors."

These six verses Cicero adequately translates by verses 190–91.

192–4. *Nam cum . . . tectam.* Ar. 413–16 :

> τῷ μή μοι πελάγει νεφέων εἰλυμένον ἄλλων
> εὔχεο μεσσόθι κεῖνο φανήμεναι οὐρανῷ ἄστρον,
> αὐτὸ μὲν ἀνέφελόν τε καὶ ἀγλαόν, ὕψι δὲ μᾶλλον
> κυμαίνοντι νέφει πεπιεσμένον,

" Wherefore I bid thee pray, when in the open sea, that that constellation wrapt in clouds appear not amidst the others in the heavens, herself unclouded and resplendent but banked above with billowing clouds."

Grotius thinks that Cicero here mistook Aratus : he would therefore read ' in nubibus ' for ' sine nubibus.' He must have assumed that Cicero was translating νεφέων εἰλυμένον by these words. On the contrary, a more careful examination shows that Cicero has omitted them entirely from the Latin version ; by ' sine nubibus ' he represents ἀνέφελον.

sub media caeli locatam. These words are, however, as Grotius saw, a mistranslation of μεσσόθι. The Greek, of course, takes μεσσόθι with ἄλλων = ' amidst the others.' A further divergence from the original occurs in the next verse, ' obscura caligine tectam,' not giving the same meaning as κυμαίνοντι νέφει πεπιεσμένον ; the Latin can only imply that the top of the Altar is invisible, whereas πεπιεσμένον supposes no more than a bank of clouds surrounding the top of the Altar.

196–7. *quem si . . . undas.* Ar. 420–22 :

> οἱ δ' εἰ μέν κε πίθωνται ἐναίσιμα σημαινούσῃ,
> αἶψά τε κοῦφά τε πάντα καὶ ἄρτια ποιήσωνται,
> αὐτίκ' ἐλαφρότερος πέλεται πόνος·

" If they heed her favouring signs (*sc.* Night's) and quickly lighten their craft and set all in order, on a sudden lo! their task is easier."

It will be seen from the above passage that Cicero changes the third person of Aratus to second, thus effecting direct relationship with the reader and making the whole a much more vivid piece of writing. No mention is made of 'lightening the craft,' whilst the paraphrase of 'their task is easier' is at once apparent. No one could deny the obvious superiority of the Latin over the Greek in the above passage.

199. *perfringit . . . malos.* Trans. " It will bring low the lofty masts of rigid strength."

Ar. 424 : αὔτως ἀπρόφατος, τὰ δὲ λαίφεα πάντα ταράξῃ.

Cicero omits the first two words and paraphrases the last five. The rhythm of this and the preceding verse is probably deliberate, the dactyls of 198 portraying the rush of the wind, the spondees of 199 the ominous cracking and downfall of the masts.

200–202. *ut res . . . Ara.* Ar. 425–30 : " sometimes they make their voyage all beneath the waves, but at other times, if they win by their prayers Zeus to their aid, and the might of the north wind pass in lightning, after much toil they yet again see each other on the ship. But at this sign fear the South Wind, until thou see'st the North Wind come with lightning."

The Latin diverges very far from the original here. One is therefore led to suppose that the Ciceronian verses were so badly mutilated (or possibly lost) in early times that some scribe wrote these three verses as a gloss on the original. Thus they were received into the text. Verse 195 points to early corruption in this passage. It has no counterpart in Aratus, *where it appears in Cicero,* but comes in verse 429 of the original, as can be seen from the translation above. Another point, not without significance, is the use of a preposition between its noun and

the dependent genitive in ' parte ex Aquilonis.' Despite
a number of examples of anastrophe of prepositions like
contra, ex, inter, propter, subter, tenus, there does not
appear to be another instance in the *Aratea* parallel to
this.

205. *caligans vestiet.* Subject, the Centaur. Ar. 433–
4 : " while behind, *Night* kindles like signs of storm upon
the gleaming Altar."

206. *Favoni.* Ar. 435 : (χρὴ) εὔροιο περισκοπέειν
ἀνέμοιο. Eurus is the east wind, Favonius the west.
Germ. 425 translates by ' Eurus,' as also does Av. 878 :
that Cicero should commit such an error is unlikely, and
it is possible that he read here ζεφύροιο.

207. *in alta sede locatus.* Ar. 436 :

$$\text{Δήεις δ' ἄστρον ἐκεῖνο δύω ὑποκείμενον ἄλλοις·}$$

Aratus goes on to say that " part in human form lies
beneath Scorpio, but the rest, a horse's trunk and tail,
are beneath the Claws." Actually the greater part of
the Centaur is situated beneath Virgo (cf. Hipp. i. 8. 21).

209. *hunc.* The MS. ' haec ' is clearly impossible
here, and the text is the suggestion of Orelli : ' hunc '
refers to the Scorpion. Cf. Ar. 436 " part . . . lies
beneath Scorpio " (note 207), and for a similar phrase
321 below, " Hunc subter . . . Leonis."

210. *subiungere.* Ar. 438 : . . . ἱππόυραια δ' ὑπὸ σφίσι
Χηλαὶ ἔχουσιν. The Aldine edition has " cedite qui
partes properat coniungere Chelis," which is corrupt.
Grotius read ' subiungere ' in conformity with the MSS.
of the *De Nat. Deor.*

211. *Quadrupes.* The identity of this beast is doubt-
ful, but in all probability it is the Wolf, Lupus. The
Centaur was said to hold in his left hand a thyrsus, upon
which was placed a hare, and in his right a ' therium.'
Eratosthenes, *Catast.* 40, however, gives a different version:
ἔχει δὲ καὶ ἐν ταῖς χερσὶ τὸ λεγόμενον θηρίον . . . τινὲς δὲ
ἀσκόν φασίν αὐτὸ εἶναι οἴνου, ἐξ οὗ σπένδει τοῖς θεοῖς ἐπὶ τὸ

θυτήριον, ἔχει δὲ αὐτὸ ἐν τῇ δεξιᾷ χειρί, ἐν δὲ τῇ ἀριστερᾷ θύρσον.

Germ. 418–20 :

> " dextra
> seu praedam e silvis portat seu dona propinquae
> placatura deos, cultor Iovis, admovet arae."

Av. 885–7 :

> " ille autem, dextram protendere visus ad aram
> caelicolum, iustae persolvit munera vitae
> agrestemque manu praedam gerit."

212. *quam . . . Graium.* Ar. 442 says : " . . . another sign, the Beast—for so men of old have named it." Cicero corroborates the meaning implicit in Aratus, that no one knew the identity of this animal.

213. *caedit.* There is little doubt that this is the correct reading which is given by the three MSS. B.C.V. of the *De Nat. Deor.* ' Cedit,' the more usual reading of D and H (followed by Buhle), is extremely harsh as a repetition of ' cedit ' in 210, besides being less suited to the sense of the passage. The Altar naturally suggests the idea of sacrifice, whilst ' truculentus ' is certainly more appropriate when used with ' caedit ' than with ' cedit.' Moreover, both the versions from Germanicus and Avienus quoted above contain this thought of ' sacrifice.' Trans. " and with grim gaze offers it as a sacrifice at the gleaming Altar."

214–22. *The Hydra.* Visible near the southern horizon on an April evening, Hydra is a long line of faint stars which has its head under the Crab and close to Procyon : from here it extends southward and eastward passing under Crater and Corvus (sometimes called its riders) and thence stretching along the entire length of Virgo. Here it disappears below the horizon in the south-east. The constellation contains one bright star, Alphard, and serves to separate the brilliant groups of winter from those of the summer. Otherwise it is of little interest.

214. *infernis de partibus*. Ar. 443 has περαιόθεν. The other passages where he uses the word (606, 645, 720) are rightly construed by the translation " from the Eastern horizon " : the difficulty here is that the Hydra runs from west to east, not east to west. The schol. on this verse of Aratus says " either from the east or from a quarter beyond and farther than the Centaur," but this does not help to overcome the difficulty. Cicero seems to have taken the word as referring, not to the Hydra's position east and west, but to its situation north and south. Hence we may here translate by " from the southern horizon," a meaning supported by ' erigit.' Germ. 426 : " Nec procul hinc " ; Av. 891 : " Desuper."

216. *Nepai*. Ar. 445–6 :

καὶ οἱ κεφαλὴ ὑπὸ μέσσον
Καρκίνον ἱκνεῖται,

Cicero here understands ' Nepa ' as the Crab, Cancer. See note F. xv. Germanicus and Avienus both use ' Cancer.'

218. *Centaurum . . . cauda*. Ar. 447 :

οὐρὴ δὲ κρέμαται ὑπὲρ αὐτοῦ Κενταύροιο.

Again Cicero's partiality for alliteration has led him to add to the original, both epithets being his own. In the next verse ' fulgens ' is also an addition.

220. *plumato corpore Corvus*. Ar. 449 : εἴδωλον Κοράκος.

222. *Procyon*. Cf. intro., verse 102.

223–36. *The Planets*. Procyon concludes the list of those stars visible south of the Ecliptic. Aratus now passes on to the planets, which he refuses to discuss in detail : " When I come to them my daring fails, but mine be the power to tell of the orbits of the fixed stars and signs in heaven." With this passage should be compared *De Cons*. verses 6–10 and note thereon.

223-5. *Haec sunt . . . cursu.* Ar. 451-3:

> ταῦτά κε θηήσαιο παρερχομένων ἐνιαυτῶν
> ἐξείης παλίνωρα· τὰ γὰρ καὶ πάντα μάλ᾽ αὕτως
> οὐρανῷ εὖ ἐνάρηρεν ἀγάλματα νυκτὸς ἰούσης.

" And all these constellations thou canst mark as the seasons pass, each returning at its appointed time : for all are unchangingly and firmly fixed in the heavens to be the ornaments of the passing night."

Considerable divergence is at once noticeable between the Latin and the Greek. " Visens nocturno tempore " seems to take the place of παρερχομένων ἐνιαυτῶν, whilst verse 224 has no equivalent in the original : no mention is made by Cicero of the fact that " all are unchangingly and firmly fixed in the heavens."

The Aldine edition transposes verses 224 and 225 and reads ' cernens caeli ' and ' voles.' In the earlier editions the verse " aeternumque . . . motum " is omitted altogether, notably by Morelius. The present order of verses is due to Grotius and appears thus in Buhle's edition.

nocturno tempore. For similar expressions, cf. verses 245, 342, 349, and *De Cons.* 26.

225. *lustrantia.* To be taken closely with ' signa,' which refers to the Fixed Stars.

226. *signorum . . . orbem.* The Zodiac. Cf. 317-19 below.

227. *quinque . . . stellae.* The five planets nearest to the sun were alone known to the ancients. Uranus was discovered on March 13th, 1781, by Herschel, Neptune simultaneously by Adams of Cambridge, and Le Verrier of the Paris Observatory, in 1846.

228. Cicero omits from Ar. 456 οὐκ ἂν ἔτ᾽ εἰς ἄλλους ὁρόων, " no longer with others as thy guide."

230. *nubila caeli.* For similar phraseology cf. Lucret. i. 6 ; *ib.* 278 ; *Georg.* iv. 166 ; *Aen.* xii. 367.

231. This verse has no actual equivalent in Aratus,

who expresses the sense of this and of verse 230 by
ἐπεὶ πάντες μετανάσται (457).

232.   Amongst his parallels taken from Lucretius and
Cicero, Munro quotes for this verse Lucret. v. 644:
" quae volvunt magnos in magnis orbibus annos."   With
this should be compared *Aen.* iii. 284 : " interea magnum
sol circumvolvitur annum."

233. *cum redeunt . . . signum.*   Ar. 458–9 :

> μακροὶ δέ σφεων εἰσὶν ἑλισσομένων ἐνιαυτοί,
> μακρὰ δὲ σήματα κεῖται ἀπόπροθεν εἰς ἓν ἰόντων.

" and long are the periods of their revolution and far
distant lies the goal of their conjunction."

This refers to the μέγας ἐνιαυτός, when the planets
moving at varying speeds in their own orbits complete
these orbits simultaneously.   Cf. Plato *Tim.* 39 ; Cic.
De Nat. Deor. ii. 20.

caeli sub tegmine.   For similar endings cf. 47, 239, 346 ;
also Lucret. i. 992 (Oxon. ed.) ; ii. 663 ; v. 1016.

234. *quarum ego . . . cursus.*   With this verse Munro
compares Lucret. iii. 316 : " quorum ego nunc nequeo
caecas exponere causas."

Although we have already been told above in verses
227–9 that the poet cannot deal with the planets in the
same way as he has accounted for the stars, Cicero here
repeats the substance of those verses as a paraphrase of
Ar. 460 : οὐ δ᾽ ἔτι θαρσαλέος κείνων ἐγώ.

235–6. *verum haec . . . orbes.*   The meaning is that
I will explain (edemus) not only the Fixed Stars (" haec
. . . fixa in orbe "), but also (simul) the orbits themselves.

237–40.   There follows a minute description of the
Circles of the Celestial Sphere.   (1) The Galaxy, more
usually called the Milky Way.   (2) The Tropic of Cancer.
(3) The Tropic of Capricorn.   (4) The Celestial Equator.
(5) The Ecliptic.

Verses 237–52 introduce this new section of the poem

and describe the Milky Way. This is an enormous zone of light (composed of millions of separate stars) extending across the sky from Cassiepia and Cepheus, through Auriga and past the eastern side of Canis Minor to the southern horizon. In the southern hemisphere it traverses Argo and attains its greatest brilliancy in the Southern Cross. From here it proceeds northwards once more, passing into the Centaur, the Altar, and Lupus, and is again visible to those living in northern latitudes in Sagittarius and Scorpio. It then branches into two paths which finally unite in the Swan and lead back to Cepheus. Thus the Milky Way completes its circuit of the heavens. On its southward journey it is best viewed on clear winter evenings : its return northward is to be seen in the summer. The structure of the Milky Way is not clearly understood, but many astronomers regard it as a vast spiral nebula. Our own solar system is estimated to lie close to the plane of the Milky Way, some 50,000 light-years from its centre. The extent of its diameter has been computed to be about 300,000 light-years.

237–9. Quattuor . . . fulti. Ar. 462–3 :

> "Ητοι μὲν τά γε κεῖται ἀλίγκια δινωτοῖσιν
> τέσσαρα, τῶν κε μάλιστα πόθη ὄφελός τε γένοιτο . . .

Except for mention of the four orbits, these verses are clearly original and owe nothing to Aratus in conception. There cannot be any doubt as to their quality : the alliteration, the heavy spondaic rhythm expressive of the vast distances traversed by these circles, the entire absence of elision producing an effect of majestic grandeur, the happy metaphor ' sub tegmine,' exhibit Cicero's technique no less than the verses themselves show him elaborating a beautiful idea.

lustrantes lumine. For similar phraseology cf. Lucret. v. 1437 ; vi. 284 ; *Aen.* ii. 754.

stelliger. Cf. note *Prog.* iii. ' tristificas.'

240. *volitantia lumina.*   Ar. 464:

μέτρα . . . κατανομένων ἐνιαυτῶν.

" measures of the waning and the waxing of the Seasons."

It is possible that Cicero here read ἄστρα for μέτρα, which would account for the use of ' lumen ' with ' annorum.'

242. *magnos.*   Taken from the Aldine edition, the ordinary reading ' multos ' being clearly unsuited to this passage.   Also the repetition ' magnos . . . magno ' is Ciceronian and effective.   Cf. verse 236 above.   Additional proof that this part of the poem refers to the Four Circles mentioned in 237, viz. the Celestial Equator, the Tropics of Cancer and Capricorn, and the Ecliptic, is given by Germ. 446 *et sqq.* and by Av. 930 *et sqq.*, both of whom specify that they are discussing these Four Belts. For rhythm cf. note 9.   Cf. too Lucret. v. 648.

243-4. *vinctos . . . duobus.*   Trans. "Connected one to the other, they are held firm by heavenly knots, and you will observe that in size two are matched with two."

The Celestial Equator and the Ecliptic are equal in size to each other, whilst the two smaller Belts of Cancer and Capricorn are also equal.

nodis caelestibus aptos.   For this verse Aratus has, 467 :

αὐτοὶ δ' ἀπλανέες (v.l. ἀπλατέες) καὶ ἀρηρότες ἀλλήλοισιν

thus giving no indication of the metaphorical ' nodis . . . aptos.'   Cicero was quick to see an opportunity of imitating Ennius here.   *Ann.* 339: " (nox) . . . stellis ardentibus apta " ; *ib.* 29, 159 " (caelum) . . . stellis fulgentibus aptum."   (Cf., too, Lucret. vi. 357: " . . . stellis fulgentibus apta " ; *Aen.* vi. 797 : " stellis ardentibus aptum," and *ib.* iv. 482 ; xi. 202 : " stellis fulgentibus aptum.")   Cf. note 17 above.

245-9. *At si . . . notatur.* Cf. notes on 155 and

190. These five verses show compression of the original :
after 247 the Latin omits Ar. 472 :

ἀλλὰ τά γε κνέφαος διαφαίνεται ὀξέα πάντα

" but they all sharply pierce the darkness "

and Ar. 473 :

εἴ ποτέ τοι τημόσδε περὶ φρένας ἵκετο θαῦμα,

" if in such an hour wonder rises in thy heart,"

whilst after 248 Cicero omits Ar. 475–6 :

(οὐρανόν), ἢ καί τίς τοι ἐπιστὰς ἄλλος ἔδειξεν
(κεῖνο περιγληνὲς τροχαλόν), . . .

" or if someone at thy side point out (that circle set with brilliants),"

Verse 245 is well rendered by Avienus, who writes 936–7 :
" . . . aurea pepli/sidera nocturni si suspectare libebit."

247. *nec . . . Luna.* Cf. Lucret. v. 707, who, speaking of the Moon deriving her light from the Sun, says : " The Moon may shine because struck by the Sun's rays . . . until just opposite to him she has shone out with full light . . ." (Munro's trans.), and undoubtedly had this verse of Cicero in mind when he wrote these words : " donec eum contra pleno bene lumine fulsit."

248. *vidisti.* Trans. " Thou hast seen a great arc of dazzling splendour (κεῖνο περιγληνὲς τροχαλόν) spreading out in the sky."

249. *candore notatur.* Cf. note *Ph. F.* ix. 2, and reference to Lucretius there cited.

250–52. *Is non . . . cavernas.* Ar. 477–9 :

τῷ δ' ἤτοι χροιὴν μὲν ἀλίγκιος οὐκέτι κύκλος
δινεῖται, τὰ δὲ μέτρα τόσοι πισύρων περ ἐόντων
οἱ δύο, τοὶ δέ σφεων μέγα μείονες εἰλίσσονται.

" A match for it in colour thou wilt find no circle wheel, but in size two of the four belts are as large, but the other two are far inferior."

It appears that Cicero seriously misunderstood the original here. In verse 250, by taking οὐκέτι closely with κύκλος, he must have thought that there was some reference in the Greek to the fact that the Milky Way, not being fully visible from northern latitudes, does not appear in the heavens as a perfect circle. He omitted πισύρων περ ἐόντων, referred οἱ δύο to the circles dealt with in Ar. 468 (*Ph.* 244 above), which caused him to write " superis duobus," and completed the verse by " et late . . . cavernas," an addition of his own. The fact that he omitted to take τόσοι (" but in size two of the four belts are as large ") led Grotius to suppose a verse missing after 250. He accordingly supplied " quattuor huic simili nitentes mole feruntur," a verse which can hardly be said to give any help to the meaning, and which has no connexion whatever with anything in the original.

So hopelessly inaccurate and obscure in meaning are these verses that one would like to imagine that they do not represent the authentic version as Cicero wrote it. If they do, one can only deplore his ignorance of the more complicated branches of astronomy, whilst remembering that he had also to deal with the difficulties of the Greek language ; for the work of a young man labouring under such disadvantages one cannot help being surprised at the general accuracy of the poem, an accuracy which makes a passage like the present one all the more noticeable.

252. *caeli . . . cavernas.* Cf. *De Cons.* 5 and Lucret. iv. 171 ; vi. 252, for similar phraseology.

253-71. *The Tropic of Cancer.* This is an imaginary circle 23½° north of the Equator, which marks the farthest point northwards reached by the sun in its annual journey through the heavens. This apparent movement of the sun into the northern hemisphere is, of course, due to the fact that the Earth's axis is inclined to the plane of the Ecliptic. There follows an enumeration of the constellations lying on or (in the case of Virgo) near the Tropic of Cancer.

253. *Quorum alter.* The Tropic of Cancer. ‘Tangens . . . auras’; cf. Lucret. iv. 933.

254. *petens.* Ar. 481 more accurately φορέονται.
genus. Cf. note F. xxii.

257. *tangit.* Ar. 483 ἐπ’ αὐτῷ, “above him.” Perseus touches neither the Tropic of Cancer nor Auriga.

257. *Andromeda . . . tenetur.* Ar. 484–6:

’Ανδρομέδης δὲ μέσην ἀγκῶνος ὕπερθεν
δεξιτερὴν ἐπέχει· τὸ μέν οἱ θέναρ ὑψόθι κεῖται,
ἀσσότερον βορέαο, νότῳ δ’ ἐπικέκλιται ἀγκών·

“ It crosses Andromeda’s right arm above the elbow. Above it is set her palm, nearer the north, and southwards leans her elbow.”

dextra de parte. “ on the right,” a freely paraphrased version of Ar. 484. Cicero has omitted Ar. 485–6.

258. *ales . . . avis.* Since Aratus asserts that the Swan rests her head *and* neck on the Belt, it seems best to punctuate after ‘ tergum ’ and not (as in Orelli) continue to ‘ connititur ’ without a stop. Cf. note 47 for ‘ ales . . . avis.’

The statements concerning Perseus, Andromeda, Virgo, Ophiuchus, Cygnus are discussed and disputed by Hipp. i. 10. 6 *et sqq.*

264–5. *in quo . . . cursus.* The interpretation of these two verses, which do not appear in the original, is far from easy.

Grotius made the remarkable assertion that the meaning intended was, “ Solem solstitii aestivi tempore medium esse inter Arcticum et Elipticam.” But, as Orelli pointed out, the Sun is always on the Ecliptic which coincides with the Tropic of Cancer at the summer solstice, and there is little point in a comparison between the Ecliptic and the Arctic Circle here ; rather does the comparison lie between the Celestial Equator and the Ecliptic. Orelli thinks the sense to be simply, “ centro semper describit viam Sol." But what exactly does he mean by ' centro ' ? If he understands by this word that the Sun traces its course along a fixed central line (i.e. the Ecliptic), ' corpore medio ' must be taken closely in translation with ' quo,' "his body being in the centre of the Belt."

A preferable explanation is that by ' medio corpore ' is meant "half his disc," for as the Sun journeys along the track marked out by the imaginary line in which the Ecliptic and the Tropic of Cancer coincide, half the disc appears above and half below this line. Trans. " But it is the mighty Lion and Crab, in gleaming splendour, which will cover the whole of the Belt wherein the Sun in summer stays his course, turning his chariot southwards as, with disc in twain, he measures out his path."

The rhythm of 264 is descriptive of the effort required to guide the Sun's great chariot, and the monosyllabic ending is especially effective, imitating the toil of slowing down and turning the huge car. Cf. Lucret. iii. 1044, " aetherius sol." The original is Ennius, cf. his well-known " simul aureus exoritur sol," *Ann.* 92.

266. *Hic, sc.* the Crab ; *iste, sc.* the Lion.
Referring to the Crab, Aratus says, 494–6 :

τέμνει, τὸν δὲ διηνεκέως ὑπένερθε χελείου
Καρκίνον, ἦχι μάλιστα διχαιόμενόν κε νοήσαις
ὀρθόν, ἵν' ὀφθαλμοὶ κύκλου ἐκάτερθεν ἴοιεν.

" and the Crab it cuts clean through by the shell where thou canst see him most clearly cut, as he stands upright with his eyes on either side of the Belt."

Another instance of omission of parts of the original. Cf. note 155. Grotius, thinking the text mutilated, supplied two verses here. The sense, however, is quite clear as the verses stand.

267. *alvo.* Ar. 493 : μέχρι παρ' αἰδῶ.
(the circle cuts the Lion beneath breast and belly) " lengthwise to the loins."

268–71. *Hunc octo . . . frequentat.* Trans. "If you can conceive this ring divided into eight parts, you will find that five of equal size revolve above the horizon, whilst the remaining three are sunk in the darkness of night below it."

After this verse editors assume a lacuna in the MSS. Ar. 499–500 has :

$$. . . \ \theta\acute{\epsilon}\rho\epsilon o\varsigma \ \delta\acute{\epsilon} \ o\acute{\iota} \ \acute{\epsilon}\nu \ \tau\rho o\pi a\acute{\iota} \ \epsilon\acute{\iota}\sigma\iota\nu.$$
$$\grave{a}\lambda\lambda' \ \acute{o} \ \mu\grave{\epsilon}\nu \ \acute{\epsilon}\nu \ \beta o\rho\acute{\epsilon}\omega \ \pi\epsilon\rho\grave{\iota} \ K a\rho\kappa\acute{\iota}\nu o\nu \ \acute{\epsilon}\sigma\tau\acute{\eta}\rho\iota\kappa\tau a\iota.$$

" In it is the Turning-point of the Sun in summer. This circle is set round the Crab in the North."

The first sentence is translated by Cicero in verses 264–5 ; the second is a somewhat pointless repetition which he presumably omitted. There seems no real reason, therefore, to suppose any loss to have occurred at this point in the poem.

272–284. *The Tropic of Capricorn.* Cf. intro. to verses 253–71. This is the imaginary circle south of the Equator corresponding to the Tropic of Cancer north of it.

272a. *Arcitenens . . . recedens.* Not represented in Aratus, this verse, whilst astronomically correct, is almost certainly a repetition which has found its way into the text. Cf. 260. The sense of it appears neither in Germanicus nor in Avienus.

The next seven verses are an interesting example of Cicero's fondness for epithets. He here inserts " distribuens," " gelidum rivum fundentis," " caeruleam," " ferae," " fulgentem," " amplam . . . claro cum lumine," none of which is present in the original. He omits Aratus's μέγα before " tergaque Centauri," and changes the Greek Τόξον ἀγαυοῦ Τοξευτῆρος (" Bow of the bright Archer ") to " Sagittari defixum . . . arcum." This constant striving after realism lends a certain romantic charm to the poem which is lacking in Aratus. Germ. 482 *et sqq.* and Av. 977 *et sqq.* should be compared with this passage. They too insert epithets, but with a choice of words which is definitely inferior to that of Cicero.

276. *pedes Canis.* Ar. 503–4 :

ἀτὰρ Κυνὸς οὐ μάλα πολλὴν
αἴνυται, ἀλλ᾽ ὁπόσην ἐπέχει ποσίν·

" It claims no great share of the Dog, but only the space which he occupies with his feet."

An instance which proves that Cicero could, on occasion, prune the original severely. He seems justified here.

277. *claro.* The Aldine edition has " crabro (crebro ?) cum lumine." The emendation is Grotius's. " Crebrum lumen " occurs nowhere else in the poem, whilst " claro cum lumine " is frequent. Cf. 298, 323, 389, and for similar phrase Cat. lxiv. 407.

Germ. 489 corrects Aratus by saying " desecat [*sc.* circulus] aplustria puppis."

280. *Hunc a . . . Solis.* Ar. 507–8 :

τὸν πύματον καθαροῖο παρερχόμενος βορέαο
ἐς νότον ἠέλιος φέρεται·

" This circle the sun passes last as he is southward borne from the bright north."

A comparison of the Latin with the Greek here shows an extremely pleasing and careful version of the former. The addition " rota fervida " is as happy as it is typical. Cf. *Aen.* vi. 748.

clarisonis. Cf. note *Prog.* iii. ' tristificas ' ; also Cat. lxiv. 320, " clarisona . . . voce," who probably borrowed this adjective from Cicero.

282. *exinde . . . flexens.* As in verses 264–5 reference was made to the longest day, June 22nd, so here

we have mention of the shortest, December 22nd. Cf.
Lucret. v. 615–17 :

> (Sol) " quo pacto aestivis e partibus aegocerotis
>   brumalis adeat flexus atque inde revertens
>   cancri se ut vertat metas ad solstitialis,"

and again, *ib.* 639–40 :

> (aer) " qui queat aestivis solem detrudere signis
>   brumalis usque ad flexus gelidumque rigorem."

Cf. too 61 above.

284. *luce dicantur*. Trans. " are allotted to the light
of day." The ablative is used here for the dative
= " superae (orbi) tres luci dicantur."

285–95. *The Celestial Equator*. The imaginary circle
on which the plane of the Terrestrial Equator cuts the
celestial sphere. It is, of course, equi-distant from the
Tropics.

285. *Hosce inter*. " Between these two," i.e. the
Tropics of Cancer and Capricorn. After verse 511
Aratus adds :

> γαῖαν ὑποστρέφεται κύκλος διχόωντι ἐοικώς.

" The Belt undergirds the Earth and with imaginary
line bisects the sphere."

287. *In quo*. . . . Referring to the spring and
autumn equinoxes on March 22nd and September 22nd
respectively. These occur when the Earth in its annual
path cuts the points where the Ecliptic coincides with the
Celestial Equator. Cf. Lucret. v. 688 : " . . . nocturnas
exaequat lucibus umbras."

auctumnali. Ar. 514 : φθίνοντος θέρεος : *lumine verno*.
ib. εἴαρος ἱσταμένοιο.

289. *Aries*. Ar. 516 :

> Κριὸς μὲν κατὰ μῆκος ἐληλάμενος διὰ κύκλου.

" The Ram being borne lengthways through it."

Actually the Ram is some distance north of the Equator. Cf. Hipparch. i. 10. 18 *et sqq.*

290. *flexo.* Ar. 517:

$$\text{Ταύρου δὲ σκελέων ὅσση περιφαίνεται ὀκλάξ.}$$

" but of the Bull just the visible bend of the knees."

291. *pectore.* Ar. 518:

$$\text{ἐν δέ τέ οἱ ζώνη εὐφεγγέος Ὠρίωνος.}$$

" In it are the Belt of the well-starred Orion. . . ."

This emendation of Morelius is certainly preferable to the MSS. ' corpore,' as Cicero uses ' pectus ' elsewhere, without exception, to render the Greek ζώνη. Cf. note 144.

Orion, in his journey across the sky, is immediately preceded by the Bull. The stars of his belt point almost directly to Aldebaran.

292. *Hydra . . . adhaeret.* The reading of this verse usually printed in early times was : " Hydra tenet flexu Crateram, Corvus adhaeret." Turnebus, who emended to the version printed in the text, realised that the original did not support the MSS., for Aratus says : " In it [*sc.* the Celestial Equator] are the Belt of the well-starred Orion and the coil of the gleaming Hydra." Hence he does not make the Hydra support the Bowl in this passage, although, of course, it actually does so. Cf. verse 219.

294. *Ales.* Ar. 522 adds : οὐ μὴν Αἰητοῦ ἀπομείρεται.
The Eagle does actually cut the Equator.

295. *propter*, i.e. facing the Eagle. Ar. 523 κατ' αὐτὸν.
The Dolphin separates the two constellations, and from northern latitudes the Horse is not on the Equator but on the Tropic of Cancer.

296–340. *The Ecliptic.* This, the apparent path of the sun in its annual journey across the sky, is an imaginary circle terminated at its extremities north and south by the Tropics of Cancer and Capricorn respectively. It cuts the Celestial Equator at the two points known as the equinoctial points (see note 287), or the First Point of Aries (in spring) and Libra, which is the other corresponding equinoctial point (in autumn). The ancients supposed these points to be fixed, but it is now known that they are slowly moving at a rate which will carry them completely round the heavens in approximately 25,800 years.

On the Ecliptic, which contains the apparent paths of the moon and the chief planets as well as that of the sun, are to be seen the twelve signs of the Zodiac, as they rise in order and cross the sky. The Zodiac is probably Babylonic in origin, and the Greeks, adopting it, divided into twelve signs, 30° wide, the belt of the heavens 8° wide on either side of the Ecliptic. This they called the Zodiac.

296–301. *Hosce . . . fertur.* Trans. " The axis issuing from the Pole through the midst of these circles maintains them in a position equidistant from each other. The extremities of a fourth radiant circle enclose the Tropics (extremos orbes), whilst its midmost point is bisected by the Celestial Equator (a medio *sc.* orbe). Its bright course is marked out slanting athwart these three circles."

296. *devinctos.* There seems no justification for ' deiunctos,' which was the suggestion of Turnebus. The two Tropics and the Equator are connected, since all three are parallel to each other, equidistant from each other, and perpendicular to the Axis of the earth. Ar. 525–6 :

Τοὺς μὲν παρβολάδην ὀρθοὺς περιβάλλεται ἄξων
μεσσόθι πάντας ἔχων.

298. *Ille . . . quartus . . . circus.* The Ecliptic, " claro . . . cum lumine," is an addition.

302. *sancta . . . Pallas.* Trans. " sacred Minerva, herself most expert in manual tasks."

302–4. *ut nemo . . . tornare . . . possiet.* Ar. 529–30 : οὔ κεν . . . ἀνὴρ . . . ἄλλη κολλήσαιτο, " not otherwise would a man join. . . ." The original gives a slightly different meaning. Cicero was followed by Germ. 518–19 :

> " non si Palladia doctus formaret ab arte,
>   distantes orbes melius religasset ab uno " ;

and by Av. 1018 *et sqq.*

303. *sollertem . . . artem.* Trans. " has imparted all the cunning of her skill in the constructive arts."

305. After this verse Cicero omits verse 533 of Aratus :

> ἐξ ἠοῦς ἐπὶ νύκτα διώκεται ἤματα πάντα.

" (just as the Belts) hasten from dawn to night throughout all time."

306–7. *terram . . . fulta.* These two verses, which express as clearly and as nobly as one could wish the majestic grandeur of the universe, are additions of Cicero.

culmine transverso. A difficult phrase presumably meaning (the constellations upheld by) " the dome of heaven lying athwart them." Grollmus (*op. cit.*, pp. 14–15) seems to think them a careless attempt to render Ar. 532 :

> ὡς τά γ᾽ ἐναιθέρια πλαγίῳ συναρηρότα κύκλῳ

" just as the Belts in the heavens, clasped by the transverse circle. . . ."

But it is perfectly clear from the context that Cicero is not referring to the Ecliptic here, but describing the Belts in general.

308. *Quattuor . . . eodem.* Ar. 534–6 :

> καὶ τὰ μὲν ἀντέλλει καὶ αὐτίκα νειόθι δύνει
> πάντα παραβλήδην· μία δέ σφεων ἐστὶν ἑκάστου
> ἐξείης ἑκάτερθε κατηλυσίη τ᾽ ἄνοδός τε.

" The three Belts rise and set all parallel but ever single, and the same is the point where in due order each rises or sets at East or West."

The τὰ μέν in verse 534 clearly refers to the three Belts (the Tropics and the Celestial Equator) ; verse 537 of the original begins αὐτὰρ ὅ γε, by which is meant the Ecliptic.

311. *quanto . . . a Capricorno.* The meaning is that the Ecliptic always extends above the horizon so much of its orbit as is equal to the distance separating the Crab from Capricorn, since each of these signs marks a half-way point on the Ecliptic. *Quanto spatio* shows attraction of the antecedent into the clause and assimilation of case to that of the relative, i.e. quantum spatium quo = (so much of its orbit) as is the distance by which . . .

313–15. *et quantos . . . partes.* The poet, in describing the length of the Ecliptic, says that six times the distance of the ray reaching from our eyes to the heavens will give the required size of this whole Belt.

From Euclid iv. 15 we know that each side of a regular hexagon is equal to the radius of the circle in which it is described. Assume the earth to be the centre of the celestial sphere : then the ray cast from an observer's eye to heaven equals the radius of the circle. Therefore six lines of this length will give the regular hexagon which subtends the whole Ecliptic. Each side of this imaginary hexagon will subtend an arc of the Ecliptic on which will be placed two signs of the Zodiac. By bisecting this side the space occupied by one sign is found.

314. *quis . . . orbem.* Ar. 541 leaves the sense of this verse to be gathered from the context. He uses merely the verb ἀποτέμνεται.

315. *sub eum succedere.* Lit. " to succeed one another on this circle." Virgil presumably had this method of describing the Zodiac in mind when he wrote :

" In medio duo signa Conon et—quis fuit alter,
    descripsit radio totum qui gentibus orbem,
    tempora quae messor, quae curvus arator haberet ? "
Ecl. iii. 40–42.

317–19. *Zodiacum . . . signa.* Ar. 544 :

Ζωίδιον δέ ἑ κύκλον ἐπίκλησιν καλέουσιν.

Cicero here expands the original into three verses. Cf. notes 114 and 155.

Signifer. Possibly coined by Cicero, and used by Lucret. in v. 691 and vi. 481. Cf. note *Prog.* iii. ' tristificas.'

320–31. The following eleven verses describe the signs of the Zodiac, each being qualified according to its brightness. The passage is remarkable for nothing but a wearisome repetition of epithets which add nothing to the meaning, whilst they retard the vigour, of the original. Aratus, who describes the list in five verses, says : " In it [*sc.* the Belt of the Zodiac] is the Crab ; after the Crab the Lion and beneath him the Maiden ; after the Maiden the Claws and the Scorpion himself and the Archer and Aegoceros, and after Aegoceros Hydrochous. Beneath him are enstarred the two Fishes and after them the Ram and next the Bull and the Twins." (545–9.)

320. *est pandens.* For ' pandit,' a usage unrestricted to any particular author or period in Latin. For ' aestifer ' cf. note 111 above.

321. *vis torva Leonis.* Lucretius uses a similar periphrasis, iii. 296 : " in primis vis est violenta leonum."

330. *proiecto corpore.* Cf. *Aen.* xi. 87 : " sternitur et toto proiectus corpore terrae."

The above passage is especially marked by archaisms, amongst others ' vis torva ' 321, ' vis magna Nepai ' 324, and the genitive in -ai, the pyrrhic in the fifth foot 325, ' inde loci ' 327, and the use of ' squamiferi ' (if this is borrowed, not coined, by Cicero) 328.

332–3. *Haec Sol . . . cursu.* Ar. 550–52 :

ἐν τοῖς ἠέλιος φέρεται δυοκαίδεκα πᾶσιν
πάντ' ἐνιαυτὸν ἄγων, καί οἱ περὶ τοῦτον ἰόντι
κύκλον ἀέξονται πᾶσαι ἐπικάρπιοι ὧραι.

" In them, twelve in all, has the sun his course as he leads on the whole year, and as he fares around this belt, all the fruitful seasons have their growth."

The compression of the original is at once apparent when the two passages are compared.

334-5. *Hic quantum . . . exit.* Ar. 553-4 says : " Half this Belt is set below the hollow of the horizon (κοίλοιο κατ᾽ ὠκεανοῖο) and half is above the earth." It would seem that as the ' convex ' of the Ecliptic sinks below the horizon, the same ' concave ' of it rises proportionately. Hence we may take ' convexus ' here as opposed to ' patens.'

exit. Grotius. Other editors ' edit ' following MSS., ' exstat,' and ' mortalibu' cedit ' (Orelli).

336. *cedunt labentia.* Cf. Lucret. iv. 144 : " lapsaque cedant."

337. *tot . . . revisunt.* Ar. 556 : τόσσαι δ᾽ ἀντέλλουσι. The horizon bisects the Belt of the Zodiac, and day continues whilst the sun is visible above the horizon. From the first appearance of the sun until its setting a half circle of the Ecliptic has risen, i.e. six zodiacal signs.

fugientia. " rising," i.e. escaping from the darkness below the horizon. The usual way of expressing this in ancient authors.

338. *caecis . . . umbris.* Cf. *Aen.* vii. 619 : " caecis se condidit umbris."

340. *ex orbi.* Archaic ablative. Owing to imperfect separation of words, the verse appears in H as, " Signifero exorbis exsignorum ordine fultum." This led Grotius to emend to " ex orbist et," which is not so good, for, as at all time six signs of the Zodiac are above the horizon, ' sex ' ought to be retained.

Germ. 570-2 :

" nullaque nox bis terna minus caelo trahit astra,
  nullaque maior erit, quam quanto tempore in auras
  orbis perfecti divisus tollitur arcus."

Av. 1056–9 :
> " omnibus iste
> noctibus inlabens pelago sex inserit astra,
> sex reparat.   Tanto nox umida tempore semper
> tenditur, extulerit quantum se circulus undis."

341–9.   The last section of Aratus's poem from verse 559 to verse 732 is concerned with those constellations which rise with a given zodiacal sign or set when the zodiacal sign is rising.   He deals with the signs of the Zodiac from the summer solstice onwards : Cancer, Leo, Virgo, Libra, Scorpio, Sagittarius, Capricorn, Aquarius, Pisces, Aries, Taurus, Gemini.

Hipparchus, ii. 1. 1 *et sqq.*, points out that Aratus treats of the actual constellations, not the ideal divisions of the Zodiac.   This leads to some inaccuracy, since the constellations do not, in every case, cover exactly the twelfth part of the Ecliptic, as they are said to do in theory.   Some even lie north of the Ecliptic, such as Leo and the more northerly of the two Fishes.

Cicero adheres to the order of the zodiacal signs as adopted by Aratus, and the nine verses commencing with 341 form an introduction to the enumeration of zodiacal signs as given above.

341. *Quod* . . .   The sense is that the rising and the course of the sun can best be determined by an examination of each sign of the Zodiac, since the sun always appears in coincidence with one of them.

vises.   The prescriptive future.

343.   After this verse Cicero appears to have omitted from Aratus τὰς δ' ἄν κε περισκέψαιο μάλιστα/εἰς αὐτὰς ὁρόων (562–3).

" One could best search out those constellations by looking on themselves."

This thought introduces the next sentence, " But if they be dark with clouds or rise hidden behind a hill, get thee fixed signs for their coming."

346. *caeli de tegmine.*   Ar. 566–7:

> αὐτὸς δ' ἂν μάλα τοι κεράων ἑκάτερθε διδοίη
> Ὠκεανός,

" Ocean himself will give thee signs at either horn " (i.e. East or West).

Ὠκεανός is rendered by ' caeli de tegmine.'   The sense is clearly the same whether the signs be observed " from the ocean " or " from the sky," i.e. the horizon.

347. *ortus atque obitus.*   Cf. *Ph.* F. x. 2, " ortus ubi atque obitus " ; *De Cons.* 58 ; *Mar.* 8 ; *Georg.* i. 257 ; iii. 277 ; Cat. lxvi. 2.

348–9. *Quae simul . . . nosces.*   Inserted as a concluding remark to the seven verses preceding, the whole of this passage being introductory to the enumeration of zodiacal signs now to be given.   After verses 566–7 (cf. translation note 346) Aratus continues : " . . . in the many constellations that wheel about him, when from below he sends forth each rising sign."

350. *Nam . . . Cancer.*   Ar. 569–71 :

> οὔ οἱ ἀφαυρότατοι, ὅτε Καρκίνος ἀντέλλῃσιν,
> ἀστέρες ἀμφοτέρωθεν ἑλισσόμενοι περίκεινται,
> τοὶ μὲν δύνοντες, τοὶ δ' ἐξ ἑτέρης ἀνιόντες.

" Not very faint are the wheeling constellations that are set about Ocean at East or West, when the Crab rises, some setting in the West and others rising in the East."

350–69.   This passage treats of those constellations which set when the Crab rises.   A convenient time to view this rising is at nine o'clock in the evening on November 20th approx.

351. *cedit delapsa.*   Ar. 572 : δύνει.

352. *et . . . Piscis.*   Trans. " And the Southern Fish sets as far as its tail."   Actually Formalhaut (cf. intro. 167) is visible until the rising of Regulus in the Lion.

Cauda tenus.   Cf. note 83 and verse 387.

355–6. nec totus . . . cedit. As these words stand in the text, they must refer to the Southern Fish, ' supero ' = ' foremost.' Ar. 575–6 writes :

αὐτὰρ ὁ γ' ἐξόπιθεν τετραμμένος, ἄλλα μὲν οὔπω
γαστέρι νειαίρῃ, τὰ δ' ὑπέρτερα νυκτὶ φορεῖται.

The reading αὐτὰρ Γνύξ ὄπιθεν (cf. Maass ' *De Ph. Ar. recensendis*' *Herm.* xix. 1884, pp. 110 *et sqq.* and Ar. 591) was certainly unknown to Cicero, and does not concern us here. It is clear that Cicero, reading αὐταρ ὅ γε, confused the meaning, and took the words to refer to the Southern Fish. That Aratus is describing Engonasin, however, is quite clear both from the meaning of the verses, " but he, backward turned, is still visible to his waist, but his upper parts are borne in night," and from similar phraseology in Ar., verse 620, ἐς κεφαλὴν ἔτι που τετραμμένος. But the abrupt transition in the original effected by αὐτὰρ ὅ γε inclines one to the belief that one or more verses were early lost. Germ. 591 has the same confusion as Cicero.

supero contectus corpore. " his upper parts plunged in night." The position of Hercules causes him to set head-foremost and to rise feet-foremost. Cf. Hygin. *Astron.* iii. 5. Manilius also refers to this peculiarity, v. 645 *et sqq.* The man born under this constellation will be a plotter and a footpad, or—a tight rope walker !

358. validis . . . a cervicibus. Ar. 578 :

. . . κατάγει δ' "Οφιν αὐχένος ἐγγύς

" . . . and brings down Ophis to the neck."

In this passage Aratus describes Ophiuchus (Anguitenens) as μογερός, this epithet being omitted by Cicero who, if the text be correct here, employs two adjectives, ' clarum ' and ' magnum,' both qualifying ' Anguem ' but without any copula.

361. Arctophylax. Cf. intro. to Ff. xvi. and xvii.

362. *Quattuor.* Actually Sagittarius, Capricorn, Aquarius, and a small part of Pisces. 'Obiens' represents in the original κατιόντα Βοώτην / Ὠκεανὸς δέχεται (581–2).

365. *post . . . noctem.* Ar. 583 :

βουλυτῷ ἐπέχει πλεῖον δίχα νυκτὸς ἰούσης,

" he takes till past midnight in the loosing of his oxen."

The length of time taken by Boötes in setting is due to the fact that he is in a perpendicular position : he rises quickly, because he is then in a horizontal position. Cf. verse 394 below. Ar. 584–5 continues : " . . . in the season when he sets with the sinking sun. Those nights are named after his late setting." These two verses are omitted by Cicero.

366. *Haec . . . tellus.* Trans. " Such the constellations which the Earth [*sc.* at the rising of the Crab] conceals from us, cloaking them in darkness." This verse is represented by ὡς οἱ μὲν δύνουσιν in Ar. 586.

367. *parte ex alia.* Ar. 586 : ὁ δ' ἀντίος. Actually the Crab rises a little after Orion ; the latter is south of the Crab, being situated on the Celestial Equator, whilst the Crab is, of course, on the Ecliptic.

368. *humeris . . . fulgens.* Ar. 587–8 :

ἀλλ' εὖ μὲν ζώνῃ, εὖ δ' ἀμφοτέροισι φαεινὸς
ὤμοις Ὠρίων,

" . . . even Orion with glittering belt and shining shoulders."

For this use of 'pectus' cf. verse 3 above and note verse 2.

369. *et dextra . . . ensem.* Ar. 588 :

ξίφεός γε μὲν ἶφι πεποιθώς.

" trusting in the might of his sword."

Aratus ends this description of Orion:

πάντα φέρων Ποταμόν, κέραος παρατείνεται ἄλλου. (589).

" and bringing all the River (Eridanus), he (Orion) rises from the other horn (the East)."

cassum luminis. Cf. *Misc. Vv.* F. ix. " sanguine cassam "; Lucret. iv. 368 ; v. 719, " cassum lumine fertur " ; *ib*. 757 and 1129 ; *Aen.* ii. 85, " cassum lumine lugent."

370–78. The constellations which set with the rising of the Lion, Aquila, and Engonasin ; those which become visible, Hydra, Lepus, and Procyon with the forefeet of the Dog.

370. *Sed . . . Leonis.* Ar. 590 : Ἐρχομένῳ δὲ Λεόντι.

371. *praeclaro.* An addition.

372. *vis magna Aquilai.* Formerly the reading of this verse was " vis maior Aquari." Ar. 591, who says that the Eagle disappears from sight with the rising of the Lion, has . . . καὶ Αἰετός, no mention being made of Aquarius. An attempt was made to correct this error by " vis maior Aëti." But this is too far from the original reading, it is unlikely that Cicero used the Greek word and, in any case, would he have written ἀητός (a rare form) rather than the usual ἀετός ? Furthermore, ' maior ' has no force here. The emendation is that of Turnebus.

373. *flexo . . . corpore.* Trans. " with bowed form." Cf. note 144.

374. *supero . . . lumine.* A substitution for κυμαίνοντος ὠκεανοῖο of Aratus, who describes Engonasin as sinking beneath the stormy ocean.

376. *clarum.* An addition : Cicero omits the Aratean epithet of the Hare, χαροπός = bright-eyed.

377. *qui . . . Ante-Canem.* An addition. Cf. 208 above and *Georg.* ii. 145, " equus campo sese arduus infert " ; *Aen.* xi. 742, " adversum se turbidus infert."

378. *vestigia prima.* Ar. 595 πρότεροί τε πόδες. Cf. 388 " pedes . . . posteriores."

379–92. There follows a list of stars which become invisible at the rising of Virgo : those which appear in their stead include more of the Hydra (cf. verse 376 "caput Hydrae "), the hind legs of the Dog, and so much of the Argo as is visible from northern latitudes.

379. *e caelo.* The usual Ciceronian substitution for Ar. 596 : γαίης ὑπὸ νείατα, " beneath the verge of the earth."

380. *pandens . . . lumina.* An addition : cf. 453 and Lucret. v. 657, " lumina pandit."

381. *Fides Cyllenia.* Mercury's lyre : Cyllene, the mountain in Arcadia where Mercury was born.

381–2. *mergitur unda . . . obtegitur depulsa.* Both these phrases are done by δύνουσι in Ar. 598, whilst Cicero omits the Greek epithet of the Arrow, εὐποίητος = shapely.

383–4. *atque Avis . . . pinnas.* Ar. 599–600 :

σὺν τοῖς ῎Ορνιθος πρῶτα πτερὰ μέσφα παρ᾽ αὐτὴν
οὐρὴν . . . (σκιόωνται).

" With them [*sc.* those constellations already set] the wing-tips of the Bird [*sc.* the Swan] up to her very tail . . . (are overshadowed)."

385. *latescit.* ἅπ. λεγ. Cf. note *Prog.* iii. ' tristificas.'

386. *longius.* Ar. 602 : ἐπὶ πλέον, " higher." Cf. intro. above and verse 376.

claro corpore. An addition.

387. *lucet mortalibus.* An addition.

388. *Inde.* Ar. 603 : φθάμενος δέ, " before her," i.e. in front of the Hydra. For the pentasyllabic ending see pp. 61 and 62.

392. *haec . . . malum.* Cf. verses 135–6. The sense of this difficult verse is that she (the Virgin) reveals the

mast in the middle (of the ship) with its gleaming pole, i.e. she reveals the ship so far as the mast in the middle of it.   Cf. Ar. 605 :

ἡ δὲ θέει γαίης ἱστὸν διχόωσα κατ' αὐτόν,

" She rises above the earth cleft right at the mast."

Cf., too, note 396 below.

393–417.   The Claws (i.e. Libra) render visible a number of constellations.   Libra can be seen to rise at approximately nine o'clock in the evening at the beginning of April.   Amongst those constellations which now wholly or partly sink are Pegasus, Cygnus, Andromeda, Cetus, whilst Cepheus " downwards bends his head, his shoulders and his hands " (417).

394. *larga cum luce*.   Lucretius uses the same phrase in ii. 806 : " larga cum luce repletast."   For ' pariter ' = Ar. 609 ἀθρόος, ' at a bound,' cf. note 365.

395. *cuius . . . fixus*.   Ar. 609 : βεβολημένος 'Αρκτούροιο, ' jewelled with Arcturus.'   Cf. intro., Ff. xvi. and xvii.

396. *totaque . . . Argo*.   Cf. verses 135–6 above.   Ar. 610 :

'Αργὼ δ' εὖ μάλα πᾶσα μετήορος ἔσσεται ἤδη·

"aloft is risen all of Argo."   The use of ' tota ' here has been questioned on the grounds that only a part of the Argo was visible in northern latitudes.   Reference to the original (where inferior MSS. and schol. have οὐ for εὖ) shows where Cicero found support for ' tota.'   The meaning is perfectly plain if understood to be the whole of Argo, which is at any time visible to us.   Cf. Germ. 626 " celsaque puppis habet " ; Av. 1133–4, " Iam celso Thessala puppis/aethere subvehitur."

398. *nondum . . . umbra*.   The first three words of this verse are an explanatory addition of Cicero's : the last four are a weakened version of Ar. 611–12 : ἀλλ' 'Υδρη . . . οὐρῆς ἂν δεύοιτο.   " But the Hydra . . . will lack her tail."

400. *vulgato nomine Nixus.* Ar. 615 adds, αἰεὶ δὲ Λύρῃ παραπεπτηῶτος, " ever crouching by the Lyre."

402. *persaepe . . . orbem.* An addition.

403. *Hic . . . alte.* A repetition of verses 399–400, faithfully copied from Aratus, who has the same repetition here.

404. *praeceps.* Cf. note 355.

obscura nocte tenetur. A rather more vigorous expression than that of Aratus, who writes, " . . . head-downward on the other side awaits the rising Scorpion . . .," ἄλλη / Σκορπίον ἀντέλλοντα μένει (620–21). For similar phraseology cf. *Aen.* ii. 420 and *ib.* iv. 461.

406–9. *nam secum . . . lucet.* The meaning of these verses is that the Scorpion will reveal the waist (medium) of Engonasin, as he rises (secum), but the Bow (i.e. the Archer) on rising will endeavour to make visible the whole body (totum) of Engonasin. So he, borne aloft by three constellations (the Claws, Scorpion, and the Archer), gleams brightly at every point (corpore toto).

Ar. 624 : ἀλλ' ὁ μὲν ὡς τρίχα πάντα καταμελεϊστὶ φορεῖται·

" Even so in three portions is he all brought up piece-meal above the horizon."

Actually Hercules is completely risen before the Archer becomes visible—to an observer in England.

409. *media de parte.* Ar. 625 : ἥμισυ δὲ Στεφάνοιο, " half the Crown." With ' at exoritur ' *sc.* " at the rising of the Claws." Astronomically incorrect, for the Corona Borealis which precedes Hercules across the sky is fully visible before the Claws are risen.

410. *caudaque . . . refulget.* Trans. " And the tip of the Centaur's tail gleams bright."

411. *Hic . . . umbras.* Ar. 627 : τῆμος ἀποιχομένην κεφαλὴν μέτα δύεται ῞Ιππος. " Then is the Horse setting after his vanished head." This is more accurate astronomically, since at the rising of the Claws almost the whole of Pegasus is set.

412. *rutila . . . pluma.* A picturesque addition of Cicero's. *Ales,* the Swan.

413–14. *et fera . . . requirens.* Ar. 629–30:

$$\tau\grave{o} \,\, \delta\acute{\epsilon} \,\, o\acute{\iota} \,\, \mu\acute{\epsilon}\gamma\alpha \,\, \delta\epsilon\tilde{\iota}\mu\alpha$$
$$K\acute{\eta}\tau\epsilon o\varsigma \,\, \mathring{\eta}\epsilon\rho\acute{o}\epsilon\iota\varsigma \,\, \grave{\epsilon}\pi\acute{\alpha}\gamma\epsilon\iota \,\, \nu\acute{o}\tau o\varsigma.$$

" And against her is brought by the misty South the mighty terror, Cetus."

The alteration in the Latin version is at once apparent on comparing the two passages ; " horribiles . . . requirens " is a typical addition of Cicero's, a touch of realism not to be foregone !

415. *Cepheus.* Ar. 631 adds : ἐκ βορέω, " from the north." Cf. intro. F. xxi.

Contra hanc. " Against the Monster " (i.e. to ward him off from his daughter).

416. *illa . . . condit.* " Whilst the dark Whale sinks, plunging up to his back beneath the horizon."

Ar. 632–3 :

$$\kappa\alpha\grave{\iota} \,\, \tau\grave{o} \,\, \mu\grave{\epsilon}\nu \,\, \grave{\epsilon}\varsigma \,\, \lambda o\varphi\iota\grave{\eta}\nu \,\, \tau\epsilon\tau\rho\alpha\mu\mu\acute{\epsilon}\nu o\nu \,\, \mathring{\alpha}\chi\rho\iota \,\, \pi\alpha\rho' \,\, \alpha\mathring{\upsilon}\tau\grave{\eta}\nu$$
$$\delta\acute{\upsilon}\nu\epsilon\iota,$$

" Cetus, neck downward, sets to his neck."

418–57. The story of Diana's vengeance upon Orion is described : this accounts for the origin of the Scorpion, whose appearance in the sky causes the setting of Orion, Andromeda, and the Whale. Part of Cepheus is lost below the horizon. Cassiepia sinks head first. The origin of this indignity is ascribed to her presumption in matching her beauty against that of the Nereids. The other half of the Crown, the Snake, the Centaur, the Serpent-Bearer's head and hands and the Snake (Anguis as compared with the Hydra above) now become visible.

418–20. *Cum vero . . . vagatur.* There is little doubt that some of the Ciceronian verses have been lost here. Ar. 634–7 [1] shows this, although Grotius supplied the missing verses,[2] asserting that they were Cicero's, but omitting to mention the codex in which he had discovered them (Orelli, vol. iv, part I. note verse 419, 1828). The passage must be regarded as corrupt, therefore ; the first edition of Lamb., 1566, says that three and a half verses are missing, and so " a nobis restituti et, paene dicam, ab inferis excitati sunt."

421–6. *ut quondam . . . nitentes.* Ar. 638–40 :

Χίῳ ὅτε θηρία πάντα
καρτερὸς Ὠρίων στιβαρῇ ἐπέκοπτε κορύνῃ,
θήρης ἀρνύμενος κείνῳ χάριν Οἰνοπίωνι.

" . . . what time in Chios he was smiting with his strong club all manner of beasts, as a service of the hunt to that King Oenopion."

A most unusual example of expansion (cf. note 156 above), for elsewhere Cicero is always careful not to insert mythology in the same way as Avienus did : this restraint accounts for the fact that the number of verses in the Ciceronian version is so nearly akin to that of the Greek.

---

1 καμπαὶ δ᾽ ἂν Ποταμοῖο καὶ αὐτίκ᾽ ἐπερχομένοιο
Σκορπίου ἐμπίπτοιεν ἐΰρρόου ὠκεανοῖο·
ὃς καὶ ἐπερχόμενος φοβέει μέγαν Ὠρίωνα,
Ἄρτεμις ἰλήκοι· προτέρων λόγος, οἵ μιν ἔφαντο
ἑλκῆσαι πέπλοιο, . . .

" The winding River (Eridanus) will straightway sink in fair flowing ocean at the coming of Scorpion, whose rising puts to flight even the mighty Orion. Thy pardon, Artemis, we crave ! There is a tale told by the men of old who said that stout Orion laid hands upon her robe . . ."

2 " Late fusa volans : in terras labitur unda
  Orionque metu perculsus conditur una ;
  pace huius liceat causam explicuisse timoris,
  Virgo, tua. Mihi, quaeso, veni placata Diana :
  Haec fama est hominum, haec per terras fama vagatur."

Cf. Germ. 644–6 ; Av. 1170–73.

excelsis . . . vitis. Trans. "As he wildly ranged o'er Chios' lofty hills—an isle fast anchored in the Ægean Sea and clothed by Bacchic vine with covering green."

Chius. Aldine edition read 'Echinus,' which gave rise subsequently to 'Echineis.' The emendation of Grotius is clearly right : the Echinades are a small group of islands at the mouth of the Achelous.

Bacchica. The MS. reading 'brachia' is harsh, and necessitates changing 'quam' to 'quae,' the reading of H 2. It must refer to the boughs of trees and the whole verse to the training of vines on the boughs of other trees as supports. Avienus adopted this reading :

> " cum sacrata Chii nemora et frondentia late
> brachia lucorum, cum silvae colla comasque
> devotae tibimet manus impia demolita est."

The reading given by Lambinus, whilst retaining the MS. 'quam,' is more poetical and is well suited as an epithet of 'vitis.' Whether the comma be placed after 'Chius,' and 'Bacchica' be taken with 'vitis,' or the punctuation placed after 'Bacchica,' thus making it an epithet to 'Chius,' seems to be of little moment, although perhaps the former alternative is preferable.

vecors amenti corde. Cf. Aratus (quoted above) στιβαρῆ . . . κορύνῃ.

Oenopionis. Oenopion was king of Chios. Orion fell in love with his daughter, Merope. His treatment of her was such as to rouse Oenopion's wrath, who, helped by Dionysus, deprived the giant of his sight. Orion afterwards regained this and lived as a hunter.

427–9. *At vero . . . luce lacunas.* Another extension of Ar. 642 :

νήσου ἀναρρήξασα μέσας ἑκάτερθε κολώνας

" But she (Artemis) forthwith rent in twain the surrounding hills of the island. . . ."

Three verses which bring to mind Virgil's description of Hercules' attack on the cave of Cacus in *Aen.* viii. 184–267.

lustravit . . . lacunas. This favourite word is of frequent occurrence in the poems. Amongst other passages, cf. 237, 332, 441 in *Phaenomena.*

430–34. *e quibus . . . terram.* Ar. 641 and 643–4 :

ἡ δέ οἱ ἐξαυτῆς ἐπετείλατο θηρίον ἄλλο

. . . . . . (642, see above)

Σκορπίον, ὅς ῥά μιν οὗτα καὶ ἔκτανε πολλὸν ἐόντα

πλειότερος προφανείς, ἐπεὶ "Αρτεμιν ἤκαχεν αὐτήν.

" And (Artemis) roused against him another kind of beast—even the Scorpion, who proving mightier wounded him, mighty though he was, and slew him, for that he had vexed Artemis."

ictu. For similar ending cf. *De Cons.* 45, " flammato fulminis ictu " ; also Lucret. iii. 488, " ut fulminis ictu " ; *ib.* v. 400, " repenti fulminis ictu."

mortiferum. Cf. note *Prog.* iii. The word is rare, but an instance occurs in Lucret. vi. 1091 : " mortiferam possit cladem conflare."

Trans. " From out this turmoil a monstrous Scorpion rises, with deadly purpose bearing its grievous sting before it. Eagerly it stabbed the huntsman with powerful stroke infusing its deadly poison through many a wound within his veins. And as he died, his massy form lay all outstretched along the earth."

438. *tota.* Cf. 413, and take ' tota ' both with ' Andromeda ' and with ' Neptunia Pistrix.' Ar. 647–9 says : " Nor does what was left of Andromeda and of Cetus fail to mark his rise but in full career they too flee."

438. *converso corpore Cepheus.* Cf. verse 417. From our northern latitudes the whole of Cepheus is, of course, always visible. ' Converso corpore,' " with form reversed," that is to say, head foremost.

441. *infera lumborum.* This use of a neuter adjective with the genitive of the noun points the way to an idiom extensively used in silver Latin. For further instances cf. 217 " inferna Leonis " and 230 " nubila caeli."

Ar. 652 specifies his " feet and knees and loins."

442. *lustrantes . . . suras.* An addition. Cf. 237 and references there given.

443. *gnatam.* Andromeda.

444. *ex caelo depulsa.* Cicero here changes the imagery. Ar. 655 says, " nor in seemly wise does she shine upon her throne," φαίνεται ἐκ δίφροιο. He then adds, 656–7 :

$$\text{ἀλλ' ἥ γ' ἐς κεφαλὴν ἴση δύετ' ἀρνευτῆρι}$$
$$\text{μειρομένη γσνάτων,}$$

" but she headlong plunges like a diver, parted at the knees."

From our latitudes Cassiepia is always and wholly visible.

447. *Nereides.* The Nereids, Doris and Panope. Cf. intro. to F. xxxi.

449. *Haec obit inclinata.* Ar. 659 : ἡ μὲν ἄρ' εἰς ἐτέρην φέρεται· Ar. 659–60 introduces the constellations now enumerated by τὰ δὲ νειόθεν ἄλλα/οὐρανὸς ἀντιφέρει, " but other signs in the east the vault of heaven brings from below "—omitted by Cicero.

Coronae. The Corona Borealis, as in 409. Grotius wrongly supposed the reference to be to the Corona Australis. This constellation was so named by Ptolemy, and was therefore unknown to Aratus under this title. Cf. verses 180–82 above.

altera. Cf. verse 409.

452–3. *linquens . . . contecta.* Trans. " e'en though the tiny tracks of his fore-feet are still obscured."

Ar. 663–4 :

$$\text{τοὶ δ' αὖθι μένουσιν}$$
$$\text{Τόξον ἐπερχόμενον πρότεροι πόδες ἱππότα Φηρός.}$$

" But the fore-feet of the Centaur-Knight await the rising of the Bow."

Φήρ. Cf. Pind. *Pyth.* iii. 6. The Φ is Aeolic for θ.

454–5. Comparison with the original suggests the possible loss of a verse, or part of a verse, here. Ar. 665–6 :

Τόξῳ καὶ σπείρῃ "Οφιος καὶ σῶμ' 'Οφιούχου
ἀντέλλει ἐπιόντι·

" At the coming of the Bow up rises the coil of the Serpent and the body of Ophiuchus."

Aratus then continues : " Their heads the rising of the Scorpion himself brings and raises even the hands of Ophiuchus and the foremost coil of the star-bespangled Serpent."

455. *inde.* At the coming of the Bow ?
(Grotius restored this lacuna by supplying " sed cetera magni/exspectant Arcus ortum.")

458–68. When Sagittarius rises Engonasin, the Lyre, and the chest of Cepheus all become visible ; Orion, the Dog, and the Hare set ; parts of Auriga and Perseus become invisible together with the Argo, save for her stern.

460. *radios laeto . . . iactans.* A pleasing addition.

461. *Sagittipotens.* Cf. note 73.

462. *Nixi caput.* Ar. 672 : ἑτέρης μετὰ χειρός.
Hence it will be seen that Aratus adds " and his other hand," a statement omitted by Cicero.

effert . . . promit. Cicero uses two verbs here where Aratus employs a phrase to serve as verb to the two subjects : ἠῴου παρελαύνεται ὠκεανοῖο, " drive up from the eastern ocean."

465. *abditus umbra.* " In darkness plunged " is Cicero's substitution for the Aratean ἀτέλεστα διωκομένοιο, " which the Dog pursues in an unending race " (678). Cicero has already described this pursuit in verses 123–5.

466–71. *inferiora cadunt . . . Navem.* The order of these verses presents difficulty. Aratus 679–82 (which four verses complete his section dealing with the movements of the constellations upon the rising of Sagittarius) says : " But not yet depart the Kids of the Charioteer and the Arm-borne (Olenian) Goat : by his great hand they shine, and are eminent beyond all his other limbs in raising storms, when they fare with the sun." Aratus then introduces the section describing the movements of the constellations at the rising of Capricorn. He continues (683–8) : " His head, hand and waist set at the rising of Aegoceros (Capricorn) : from waist to foot he sets at the *rising of the Archer.* Nor do Perseus and the end of the stern of jewelled Argo remain on high, but Perseus sets all save his knee and right foot and Argo is gone save her curved stern."

Thus it is clear that Aratus mixed the movements of constellations under Sagittarius with those under Capricorn. Cicero preferred to distinguish those signs setting under (1) Sagittarius, (2) Capricorn, if indeed the order in the *Phaenomena* is Cicero's own, and not due to the text of Aratus which he was using, and in which the transposition of verses might have been already effected by some earlier grammarian.

Upon the assumption that this alteration is due to Cicero himself there seems no justification for changing the order back to that of Aratus, and thus destroying a carefully planned piece of work.

469–74. Capricorn's setting banishes the Charioteer, the Goat, and the Kids : Argo and Procyon set. There rise the Eagle, the Swan, and the Arrow.

469. *obiens Capricornus.* Ar. 684 : Αἰγόκερος ἀνιών, " at the rising of Aegoceros." If Capricorn upon rising causes the setting of these constellations, still more so will he when he himself sets. Thus the sense is retained although the translation is not accurate.

473. *Volucres.* The Swan and the Eagle.

474–82. The rising of Aquarius brings up the feet and head of Pegasus and causes the setting of the Centaur's tail and the disappearance of the head and neck of the Hydra.   The rising of the Fishes causes the Hydra to set completely.

477. *cedit . . . fugiens.* Ar. 693–4 :

"Ιππος δ' . . .
ποσσί τε καὶ κεφαλῇ ἀνελίσσεται.

" . . . up wheel the feet and head of the Horse."

These two words are almost invariably used by Cicero of the *setting* of a constellation (but cf. 337 ' fugientia ') : if the MS. reading here be correct, they must be taken as referring to the Horse's departure and flight from below the horizon into the heavens.   Some such variant as " exit . . . oriens " would be much nearer the original in meaning and in phraseology.   But in the absence of any evidence to the contrary it has not been thought justifiable to alter the text.

signipotens.   This beautiful epithet is ἅπ. λεγ.   Ar. 695 uses ἀστερίη.   The force of the word is, of course, denoting that the whole power of night lies in her constellations.   Cf. note *Prog.* iii.   Trans. " but opposite " (i.e. the Horse) " star-enwrought night draws the Centaur, tail-first, beneath the horizon."

478. *ad se.*   For the more usual " ad infera."

479. *caput . . . latos.*   Ar. 697 adds αὐτῷ σὺν θώρηκι, " breast and all."

481.   After this verse Aratus continues 699–701 :

ἡ δὲ καὶ ἐξόπιθεν πολλὴ μένει· ἀλλ' ἄρα καὶ τὴν
αὐτῷ Κενταύρῳ, ὁπότ' 'Ιχθύες ἀντέλλωσιν,
ἀθρόον ἐμφέρεται·

" Yet many a coil of the Hydra remains, but Night engulfs her wholly with the Centaur, when the Fishes rise,"

481. *ardentia lumina.* Cf. *Aen.* ii. 405, "tendens ardentia lumina frustra." If Cicero ever completed his translation of the *Phaenomena* the remaining verses are lost. There are thirty-one more verses of the original in which Aratus ends his account of the movements of the constellations at the rising of Pisces, Aries, Taurus, and Gemini (cf. intro. verses 341–9).

He wrote a true epitome of his work when he concluded the poem with one forceful hexameter :

πάντη γὰρ τά γε πολλὰ θεοὶ ἄνδρεσσι λέγουσιν.

" For on every hand signs in multitude do the gods reveal to man."

PROGNOSTICA

F. I. Ar. 130 *et sqq.*, discussing the signs given by the Sun, says : " Fear the coming rain when suddenly the Sun's rays seem to thin and pale—just as they often fade when the Moon overshadows them as she stands straight between Earth and Sun."

means. Cicero's version of κατ' ἰθύ/ἱσταμένη γαίης τε καὶ ἠελίοιο (σελήνη).

Hyperionis officit orbi. Greek σκιάῃσι. For similar (cf. F. iii. 'Neptuno') examples of metonymy cf. *De Nat. Deor.* iii. 16. 41.

stinguuntur . . . tecti. Greek ἀμαλδύνονται. 'Stinguo,' used here and in *Ph.* F. ii. does not seem to have been employed by the earlier poets, and, but for a few examples in Lucretius (i. 667 ; ii. 828), soon fell into an oblivion from which it was never rescued.

caeca caligine. Cf. *Ph.* 345, " caeca caligine nubes " ; 480, " caligine caeca " ; Lucret. iv. 456, " noctis caligine caeca " ; *Aen.* iii. 203, " caeca caligine solem " ; *Aen.* viii. 253, " caligine caeca." Cf. also Lucret. iii. 304 ; Cat. lxiv. 207 ; Sil. Ital. v. 34, and Cicero *Ph.* 194.

F. II. Ar. 160 *et sqq.* mentions the Manger and the

Asses, two bright stars, one to the north, the other to the south of the Manger. The group can be seen in the early evening hours of April close to the Crab, although little more than a faint, nebulous cloud of light is visible to the naked eye.

Ast . . . Phatne. Ar. 160–1 :

> Σκέπτεο καὶ Φατνήν.   ἡ μέν τ᾿ ὀλίγη εἰκυῖα
> ἀχλύϊ βορραίη ὑπὸ Καρκίνῳ ἡγηλάζει.

The text is the emendation of editors for " candent lumine Phatnae." Through some scribal error the Manger and the Asses were associated as a plural constellation. Cf. Av. 1651–1669 and 1735 :

> " Convenit hic etiam parvum Praesepe notare.
>
> .   .   .   .
>
> . . . Duo propter denique asellos
> suspice, quorum alius septem vicina trioni
> astra adolet, tepidum procul alter spectat in
>   austrum."

For the phrase cf. Lucret. v. 721, " candenti lumine tinctus."

F. III. Ar. 177–80 continues (after discussing the Manger and the Asses) with indications which foretell wind and storms.

> σῆμα δέ τοι ἀνέμοιο καὶ οἰδαίνουσα θάλασσα
> γινέσθω, καὶ μακρὸν ἐπ᾿ αἰγιαλοὶ βοόωντες,
> ἀκταί τ᾿ εἰνάλιαι ὁπότ᾿ εὔδιοι ἠχήεσσαι
> γίγνωνται, κορυφαί τε βοώμεναι οὔρεος ἄκραι.

An examination of this passage exhibits Cicero's usual tendency to expand the original, particularly if such expansion improve the poetic imagery.

cum . . . tumescit. This clause finds no place in Aratus. Pease (ed. *De Div.*) points out, on the authority of Atzert (*De Cic. interprete Graecorum*, 1908, 3–11), that

Cicero is here following a scholiast. He also compares Maass (*Comment. in Arati Reliq.*, 1898, 509. 1. 3) :

ὅταν ἐξαίφνης . . . ἀνοιδαίνη ἡ θάλασσα.

tumescit. Cf. *Georg.* i. 357 ; ii. 479 ; Ovid *Met.* i. 36 ; Lucret. x. 224. The rhythm of this verse with the repetition of 't,' 'p,' and 'u' well represents the surging waters of the sea. The alliteration on 's' throughout the whole Fragment is almost certainly intentional in imitation of the whistling of the wind.

tristificas. Many words, mostly compound adjectives, appear for the first time in Cicero's verse. These were either coined by him or drawn from the works of early poets which are now no longer extant. Some of them were adopted by succeeding poets, others perished with their author. Amongst the former were : 'aurifer.' Soph. Trans. 44 ; 'horrisonus' Aesch. Trans. F. ii. 3 ; 'luctificus' *ib.* 26 ; 'tristificus' above and *De Cons.* 48 ; 'umbrifer' *De Cons.* 73 and *Il.* F. i. 10 ; 'auriger' *ib.* 9 ; 'auctifer' *Ody.* F. ii. 2 ; in *Ph.* occur 'pulverulentus' 25 ; 'aestifer' 111 ; 'spinifer' 178 ; 'stelliger' 238 ; 'clarisonus' 280 ; 'squamifer' 328 ; 'mortifer' 433 ; also the verb 'claro' used in its transitive sense in *De Cons.* 63 and *Ph.* 39. Amongst the latter were : 'vastificus' Soph. Trans. 40 ; 'multiplicabilis' *ib.* 43 ; 'fluctiger' *Marius* F. ii. ; 'mollipes' and 'umifer' *Prog.* vii. below ; 'anxifer' *De Cons.* 77 and Soph. Trans. 33 ; 'herbigradus' and 'domiportus' in *Misc. Vv.* In *Ph.* occur 'sagittipotens' 73, 325, 461 ; 'levipes' 121 ; 'signipotens' 477 ; also the verb 'clino' 53, 86, 259 ; 'latesco' 385.

certant . . . reddere voces. The infinitive after 'certo' is not found in Ciceronian prose. Cf. Lucret. iv. 300, "loca vidi reddere voces" ; Cat. lxiv. 166, "nec missas audire queunt nec reddere voces."

aut densus . . . repulsus. Cicero omits εὔδιοι from his version.

For comparisons of phraseology see Virg. *Aen.* v. 35, xi. 526; Av. 1671–5, which is inferior to Cicero.

> " . . . Nam cum traxere tumorem
> aequora prolixum, cum litora curva resultant
> sponte procul neque caeruleus colliditur aestus,
> aut cum proceris vertex in montibus ultro
> perstrepit aerium, ventos instare docebunt."

densus. "Continual" has been suggested as a translation, and in support of this one can refer to *Aen.* v. 459 and Hor. *Od.* iii. 5. 31. But I prefer "muffled" in accordance with the word's common usage. Amongst many examples denoting 'material' cf. Quint. xi. 3. 63 : "Vox atrox in ira et aspera ac densa." The heavy rhythm is illustrative of the sound.

saepe repulsus. MSS. 'repulsus' : hence 'saepe' is presumably the ablative of the noun upon which depends 'scopulorum.' Editors usually read 'repulsu' and take 'saepe' as an adverb. There seems to be no justification for this. For the use of 'saepes' as a noun cf. the verse quoted in *De Nat. Deor.* i. 119 : "silvestribus saepibus densa"; Ovid *Tr.* iv. 1. 81 : "portarum saepe." Trans. "row of cliffs."

It is suggested that 'montis' refers to the upper, 'scopulorum' to the lower part of the cliffs.

F. IV. Ar. 181–3. In the original these three verses form a continuous passage with the four already translated in F. iii. The heron foretells stormy weather when it flies inland with loud cries.

Cana fulix. An earlier reading was 'rana fulix,' which Camerarius emended to 'rava fulix.' Aratus denoted this colour by the word ξουθός. The suggestion was made that Cicero read not ἐπὶ ξηρὴν ὅτ' ἐρωδιός but ἐπὶ ξουθὸς ὅτ' ἐρωδιός. The reading here printed is Baeh. (1879) from B. (Cod. Leid. Voss. 86. S. X.). The coot's forehead is hoar-white, almost snow-white. Avienus 'parva fulix.' This word 'fulix' has been identified with the coot.   Aratus, however, uses the word ἐρωδιός (ardea), the heron, not φαλαρίς, the coot.   Perhaps Cicero misunderstood the original.   For 'fulix' (fulica), the coot, cf. Pliny *N.H.* xi. 37. 44; *Georg.* i. 363.   A further difficulty is that the coot is a bird of fresh waters. Possibly the increase of its numbers on ponds in autumn when it is on migration gave rise to a belief in arrivals from the sea.

fugiens.   The translation of the whole Fragment is very free.   Of the Greek, ἐπὶ ξηρὴν and οὐ κατὰ κόσμον are not translated, while verses 2 and 3 of the Latin, apart from the phrase "horribiles . . . instare procellas," are represented in Aratus by φωνῇ περίαλλα λεληκώς.   Munro has a note on the omission of conjunctions between participles and verbs (i.e. 'fugiens,' 'clamans,' 'fundens'), Lucret. v. 692–3.   For the phraseology cf. *ib.* 387, " ex alto gurgite ponti."

haud . . . cantus.   As mentioned above, this verse is an extension of 'nuntiat clamans,' a device which Cicero was fond of adopting, especially when it enabled him, as here, to achieve an onomatopoeic line.   The repetition of 'o' and 'u' is surely intentional.   For 'fundere' cf. note *De Cons.* 74.

F. V. Ar. 214 *et sqq.* mentions frogs as giving signs of rain.

ἢ μᾶλλον (δειλαὶ γενεαί, ὕδροισιν ὄνειαρ)
αὐτόθεν ἐξ ὕδατος πατέρες βοόωσιν γυρίνων,

The words πατέρες γυρίνων are omitted by Cicero.   He expands into two lines (in the same way, and for the same purpose), as he expanded 'nuntiat clamans' above, the word βοόωσιν.   It is possible that Cicero mistook the meaning of the parenthesis which he renders by " aquai dulcis alumnae."   Av. 1696 " Si repetant veterem ranae per stagna querellam."   'Alumnae,' of course, refers to the frogs.   For frogs as signs of rain, cf. *Georg.* i. 378; Pliny *N.H.* xviii. 361 ; Frazer, *Golden Bough* i., 3rd ed., 1911, pp. 292–5.

F. VI. Ar. 216–21. The original of these six verses, together with the two verses translated by F. v., forms a continuous passage. The first four verses of the Latin are represented by one in Aratus :

ἢ τρύζει ὀρθρινὸν ἐρημαίη ὀλολυγών.

Cicero omits ἐρημαίη. Isidore (*Etym*. xii. 7. 37) quotes a one-line translation of Cicero's for this passage. " Eadem [*sc*. luscinia] et acredula de qua Cicero in Prognosticis, ' et matutinos exercet acredula cantus.' " Pease (ed. *De Div*.) mentions this, and adds that it helps to support the theory that Cicero did two versions of this poem, an earlier and a later one about 60 B.C., as a rhetorical exercise. Cf. Pease, *Class. Philol*. 12, 1917, pp. 302–4.

acredula. The identity of this animal is not certain. Aratus seems to be using ὀλολυγών in the sense of a frog, and Theocritus vii. 139 supports this meaning. (Some have supposed it to denote the nightingale, others the long-tailed tit, whilst according to one explanation of a scholiast on Aratus it is " a bird like a turtle dove.") Av. 1703 translates : " Si matutinas ululae dant carmine voces," thus lending support to those who would identify the word with the owl. Another explanation suggests that the creature may have been some kind of an insect like the cicada.

vocibus instat. Epanalepsis—or the repetition of the end of one verse at the beginning of the next—is found as early as Homer. Cf. *Il*. xxii. 127–8. Cf. Lucret. v. 298–9, 950–1. Cicero uses this figure to imitate the repeated cries of the ' acredula.'

For modern usage cf. Milton, *Lycidas* :

> " But, O the heavy change now thou art gone,
> Now thou art gone, and never must return ! "

acredula . . . querellas. The repetition of ' o,' ' u,' and ' s ' seems to be intentional for onomatopoeic effect.

Cf. F. iv. 3. For phraseology cf. *Aen.* v. 842, " funditque has ore loquellas," and Lucret. i. 39, " suaves ex ore loquellas."

rores . . . remittit. A somewhat purposeless alliteration.

Fuscaque . . . cornix. λακέρυζα . . . κορώνη : the chattering crow. κορώνη is the Carrion Crow (black) : *Cornix* may be the Hooded Crow (head, wings, and tail black : the rest of his body is dusky-grey. Hence, perhaps ' fusca.' He is fond of the shore in winter). ' Fuscus ' usually ' dusky,' can sometimes be used of the voice meaning ' hoarse.' Cf. *De Nat. Deor.* ii. 58. 146 ; Pliny *N.H.* xxviii. 6. 171 ; cf. too Virgil's description in *Georg.* i. 388–9 :

> " Tum cornix plena pluviam vocat improba voce
> et sola in sicca secum spatiatur arena."

Av. 1704–6 translates :

> " Improba si cornix caput altis inserit undis,
> flumine terga rigans, si saevit gutture rauco,
> plurimus abruptis fundetur nubibus imber."

cursans . . . litora. This represents χέρσῳ ὑπέτυψε of Aratus, but his παρ' ἠϊόνι προυχούσῃ does not appear in Cicero.

demersit. No rendering is given of Ar. 220–21 :

> . . . ἢ καὶ μάλα πᾶσα κολυμβᾷ,
> ἢ πολλὴ στρέφεται παρ' ὕδωρ παχέα κρώζουσα.

This strict condensation, unlike Cicero, supports the theory that he wrote two versions. It is natural that a more mature translation would be less verbose than a youthful attempt at the same passage. Cf. note at the beginning of this Fragment.

The perfect (also ' recepit ') is gnomic. Cf. Ar. 219 ἐβάψατο.

cervice. Cf. note *Marius* 4.

F. VII. Ar. 222–3. These two verses in the original immediately follow those translated in F. vi.

καὶ βόες ἤδη τοι πάρος ὕδατος ἐνδίοιο
οὐρανὸν εἰσανιδόντες ἀπ’ αἰθέρος ὠσφρήσαντο.

Cicero omits in his translation the words καὶ, ἤδη, ἐνδίοιο, whilst the phrase πάρος ὕδατος is differently represented by " umiferum . . . succum." " Lumina caeli " takes the place of οὐρανόν. The expressive ‘ mollipedes ’ is an addition of Cicero's, for which, together with ‘ umiferum,’ cf. note F. iii. 4. For this prognostic cf. Pliny *N.H.* xviii. 364 ; *Georg.* i. 375–6 :

> " aut bucula caelum
> suspiciens patulis captavit naribus auras."

Av. 1707–8 thus translates :

> " imber erit, latis cum bucula naribus auras
>   concipit,"

mollipedes. Trans. " slow-footed," " lazy-footed."
lumina caeli. These words end verses 113 and 405 of the *Phaenomena.* Cf., too, Cat. lxvi. 59.
F. VIII. Ar. 319–21. Aratus is dealing with the times for sowing and reaping. The hundred verses separating the original of this Fragment from that of the preceding Fragments enumerated various prognostics, including the ways of foretelling the weather from the flame of lamps and fires.
lentiscus. The mastich tree. For an account of this as a prognostic cf. Theophr. *De Sig. Tempest.* 55. " Semper viridis . . . gravata " is a pleasing addition of Cicero's.
solita. In Pliny these three verses are quoted, but with the reading ‘ solita est,’ which Grotius adopted.
triplici . . . ter . . . tria. Cf. Lucret. v. 93–4 :

> " Triplicem . . . tria . . .
>   tres . . . tria."

The double alliteration seems to have no justification here.

Av. 1785–7 :

"Ter fetum concipit arbos
terque novos genetrix fructus alit ipsaque trino
flore renidescens tria tempora prodit arandi."

F. IX. Ar. 366–7 or 372. This Fragment may be a translation of either of these original verses :

χαίρει δέ που αἰπόλος ἀνὴρ
αὐταῖς ὀρνίθεσσιν,

or

Ἀρνάσι μὲν χειμῶνας ἐτεκμήραντο νομῆες.

Neither passage includes the equivalent of " de gurgite vasto."

For the phrase ' Caprigeni pecoris ' cf. *Aen.* iii. 221. And for similar ending cf. F. iv. 1 above.

HOMERIC TRANSLATIONS

The Iliad

F. I. Cicero is attempting to dispel the superstitious fear with which the average Roman regarded the occurrence of omens. He postulates a primary cause, the discovery of which will result in a logical explanation of physical phenomena. Celebrated portents are noted, and the passage continues, " Nam illud mirarer [*sc.* Cicero], si crederem, quod apud Homerum Calchantem dixisti ex passerum numero belli Troiani annos auguratum : de cuius coniectura sic apud Homerum, ut nos otiosi convertimus, loquitur Agamemnon " (cf. *Tusc. Disp.* ii. 26 : " studiose equidem utor nostris poetis : sed sicubi illi defecerunt, verti ipse multa de Graecis, ne quo ornamento in hoc genere disputationis careret Latina oratio "). These verses are given to Agamemnon : in the *Iliad* (Bk. ii. 278–83) the speaker is Odysseus. A similar confusion occurs in F. iii. Such inconsistencies are natural enough when one realises that these verses, almost certainly composed in the author's youth, are being quoted in a work written years later, probably without further reference to the originals.

Although we have only 29 Latin verses to represent 32 of Greek, the translation of this passage is free. This incident of the sparrow was popular amongst Roman writers, and imitations are to be found in Ovid *Met.* xii. 10–23 ; *Ilias Latina* 144–53 ; Apollod. *Ep.* iii. 15 ; Petr. 89 ; Lycophr. *Alex.* 202–3. The following is the version given in the *Ilias Latina* :

" Tandem sollertis prudentia Nestoris aevo
    compressam miti sedavit pectore turbam
    admonuitque duces dictis, responsa recordans
    temporis illius, quo visus in Aulide serpens
    consumpsit volucrum bis quattuor arbore fetus
    atque ipsam invalido pugnantem corpore contra
    addidit extremo natorum funere matrem.
    Tunc 'sic deinde,' senex, 'moneo remoneboque, Achivi;
    in decimo labor est, Calchas quem dixerat, anno,
    quo caderet Danaum victricibus Ilion armis.' "

2. *auguris . . . orsus.* He is not named as augur in the Greek, but cf. *Il.* i. 69. These two verses are a considerably expanded version of ἢ ἐτεὸν Κάλχας μαντεύεται ἦε καὶ οὐκί.

Notice the imitation of the Greek idiom (although not occurring in the original) whereby the subject of an indirect question precedes the question as object of the main verb, e.g. " I know Thee who thou art," etc.

fata : " predictions " (of destiny). Cf. *De Div.* i. 66 ; ii. 98 ; *In Cat.* iii. 9.

pectoris orsus. 'Orsus' found only here and in *Culex* 2. Trans. : " utterance of his heart." Cf. *Aen.* vi. 48 ; Ovid *Ex Pont.* iii. 4. 93.

4. *memori.* An ingenious trans. of : ἐστὲ δὲ πάντες μάρτυροι.

portentum . . . retentant. Note the internal alliteration, and see note on *De Cons.* 5.

5. *funestis . . . fatis.* Cf. original, κῆρες θανάτοιο. The Romans had no exact equivalent for this phrase. The Parcae could bring happiness as well as death ; κῆρ signified the power of death only.

liquerunt lumina. Cf. *De Cons.* 24, " vitalia lumina liquit."

6. *primum . . . est.* A free rendering of the proverbial expression χθιζά τε καὶ πρωιζά (more commonly πρώην τε καὶ χθές) which has no parallel in Latin.

vestita est. A happy paraphrase of the more prosaic ἠγερέθοντο. The word is a favourite one with Cicero (cf. *Ph.* 60, 205, 262, 332, 366, 424, 441, 475, 481). Of these nine instances all except 424 are connected with light. This metaphor of light as a garment seems not to appear in earlier Latin or in Greek. Lucretius uses it in ii. 148 of the sun which is wont, at dawn, " convestire sua perfundens omnia luce." Virgil has an example of the Ciceronian use, where the metaphor is not mixed by such an addition as " perfundens," in *Aen.* vi. 640 :

" Largior hic campos aether et lumine vestit
   purpureo, solemque suum, sua sidera norunt."

Modern poets have adopted this metaphor also. Wordsworth, in *Laodamia*, has, " And fields invested with purpureal gleams." Cf., too, Milton, *Par. Lost* iii. 10.

8. *fumantibus.* This appears to be substituted for the Greek ἱερούς. Probably Cicero knew another reading in his copy of the original.

9. *aurigeris . . . tauris.* " Auriger " is first found here : it was later borrowed by Val. Flac. 8. 110, who has " aurigera arbor " of the tree on which was hung the golden fleece. Cf. note on *Prog.* F. iii. 4. Homer does not mention the gilding of the horns, but Cicero was

probably thinking of the customary practice. Cf. Pliny *N.H.* xxxiii. 39 ; *Aen.* ix. 624 ; Livy iv. 16. 2 ; vii. 37. 1. The original τελήεσσας is not translated.

divom. For this, ' aquai ' in 10, ' divom versarier ' in 21, see intro.

10. *umbrifera.* An expansion of καλῇ. Cf. *De Cons.* 73.

11. *inmani . . . draconem.* Cf. *Il.* ii. 308–9 :

> ἔνθ' ἐφάνη μέγα σῆμα· δράκων ἐπὶ νῶτα δαφοινός,
> σμερδαλέος, τόν ῥ' αὐτὸς 'Ολύμπιος ἧκε φόωσδε.

There is considerable divergence between the two descriptions. The dramatic introduction to the omen is omitted, and " inmani specie tortuque " (" writhing its twisted coils of monstrous shape ") takes the place of δαφοινός. It is unfortunate that we thus gain no clue to the interpretation of the Greek word. (See *Il.* ii. 308 note, ed. Leaf & Bayfield, 1908.)

Cf. Cicero's trans. in the *Trachiniae* 43–4 : " tortu multiplicabili Draconem."

13–16. *qui platani . . . morsu.* Either Cicero did not translate every line of the original, or at least two lines of his translation have perished. No mention is made of :

> . . . πρός ῥα πλατάνιστον ὄρουσεν.
> ἔνθα δ' ἔσαν στρουθοῖο νεοσσοί, νήπια τέκνα.

Verse 16 can hardly pretend to be even a paraphrase of the original : τὴν δ' ἐλελιξάμενος πτέρυγος λάβεν ἀμφιαχυῖαν. These four verses entirely lack the intensity of the Homeric passage which is marked by real poetic feeling. Note (310–16) στρουθοῖο νεοσσοί : νήπια τέκνα : πετάλοις ὑποπεπτηῶτες : μήτηρ . . . ἥ τέκε τέκνα : ἐλεεινά . . . τετριγῶτας.

foliorum tegmine. For the same phrase in the same position cf. *Ph.* 114.

corripuit pullos. Ovid *Met.* xii. 17, " corripuit serpens."

nona . . . genetrix. A scholiast on *Il.* ii. 305 says : ἐννέα δὲ καὶ οὐ δέκα ὁ ἀριθμὸς ὅτι τοῦ πολέμου ὁ χρόνος ἀριθμεῖται, οὐ τῆς ἁλώσεως.

inmani morsu. A characteristic expansion of τὴν δ' . . . λάβεν (above).

18. *genitor Saturnius.* Cf. Κρόνου παῖς ἀγκυλομήτεω.

19. *abdidit.* The Greek phrase τὸν μὲν αἴζηλον θῆκεν θεός gives difficulty. A scholiast on *Il.* ii. 318 says : ἀρίζηλον· ὅτι Ζηνόδοτος γράφει ἀρίδηλον καὶ τὸν ἐχόμενον προσέθηκεν. τὸ γὰρ ἀρίδηλον ἄγαν ἐμφανές, ὅπερ ἀπίθανον· ὁ γὰρ ἐὰν πλάσῃ, τοῦτο ἀναιρεῖ· λέγει μέντοι γε ὅτι ὁ φήνας αὐτὸν θεὸς καὶ ἄδηλον ἐποίησεν.

αἴζηλον = invisible, by turning him into a stone.

ἀρίζηλον = conspicuous, i.e. as a monument in stone.

Cicero evidently takes the meaning 'invisible,' and stresses the contrast between the two compounds of ' do '—' ediderat ' and ' abdidit.'

20. *timidi.* An addition : verses 20 and 21 are a free translation of the Greek. Note the omission of verse 321 of the original in Cicero :

ὡς οὖν δεινὰ πέλωρα θεῶν εἰσῆλθ' ἑκατόμβας.

22–4. *fidenti voce.* Cf. θεοπροπέων ; *Achivi,* κάρη κομόωντες Ἀχαιοί ; *deum ipse creator,* μέγα μητίετα Ζεύς.

Cf. *Aen.* iii. 320 ' voce locuta est.' It has been suggested (Norden, 2nd ed., 1916) that this may be an archaic form of expression like that in Pind. *Ol.* vi. 13–14, ἄπὸ γλώσσας . . . φθέγξατο.

25. *tarda . . . nimis.* The MSS. here have ' sera animis,' clearly a scribal error. The Latin is a skilful translation of ὄψιμον ὀψιτέλεστον. Trans. " Though late they be and overlong delayed."

26. *Nam . . . videtis.* Verse 326 is almost identical with verse 317 in the *Iliad,* and 327 is a repetition of 313. Rhetorical taste of Cicero's times deprecated this doubling of similar statements. He therefore gives a condensed version in this verse which serves as an introduction to

the following line about the duration of the Trojan war.

27. *exanclabimus.* An archaic word. Cf. Ennius *Androm.* 102 ; *Eumen.* 147. Nonius remarks of this word : " exanclare etiam significat perpeti."

28. *quae . . . Achivos.* Note the omission of εὐρυά-γυιαν. 'Poena satiabit Achivos' does not appear as part of the original.

29. *matura.* A clever rendering of τελεῖται.

F. II. Cicero is saying that men sometimes lament the loss of those dear to them because they feel it to be their duty : they could spare themselves much sorrow if they would. Some exhibit outward signs of grief, others " when in sorrow, betake themselves to deserts, as Homer says of Bellerophon " :

1. *in campis . . . Aleis.* " On the plains of wandering." Cf. original, κὰπ πεδίον τὸ 'Αλήιον. The scholiast on Homer says : 'Αλήιον . . . πεδίον τῆς Κιλικίας καλούμενον ἀπὸ τῆς τοῦ Βελλεροφόντου ἄλης τοῦτ' ἔστι πλάνης. Cf. Herod. vi. 95 ; Auson. *Epit.* xxv. 69.

2. *ipse . . . vitans.* Cf. *Il.* vi. 202 :

ὃν θυμὸν κατέδων, πάτον ἀνθρώπων ἀλεείνων.

An exact translation of this verse, even to the extent of securing the alliteration of 'Αλήιον (in preceding verse) and ἀλεείνων by ' vestigia vitans.' Trans. " shunning the busy haunts of men."

F. III. These verses come from Cicero's *de Gloria*, 2 (*ap.* Gell. xv. 6). Gellius points out a further inconsistency as to the speaker of the lines. He says : " Apud eundem poetam Aiax cum Hectore congrediens depugnandi causa agit ut sepeliatur, si sit forte victus, declaratque se velle ut suum tumulum etiam post saeclis praetereuntes sic loquantur : ' Hic . . . vivet.' " Then Gellius adds : " Huius autem sententiae versus quos Cicero in linguam Latinam vertit, non Aiax apud Homerum dicit neque Aiax agit ut sepeliatur, sed Hector dicit et Hector de sepultura agit priusquam sciat an Aiax secum depugnandi causa congressurus sit." (Cf. note intro. F. i.)

1. *lumina linquens.* Cf. F. i. 5 ; *De Cons.* 24.

2. The two Homeric epithets in the verse, ὅν ποτ' ἀριστεύοντα κατέκτανε φαίδιμος Ἕκτωρ, are omitted by Cicero. Similar omissions are characteristic in the rest of the poems.

3. *Fabitur.* An uncommon form of this verb. Cf. Prop. iv. 4. 2.

F. IV. Cicero here continues the argument mentioned in the introduction to F. i. In the *Iliad*, Odysseus comes to Achilles and prays him have pity on the Greeks and return to the battle, because " Jove sends forth his lightning with signs propitious for the Trojans." Cicero writes : " At Homericus Aiax apud Achillem querens de ferocitate Troianorum, nescioquid hoc modo nuntiat : ' Prospera . . . edit.' " The speaker in the *Iliad* is Odysseus, not Ajax, who, however, is mentioned in the same verse. Similar confusions occur in Ff. i. and iii.

Note the omission of Κρονίδης in Latin. Cicero retains ἐνδέξια in the word ' dextris,' although he explains in this passage that the Romans regarded the left as the favourable side in augury, the Greeks and barbarians the right. (The Roman when taking auspices faced south, having the east, the lucky side, on his left.) Cf. *De Rep.* vi. 17, " Est hominum generi prosperus et salutaris ille fulgor qui dicitur Iovis."

F. V. In this passage the nature of dreams is discussed. Cicero turns to the dreams of philosophers : " Est apud Platonem Socrates, cum esset in custodia, dicens Critoni, suo familiari, sibi post tertium diem esse moriendum, vidisse se in somnis pulchritudine eximia feminam quae se nomine appellans diceret Homericum quendam eius modi versum."

Cf. Plato, *Crito* p. 44 a–b : Ὦ Σώκρατες, ἤματί κεν τριτάτῳ Φθίην ἐρίβωλον ἵκοιο. Homer (*loc. cit.*) : ἤματί κε τριτάτῳ Φθίην ἐρίβωλον ἱκοίμην. Note that Cicero translates Plato's ἵκοιο, not the Homeric ἱκοίμην (speaker Achilles). Pease remarks (ed. *De Div.*) : " A different Latin version appears in Chalcidius. In Plat. *Tim.* 252 (in Mullach *F.P.G.* 1867, 235) : ' terna luce petes Phthiae praefertilis arva.' " The Socratic verse is explained as meaning, either (1) that the return home signifies death, or (2) that there is a play on the words Φθίην and φθί(ν)ειν.

tempestas. Trans. " day " : for the use of this word with a similar meaning cf. Plaut. *Most.* 18–19 ; Hor. *Sat.* i. 5. 96.

Phthiae. Note the omission of ἐρίβωλον and the change of construction from the original Φθίην to the locative, necessitated by the use of ' loco ' for the Homeric verb ἱκνέομαι.

F. VI. The truly wise are free from all mental worry and emotion. Cicero says that Dionysius of Heraclea rightly discussed this with reference to the words of Achilles in Homer, which (adds Cicero) " run, I believe, like this."

2. *cum . . . laude.* Hardly even a free paraphrase of :

. . . ὥς μ' ἀσύφηλον ἐν Ἀργείοισιν ἔρεξεν
Ἀτρείδης ὡς εἴ τιν' ἀτίμητον μετανάστην.

Cicero does not claim to be translating literally, as his own remark (intro. F. iv. : " . . . nescioquid hoc modo nuntiat ") testifies.

F. VII. Grief and the outward signs of mourning become largely conventionalised by habit. True wisdom should control the emotions, but grief can be temporarily dispelled by expediency or some other more powerful feeling, such as fear. Cf. F. ii. Cicero quotes Odysseus as refuting Achilles' suggestion of an immediate attack upon the enemy before the Greek forces have taken food. Let them be fed, " for," says Odysseus, " the Greeks cannot mourn their dead by fasting."

1. *nimis multos*. This contains no suggestion of the original ἐπήτριμοι, ' in succession.'

omni luce cadentes. There is a variant reading here, ' carentes,' which is clearly a corruption. The reading in the text was restored by Manutius, and represents the original πίπτουσιν : hence ' omni luce ' can be translated daily (cf. ἤματα πάντα). ' Carentes ' would necessitate ' luce,' meaning life, on analogy with such phrases as ' corpora luce carentum ' (*Georg.* iv. 255), but ' omni ' would be intolerably harsh.

2. *maerore*. Commentators translate the original, πότε κέν τις ἀναπνεύσειε πόνοιο, " when could a man, in that case, take respite from fasting."

Cicero certainly did not take πόνοιο in this sense, but in that of ' maeror,' mourning.

4. *firmo . . . diurnis*. An exact translation of the original :

νηλέα θυμὸν ἔχοντας, ἐπ' ἤματι δακρύσαντας.

" Steeling our hearts and weeping but a day."

THE ODYSSEY

F. I. Cicero is discussing the universal desire for knowledge, and quotes his translation of this passage in the *Odyssey* in order to show that it was not the sweetness of the Sirens' voices nor any novelty in their songs which lured men to destruction, but their claim to know " all that passes on the boundless earth." Consequently the original verses bearing on this thought are expanded by Cicero with considerable freedom (note verses 5–6).

1. *Argolicum*. Archaic gen. pl.—a form which occurs frequently in the poems.

Ulixes. Cf. πολύαιν' 'Οδυσεῦ, μέγα κῦδος 'Αχαιῶν ; Greek epithets are often omitted by Cicero. In some cases

Latin would be unable to provide suitable equivalents, but in others, where there existed one ready to hand, it was seldom used. This verse provides an example of each in the omission of πολύαινε and μέγα.

quin . . . flectis. By the use of 'quin' the original jussive (νῆα κατάστησον) is skilfully converted into an interrogative sentence, suggestive of the pleading of the Sirens.

2. *auribus . . . agnoscere.* The translation of ἀκούσῃς: cf. verse 7 'tenemus' [*sc.* 'in mente'] for original ἴδμεν.

3. *haec . . . caerula cursu.* A loose paraphrase of the original τῇδε παρήλασε νηὶ μελαίνη. The phrase 'caerula cursu' (a typically Ciceronian alliteration) may have been derived from Ennius. In a fragmentary verse, *Ann.* 143, occur the words ". . . i caerula cursu," which have been emended to 'Neptuni caerula cursu." If this be the true reading, Cicero can no longer be regarded as the first poet to use this word to describe the sea. (Lucret. v. 481 and Virg. *Aen.* iv. 583, vii. 198 both adopted it.)

The spondaic rhythm of this verse seems to be fortuitous, whilst the two elisions, together with that in verse 9, are the only ones in the whole Fragment.

4. *vocum . . . captus.* A happy rendering of μελίγηρυν ἀπὸ στομάτων ὄπ' ἀκοῦσαι.

5–6. *post . . . oras.* The original is certainly neater and more effective than Cicero's expansion : ἀλλ' ὅ γε τερψάμενος νεῖται καὶ πλείονα εἰδώς.

7. *tenemus.* Cf. note 2 and, with this whole verse, the original 189–90 :

ἴδμεν . . . πάνθ' ὅσ' . . .
'Αργεῖοι Τρῶές τε . . . μόγησαν·

9. *omniaque . . . terris.* A free rendering of ὅσσα γένηται ἐπὶ χθονὶ πουλυβοτείρη. Lucretius may have borrowed his familiar 'vestigia rerum' from here. Notice 'latis' as a translation of πουλυβοτείρη.

F. II. The only evidence that these verses are Cicero's is to be found in St. Augustine (*De. Civ. Dei*, v. 8), who is speaking " of those who give the name of ' fate,' not to the position of the stars, but to the chain of causes which depends upon the will of God." God's will is omnipotent : men are dependent upon Him. Then the author continues : " Illi quoque versus Homerici huic sententiae suffragantur quos Cicero in Latinum vertit, ' Tales . . . terras.' "

Cicero's translation of the Greek is free. (Aristotle, *De Anim.* iii. 3. 2 refers to the Homeric passage here translated.) St. Augustine himself possibly drew this quotation from the part of the *De Fato* no longer extant, or from the lost chapters of the *Academica Priora*.

1. *hominum.* The Latin version omits ἐπιχθονίων, since ' homo ' is the equivalent of ἐπιχθόνιος ἄνθρωπος ; but ἄνθρωπος used alone in Greek could be applied even to those who had died and departed to the Isles of the Blest. Cf. *Od.* iv. 565.

pater ipse. This is the only example (except those in the *Phaenomena*) of the double dissyllabic ending. Cf. intro. p. 63. For the phrase, which is possibly Ennian in origin, cf. *Marius* 12 ; *De Cons.* 36–7 ; *Georg.* i. 121, 353 ; Catull. lxiv. 21.

2. *Iuppiter . . . terras.* The extent to which Cicero departed from his original is best seen by examining the Homeric passage :

τοῖος γὰρ νόος ἐστὶν ἐπιχθονίων ἀνθρώπων
οἷον ἐπ' ἦμαρ ἄγῃσι πατὴρ ἀνδρῶν τε θεῶν τε.

Free translation as it is, one cannot help but notice the beauty of the second verse. ' Auctiferas ' is purposely used to produce an archaic effect and is ἅπαξ λεγόμενον. (See note *Prog.* 3 ' tristificas.') For the phrase ' lustravit lumine terras,' cf. *Ph.* 332, 429, 442 : also *De Cons.* 2, and *Ph.* 237.

MISCELLANEOUS VERSES

F. I. ALCYONES.

In Capitolinus's life of the first Gordian, the MSS. have the following sentence which is clearly corrupt : " Adulescens cum esset Gordianus de quo sermo est poemata scripsit, quae omnia exstant, et quidem cuncta illa quae Cicero et demerio et arathum et balcyonas et Nilum, quae quidem ad hoc scripsit, ut Ciceronis poemata nimis antiqua viderentur." The words " et demerio . . . et Nilum " have been variously emended. Casaubon proposed " quae Cicero edidit, Marium et Aratum et Alcyonas et Uxorium et Limona." This was finally emended by his pupil, Salmasius, to the reading now generally accepted : " quae Cicero edidit, Marium et Aratum et Alcyonas et Nilum." See intro. essay, p. 25.

Nonius quotes sufficient to show that the poem was written in hexameters, and in an attempt to supply the first foot of the first verse, editors formerly wrote " Alcyonem genuit."   But if, as is probable, Cicero here refers to Lucifer, this suggestion must be abandoned, as Lucifer was the father of Alcyone's husband, Ceyx.   On the whole, the most satisfactory conjecture is Onions's. He would read ' Lucifer ' and understand ' hunc ' as referring to Ceyx.   The story of the metamorphosis of Alcyone and Ceyx into kingfishers is related at length by Ovid *Metam.* xi. 270 *et sqq.*   Ceyx is there described as son of Lucifer.

> " Hic regnum sine vi, sine caede regebat
> Lucifero genitore satus, patriumque nitorem
> ore ferens Ceyx."

Virgil may have had the first of these two verses in mind when he wrote : " cum levis aetheriis delapsus Somnus ab astris " (*Aen.* v. 838).

F. II. Limon. " The Meadow." (λειμών)

The only reference to this poem is in Suetonius (*loc. cit.*), where we read : " Cicero in Limone hactenus laudat : ' Tu quoque. . . .' " The word ' Limon ' was not infrequently used as a title for books, as Pliny (*N.H.* pref. 24) and Gellius (*N.A.* pref. 6) mention. Probably this was a collection of epigrams and poetical criticisms compiled by Cicero at various times. It has been suggested that Caesar imitated these Ciceronian verses (Suet. *loc. cit.*) when he wrote his own epigram on Terence :

" Tu quoque, tu in summis, O dimidiate Menander,
   poneris et merito, puri sermonis amator. . . ."

Another imitator was found in the person of Ausonius who, in his *Protrepticon*, has these verses :

" Tu quoque, qui Latium lecto sermone, Terenti,
   comis et adstrictus percurris pulpita socco,
   ad nova vix memorem diverbia coge senectam."

That Cicero should thus praise Terence is not surprising when one remembers his affectionate respect for the older school of poets. He quotes verses from Terence in his own works some thirty times.

F. III. Thalia Maesta (?).

The only reference to this verse occurs in Servius *Ad Ecl.* i. 58, where the following note is found : " ' palumbes '/columbae quas volgus tetas vocat : et non dicuntur Latine, sed multorum auctoritas Latinum facit : Cicero in elegia (Fabricius : MSS. egia L ; aegia PH ; egidia R ; eia M.) quae Thalia Maesta (Heinsius) [Talea Masta Cod. Leidensis (V) : Taliamastas Cod. Regius (R) and Voss] inscribitur : ' iam . . . reliquit.' "

It is useless to attempt any explanation of this verse. Many have been the attempts to restore its title, of which the most probable appear to be that of Heinsius ; 'Italia maesta' of Urlichsius ; 'τὰ ἐν ἐλάσει' of Nobbe. Hertz proposed θαυμαστά.

F. IV*a* (1). ELEGIAC COUPLETS.

The meaning of the first couplet seems to be that a small piece of ground may be called a farm, but Vettus's definition is absurd when he says that this can be such as a sling can hurl—provided that it does not fall out through the opening in the sling. 'Vettus' (Leo *Hermes*, 49, p. 194. 2) is conjectured for MS. 'Vetto,' of whom nothing is known. Some editors have read 'Varro,' assuming that Cicero was illustrating some etymology given by that author and no longer extant. But against this suggestion we have the following etymology in *De L. L.* iv. 4 : " Ager quod videbatur pecudum ac pecuniae fundamentum esse, 'fundus' dictus aut quod fundat quotannis multa." It is also unlikely that Varro used elsewhere in his work an etymology already repudiated by Cicero, and equally unlikely that the latter would have composed an epigram against one who dedicated his work to him (Cicero) from the fifth book onwards.

Voss (Etym. *v.* 'fundus ') and others have attributed this epigram to Tullius Laurea, Cicero's freedman— apparently because Pliny *N.H.* 31. 7 remarks that Laurea practised this kind of versifying. Also Quint. (*loc. cit.*) says : " Nec pauciora sunt (*sc.* hyperboles) genera minuendi : ' vix ossibus haerent ' et quod Ciceronis est in quodam ioculari libello " ; and here no praenomen is mentioned. But if one is to reject a Ciceronian authorship on this score, many other fragments must be regarded with suspicion, such as Alcyones and Limon. It seems more likely that if any other but Cicero himself were meant, ancient authors would have certainly added the praenomen. Therefore just because it is omitted here, the authenticity of the Fragment is supported rather than denied.

For this use of ' mittere ' cf. Ovid *Fasti* iii. 584.

F. IV*a* (2).

Burmann and other editors connect this second epigram with the former one. There seems to be no reason for so doing, other than a certain similarity of subject-matter. It has also been pointed out that this couplet detracts from the force and vigour of the first if joined to it. Whether the ' Iocularis Libellus ' referred to above, in the quotation from Quintilian, was actually written by Cicero or was a commonplace book in which he collected the poetical *jeux d'esprit* of others is unknown. In the latter case, of course, one would have to reject a Ciceronian authorship for the first of these two Fragments, but there seems no justifiable reason for so doing in the absence of any direct evidence to the contrary.

F. IV*b*.

What is more desirable, asks Cicero, than death, if it bring not extinction, but merely a change in our surroundings ? If thereby we are destroyed, what is better than a sleep of perpetual oblivion ? If the second alternative be true, then the words of Ennius have more to recommend them than those of Solon. For our Ennius wrote :

> " Nemo me lacrumis, ' inquit,' nec funera fletu
> faxit."

But the philosopher, Solon, said :

> " Mors . . .
>
> . . . gemitu."

The original (Sol. F. 22, 5 D) runs :

μηδέ μοι ἄκλαυστος θάνατος μόλοι, ἀλλὰ φίλοισι
καλλείποιμι θανὼν ἄλγεα καὶ στοναχάς.

It will be seen that the translation is close, but for the introduction of an additional idea by the words, ' ut celebrent,' some modification was necessitated in the pentameter.

F. IV*c*.

Cicero is speaking of those who die nobly in battle. He gives this Latin version of Simonides' well-known epitaph, composed on the Spartans who fell at Thermopylae.

The original (quoted from Herod. vii. 228 ; also Sim. F. 92 b D) runs :

> ὦ ξεῖν', ἀγγέλλειν Λακεδαιμονίοις ὅτι τῇδε
> κείμεθα τοῖς κείνων ῥήμασι πειθόμενοι.

Expansion has marred the terse tragedy of the original : the Latin is but a pale reflection of the Greek.

F. V.

Not to be born at all is by far the best lot which can befall one : next best to this is the speediest possible death. This opinion is also found, says Cicero, in the *Cresphontes* of Euripides (see Cicero's trans. in Ff. Eur.). He then continues : " There is something like this in Crantor's *Consolation* : for he says that Terinaeus, of Elysia, lamenting the death of his son . . . was told : ' Ignaris . . . tibique.' " The original (ps-Plutarch, *Cons. ad Apollon* 109) runs :

> † ἤρου, νήπιε 'Ηλύσιε, φρένας ἀνδρῶν.
> Εὐθύνοος κεῖται μοιριδίῳ θανάτῳ.
> οὐκ ἦν γὰρ ζώειν καλὸν <οὔτε οἱ> οὔτε γονεῦσι.

Except for the paraphrase in the first verse, the Latin is a faithful translation of the original. There is no direct evidence that this is Cicero's own version, but, no other author being indicated, editors include it amongst the Fragments. It will be seen that the pentameter of the original is represented by a Latin hexameter.

potitur. For ĭ cf. *Aen.* iii. 56:

" vi potitur. Quid non mortalia pectora cogis,"

finiri. For the use of this word in the sense of ' mori ' cf. Tac. *Ann.* vi. 50 : " Sic Tiberius finivit octavo et septuagesimo aetatis anno " ; Pliny *Ep.* i. 12. 2 : " qui morbo finiuntur."

F. VI.

A comparison of the noble and the ignoble ways of life leads one, says Cicero, to the following conclusion : " Nec in misera vita quidquam est praedicabile aut gloriandum, nec in ea quae nec misera sit nec beata. Et est in aliqua vita praedicabile aliquid et gloriandum ac prae se ferendum, ut Epaminondas. . . ."
The metaphor implied in the Greek verb is carefully retained in the translation by ' attonsa.'
The original (Paus. ix. 15. 6) runs : Ἡμετέραις βουλαῖς Σπάρτη μὲν ἐκείρατο δόξαν.

F. VII.

Here is suggested the commonplace thought that if life be controlled by destiny the gods must be powerless. Cicero continues : " Hoc sentit Homerus cum querentem Iovem (*Il.* xvi. 431–8) quod Sarpedonem filium a morte contra fatum eripere non posset. Hoc idem significat Graecus ille in eam sententiam versus. . . ."
The original of this verse is not preserved, but the same idea is frequent in ancient writers. Pease (ed. *De Div. ad loc.*) gives full references : amongst the more familiar are Aesch. *Prom.* 517–18 ; Herod. i. 91 ; Soph. *Antig.* 1106 ; *Oed. Col.* 191 ; Eur. *Hel.* 514 ; *Alc.* 965–6 ; *Or.* 488 ; in Latin Ovid *Met.* ix. 434–5 ; Sil. Ital. v. 76, and Livy ix. 4. 16. Statius, however,

definitely asserts (*Theb.* i. 213) Jupiter's supremacy to Fate, " vocem Iovis fata sequuntur."

F. VIII.

The folly of trusting to oracles. " Nam cum sors illa edita est opulentissimo regi Asiae ' Croesus . . . vim,' hostium vim sese perversurum putavit, pervertit autem suam."

The original (Aristid. *Rhet.* iii. p. 1407, a 39) runs :

Κροῖσος ῎Αλυν διαβὰς μεγάλην ἀρχὴν καταλύσει.

Cf. Herod. i. 53-4, 71, 75, 86. The oracle is also quoted in Diod. ix. 31. 1. See, too, Schol. Soph. *Trach.* 1 ; Schol. Eur. *Or.* 165. Another Latin version exists in verse (cf. Chalcid. *in Plat. Tim.* 169, p. 221, Wrobel) :

" perdet Croesus, Halyn transgressus, maxima regna."

penetrans. Pease (ed. *De Div. ad loc.*) thinks this may be taken as a free rendering in which Cicero thinks of Croesus " as passing within the boundary which that river constituted."

opum vim. The only instance, apart from the nine in the *Phaenomena*, of a monosyllabic ending in Cicero. (Cf. intro. essay, p. 62)

Virgil twice borrows this ending : *Aen.* ix. 532 has :

" expugnare Itali summaque evertere opum vi " ;

and again, *Aen.* xii. 552 :

" pro se quisque, viri summa nituntur opum vi."

The ending is archaic, and was borrowed by both poets from Ennius. Cf. *Ann.* 161, 412.

F. IX.

Discussing obscurity in speech Cicero here gives a verbose equivalent for what most men are content to call a snail. The verse appears to have been translated from each of the following lines. The first occurs in Hesiod, *Opp.* 569, the second in *Aenigma Athen.* ii. 63B :

(1) ἀλλ' ὁπόταν φερέοικος ἀπὸ χθονὸς ἂμ φυτὰ βαίνῃ.
(2) ὑλογενής, ἀνάκανθος, ἀναίματος, ὑγροκέλευθος.

Cicero combined these two originals, reading φερέοικος for ἀνάκανθος and ἂμ φυτὰ βαίνων for ὑγροκέλευθος. The result reminds one of the notorious line of Pacuvius :

" Nerei repandirostrum incurvicervicum pecus."

(Cf. Pers. i. 77.)

For these compound adjectives cf. note *Prog.* iii. ' tristificas.'

cassam. Cf. *Ph.* 369 : " retinens non cassum luminis ensem."

F. X.

No life can be happy, says Cicero, which is not regulated by self-control and clear thinking. " Ex quo Sardanapali, opulentissimi Syriae regis, error agnoscitur qui incidi iussit in busto ; ' Haec . . . relicta.' (Quid aliud, inquit Aristoteles, in bovis, non in regis, sepulcro inscriberes ?) "

The original (*Anth. Pal.* vii. 325 ; cf., too, Strabo xiv.) runs :

τόσσ' ἔχω ὅσσ' ἔφαγόν τε καὶ ἔμπιον καὶ μετ' ἐρώτων
τέρπν' ἐδάην, τὰ δὲ πολλὰ καὶ ὄλβια πάντα λέλειπται.

F. XI.

This famous verse occurs in a letter to Atticus, written November 26th, 50 B.C. Cicero, having arrived at Brundisium after a favourable crossing, quotes this verse, and then continues : " There, that verse with its spondaic ending you can pass off on any of our new school of poets as your own ! " The only other example of a spondaic verse occurs in the *Ph.* 3 (cf. intro. essay, p. 60).

Onchesmites. A wind that blew from the harbour of Onchesmus in Epirus. It should be noted that the form is (1) a learned word, (2) Greek—as is so often the case with spondaic hexameters.

VERSES OF DOUBTFUL AUTHENTICITY

F. I.

Mortals are not to fear death as an evil. Epicharmus is quoted in support of this opinion (F. 247 K) : ἀποθανεῖν ἢ τεθνάναι οὔ μοι διαφέρει. Diels corrected (presumably from the Latin version) to : ἀποθανεῖν ⟨μη εἴ⟩η, τεθνάκειν δ' οὐκ ἐμίν ⟨γα⟩ διαφέρει. There is no reason for supposing this Fragment Cicero's, except that he names no author in the text. Morel suggests that the line may have been Ennius's.

F. II.

" Besides this, forms often come across us having no real existence, but having, however, a distinct appearance. Such an apparition is said to have appeared to Brennus and to his Gallic troops when he was waging an impious war upon the temple of Apollo at Delphi. For then it is reported that the Pythian priestess said these words : ' I and the white virgins will provide for the future.' So it happened the Greeks fancied they saw white virgins bearing arms against them and that their entire army was overwhelmed in the snow " (Trans. Loeb Class. Libr.). Cf. Suidas s.v. Ἐμοὶ μελήσει ταῦτα καὶ λευκαῖς κόραις. The verse also appears in Schol. on Ar. *Nub.* 144 ; Aristid. *Or.* 4, p. 338, fin. Cf., too, Diod. 22. 9.

Cicero interprets the white virgins as meaning snowflakes. Cf. Justin. xxiv. 8. 10 ; Paus. x. 23. 4. For the comparison between maidens and snowflakes, see Serv. *Aen.* iv. 250. Justinian (*loc. cit.*) says : " Dum omnes opem dei suppliciter implorant, iuvenem supra humanum modum insignis pulchritudinis comitesque ei duas armatasque virgines ex propinquis duabus Dianae Minervaeque aedibus occurrisse." Thus he furnishes a second explanation. (For further information, see Pease ed. *De Div. ad loc.*)

F. III.

" Vide, igitur, ne nulla sit divinatio." Cicero continues by remarking that there is a common Greek proverb to this effect : ' the wisest prophet's he who guesses best.' Cf. Nauck. *Trag. Gr. Fr.*, 2nd ed. (1889), 674, note 973 :

μάντις δ' ἄριστος ὅστις εἰκάζει καλῶς.

Plut. *De Def. Orac.* 40 and Arr. *Alex.* vii. 16. 6, ascribe this verse to Euripides. Cicero, *Ad Att.* vii. 13. 4, quotes the first three Greek words, but leaves the author unnamed. His introductory words ("Est quidam Graecus vulgaris in hanc sententiam versus") suggest that he considered the verse anonymous. Cf. Eur. *Tr.* (*De Nat. Deor.* ii. 25) " hunc perhibeto Iovem."

F. IV.

Cicero is arguing that Theophrastus was wrong in asserting that external evil can destroy man's happiness. Therefore Theophrastus is blamed for commending this sentence in his Callisthenes. Never did philosopher assert anything so feeble. Cf. Plutarch περὶ τύχης (in exordio) :

τύχη τὰ θνητῶν πράγματ' οὐκ εὐβουλία.

The verse is attributed to the comic poet, Chaeremon.

F. V.

Aristoxenus, who believed the soul to be a harmony, had better have followed his own out of music and left philosophy to Aristotle ! Good advice is given him in that Greek proverb (cf. Arist. *Vesp.* 1431) :

Ἕρδοι τις ἣν ἕκαστος εἰδείη τέχνην.

For a similar sentiment, cf. Hor. *Ep.* i. 14. 44 :

" Quam scit uterque, libens, censebo, exerceat artem."

F. VI.

Caesar was indifferent to the existence or non-existence of magistrates. " In 47, for example, he had omitted to nominate them at all . . . while by appointing a ' consul suffectus ' for a few hours only at the end of 45 . . . he seemed to show that these were now only complimentary titles " (Myres, *Hist. of Rome*, 1910, p. 521).

Q. Fabius Maximus, having died on December 31st, C. Caninius Rebilus was appointed for the remainder of the day. Cicero gives an account of the unfortunate Caninius, *Ep. ad Fam.* vii. 30 : " Ita Caninio consule scito neminem prandisse. Nihil tamen eo consule mali factum est. Fuit enim mirifica vigilantia qui suo toto consulatu somnum non viderit ! " Cf., too, Macr. vii. 3. 10 where the same joke reappears :

" Vigilantissimus est consul noster, qui in consulatu suo somnum non vidit."

The above six Fragments are attributed to Cicero for want of any direct evidence to the contrary. In their editions of Cicero, some editors include some, others different ones, of the Fragments. It seems most satisfactory to include all or none. In Morel's edition of the *Fr. Poet. Lat.* 1927, Ff. iii., iv., v., vi., are all omitted without comment. Of the eleven *Misc. Vv.*, he omits the second couplet of iv*a* and xi.

TRANSLATIONS OF ÆSCHYLUS

F. I.

There are many ways of assuaging grief. Chrysippus thought that the most efficacious was to remove from him who mourned the idea that such grief was his bounden duty. " But it is as important to seize the right moment

when dealing with diseases of the mind as with those of
the body : as Prometheus answers, in Aeschylus, when
these words are said to him. . . ."

Atqui . . . Oceanus speaks to Prometheus. The
Latin version is a paraphrase of the first verse of Aeschylus,
which is written as an interrogative sentence :

οὐκ οὖν, Προμηθεῦ, τοῦτο γιγνώσκεις, ὅτι
ὀργῆς νοσούσης εἰσὶν ἰατροὶ λόγοι ;

rationem. Lambinus read ' orationem ' here. It is
clear, however, that λόγοι in the original is used in the
sense of ' reason,' as so often, and no emendation seems
justified.

Si quidem. " Yes, if."

non . . . manus. A somewhat free translation, inter-
preting the spirit rather than the phraseology of the
original :

καὶ μὴ σφυδῶντα (v.l. σφριγῶντα) θυμὸν ἰσχναίνῃ βίᾳ.

vulnus. For the use of this word in the sense of mental
anguish, grief, cf. Lucret. ii. 639 :

" (ne Saturnus) . . . aeternumque daret matri sub
pectore vulnus."

F. II.

Preceding this second Fragment there occur four
verses in *Tusc. Disp.* ii. 10. 23. They were originally
written as a part of the prose text. But scholars of all
periods have emended in the belief that they were verse.
The following arrangement is that of Bentley :

Unde ignes cluet immortalibus
clam divis doctu' Prometheus
clepsisse dolo, poenasque Iovi
furti expendisse supremo.

Varro (*De L.L.* vii. 11) says that these verses come from the *Philoctetes* of Accius. See, however, p. 226 and Cicero's own remarks, *Tusc. Disp.* ii. 11. 26, where he says : " . . . I have been very fond of quoting our poets, and where I cannot be supplied from them, I translate from the Greek."

cluet.=' dicitur.' On this word depend the two succeeding infinitives.

There is no Greek original extant, and this Fragment is generally assumed to be translated from the *Prometheus Freed,* probably the second of the Aeschylean trilogy. The chorus of that play consisted of Titans (cf. Arrian, *Periplus Ponti Euxini,* p. 19, quoted Dougan ed. *Tusc. Disp., ad loc.*), and this speech of Prometheus was, in all probability, an answer to an introductory ode of theirs. The Latin version is especially interesting as presenting part of an otherwise lost play of which it has been said, " There is perhaps no piece of lost literature that has been more ardently longed for than the *Prometheus Freed* " (*Ancient Gk. Lit.,* G. Murray, p. 221).

1. *Titanum suboles.* The Titans forming this chorus were Coeus, Crius, Hyperion and Iapetus. The last named was the father of Prometheus : thus his son claims kinship at the outset by the words ' socia nostri sanguinis.' The Titans themselves were descended from Uranus (cf. ' generata caelo ' 2) and Ge.

3–4. *navem . . . navitae.* This is not a particularly happy simile. The sailor fastens his ship for safety, Prometheus is bound to the rocks for torture. For ' horrisono ' cf. note *Prog.* 3.

6. *adscivit.* A word used of admitting recruits to a legion. So here Jupiter has ' enrolled ' the strength of Vulcan in his war against Prometheus. Trans. " availed himself of."

With this verse, cf. *Prom. Bound* (ed. Blomfield), verse 113 :

ὑπαίθριος δεσμοῖσι πασσαλευτὸς ὤν,

7. *ille*. Vulcan, not Jupiter. Cf. verses 1–87 of
Prom. Bound (ed. Blomfield).

10–12. *Iam tertio . . . fero. Iam,* "furthermore."
' *quōque*,' the pronoun. ' *Iovis satelles*,' the eagle. Cf.
Marius ii. 1 : " Hic Iovis altisoni subito pinnata satelles,"
and with these three verses, *Prom. Bound* 1021-5 :

Διὸς δέ τοι
πτηνὸς κύων, δαφοινὸς ἀετός, λάβρως
διαρταμήσει σώματος μέγα ῥάκος,
ἄκλητος ἕρπων δαιταλεὺς πανήμερος,
κελαινόβρωτον δ' ἧπαρ ἐκθοινήσεται.

15. *adulat.* "cleanses away the gore." A very rare
meaning of this word. For the active use, cf. Lucret.
v. 1070.[1]

16. *inflatu renovatumst iecur.* "swells and grows
again." ' Inflatu ' is here used in the sense of
' intumesco.'

18. *hanc . . . quae.* The reading printed is the
emendation of Bentley for the words ' hunc . . . qui '
(vulgo), which are clearly a scribal error for the feminine
necessitated by the preceding lines.

22. *me viduus.* "powerless" : lit. "deprived of
myself." For further uses of a similar nature cf. Hor.
Od. i. 10. 11 : " . . . viduus pharetra/risit Apollo."

Also *Culex* 372 : " cogor adire lacus, viduos a lumine
Phoebi."

anxias. Used here in an active sense, " agonising."
Cf. *De Cons.* 77; Soph. 33 ; also *Aen.* ix. 89, ' timor
anxius,' and Lucret. iii. 993, ' anxius angor.'

23. Translate : " Looking to longed-for death to

---

[1] *Sublime . . . sanguinem.* Non. Marcell. (Linds. p. 25, 17 M)
quotes these words as coming from the ' *Prometheus* ' of Accius. It
seems (cf. intro. to this F., p. 249) that Cicero claimed this translation as
his own. Nonius may have been misled by the fact that the short quota-
tion preceding this Fragment is probably by Accius—on the other
hand, Cicero himself may have copied this passage from Accius.

loose my torture." This preserves, to some extent, the alliteration of the original.

25. *saeclis glomerata horridis.* "amassed through the awful ages," i.e. ages of awful suffering. For the further use of the verb ' glomero ' cf. *De Cons.* 35 : " omnia fixa tuus glomerans determinat annus."

26. *luctifica.* See note *Prog.* iii. ' tristificas.'

27. *e quo. Sc.* ' corpore.'

28. *assidue instillant.* " ceaselessly drip upon."

SOPHOCLES

F. III.

As in the two translations made from Aeschylus, this also deals with the endurance of suffering. " But let us," says Cicero (in the text M.), " look at the great Hercules. At that time, when he was seeking immortality through death, he was racked with pain. What (bitter) words he uttered in the Trachiniae of Sophocles when Deianeira had caused him to wear the robe dyed in the Centaur's blood, which had clung to his flesh."

With this passage should be compared Ovid *Met.* ix. 101 *et sqq.*

2. *animo.* T. 1047 : καὶ χερσὶ καὶ νώτοισι μοχθήσας ἐγώ.

Despite the rarity of the uncontracted form of νοῦς in Attic and of its use in the plural, Cicero appears to have read here νοόισι or νόεσσι. μοχθήσας is translated by ' exanclata,' whilst the original has nothing corresponding to ' animo pertuli.'

3. *Iunonis terror implacabilis.* A considerable expansion of ἄκοιτις ἡ Διός. *Terror*, " the dread wrath of relentless Juno." For a similar use of ' terror ' cf. Cic. *Brut.* 11. 44 " (Periclis) vis dicendi terrorque," where it seems to denote ' awful power.' Greek δεινότης.

4. *tristis.* The original has : ὁ στυγνὸς Εὐρυσθεύς. Trans. ' dark,' ' sullen.'

5. *una vecors . . . edita.* T. 1050 : οἷον τόδ' ἡ δολῶπις Οἰνέως κορή.

vecors. According to Festus the word is used "(est) turbati et mali cordis." Trans. "malignant." But δολῶπις, the word in Sophocles, is rather "treacherous."

Oenei partu edita. "the daughter of Oeneus." The use of 'partus' here is very unusual, the word being restricted to women. Cicero probably had in mind the Greek word τόκος, which is frequently employed of either sex. Quint. *Inst. Orat.* viii. 6. 34 speaks of 'pario' being used of males : "apud tragicos etiam leo pariet." For examples of τόκος cf. *Oed. Col.* 1315, *Phil.* 614 and 1230.

6. *inscium.* T. 1051 : καθῆψεν ὤμοις τοῖς ἐμοῖς . . . The last three words are omitted in the translation, which, however, adds 'inscium.'

irretivit veste furiali. T. 1051–2 : Ἐρινύων / ὑφαντὸν ἀμφίβληστρον. The translation of ὑφαντόν is aptly done by ' irretivit '—a word rare except in Cicero.

7. *latere inhaerens.* So the best MSS. ' Lateri,' in conformity with the normal prose usage, Orelli and Baiter. For this ablative Dougan in his edition quotes references to Ovid *Met.* xi. 403, "inhaerentem lacerae cervice iuvencae," and *Aen.* x. 361 ; Ovid *Met.* v. 38.

7. *lacerat viscera.* T. βέβρωκε σάρκας.

8. *graviter.* An addition.

9. *decolorem.* T. 1055 has χλωρὸν αἷμα. Jebb (*Tragedies of Sophocles,* Cambridge, 1904) takes χλωρόν as ' fresh.' This makes ' decolorem ' an incorrect translation. May it not have been understood by Cicero in its more usual sense of ' pale ' ? Cf. *Il.* x. 376, xv. 4 ; Aesch. *Supp.* 566.

11. *illigatus . . . textili.* i.e. "illigatus tunica texta perniciosa." For similar transference of ideas, cf. verse 6 above.

12–13. *terra . . . Gigantum.* T. 1058–9 : ὁ γηγενὴς στρατὸς Γιγάντων. ' Moles ' is uncommon in this connexion ; cf. Tac. *Ann.* xii. 66 : "moles curarum." *' Terra edita,'* γηγενής.

13–14. *non biformato . . . Centaurus.* T. 1059 : οὔτε θήρειος βιά. " nor the might of savage beasts " (Jebb). But does the Greek refer to animals in general ? Cicero seems to have been right here in taking θήρειος as Centaur —a common meaning of the word. Cf. in this play 1095, ἱπποβάμονα στρατὸν θηρῶν. Also *Il.* i. 267, ii. 743 ; Pind. *Pyth.* iii. 8.

biformato. A transferred epithet and ἅπαξ λεγόμενον.

14. *ictus . . . meo.* T. 1058 and 1061 : κ' οὐ ταῦτα . . . ἔδρασέ πω. This (as ' terra edita ' above) shows the greater flexibility of Greek over Latin. Cf., too, the compactness of T. 1060–1 : οὔθ' ὅσην ἐγὼ|γαῖαν καθαίρων ἱκόμην . . . with verses 16 and 17 below.

15. *non . . . immanitas.* Another expansion. T. 1060 ἄγλωσσος. Cf. verse 17 below, where ' omnem . . . expuli ' represents only καθαίρων of the original.

16. *terris . . . ultimis.* T. 1100 : ἐπ' ἐσχάτοις τόποις. Orelli would refer this to Africa or Libya, but more likely is the suggestion that it denotes the Pillars of Hercules.

17. *ecferitatem.* This is the emendation of Klotz, indicated by the best MSS. Several other MSS. and early editions have ' hinc feritatem.' Davisius and Orelli read ' hic feritatem.' For ' ecferitas ' Dougan refers to Cic. *Pro Sest.* 42. 91. The reference here, of course, is to the destruction of such monsters as the Stymphalian Birds, etc.

18. *sed . . . manu.* The reading here printed is Bentley's emendation for the MSS. ' feminea . . . feminea.' This verse is a notable example of Cicero's skill as a translator. T. 1062–3 :

> γυνὴ δὲ, θῆλυς οὖσα κ' οὐκ ἀνδρὸς φύσιν
> μόνη με δὴ καθεῖλε φασγάνου δίχα.

Cicero obtains an effect stronger than that of the original by transferring the phrase " born not to the strength of men " (Jebb) from Deianeira to Hercules by use of the word ' vir.' This forms a well-balanced antithesis to ' feminae . . . manu,' whilst the repetition of ' feminae ' adds dramatic point to the verse, at the same time translating both γυνή and θῆλυς. " Without stroke of sword " (Jebb) is omitted in the Latin.

19. *O nate*. Hyllus, the son of Hercules and Deianeira.

usurpa. Lit. " employ this name of son truly for thy father," i.e. " prove a true son to your father now."

20. *ne . . . caritas*. A paraphrase of T. 1065 :

καὶ μὴ τὸ μητρὸς ὄνομα πρεσβεύσῃς πλέον.

me superet. " outweigh (thy regard for) me."

21. *manibus . . . piis*. The adjective is an addition. T. 1066 : χεροῖν σαῖν. ' Piis ' because Hyllus would be avenging his father.

22. *Iam . . . putes*. Two and a half verses of the original are here condensed into one :

ὡς εἰδῶ σάφα
εἰ τοὐμὸν ἀλγεῖς μᾶλλον ἢ κείνης ὁρῶν
λωβητὸν εἶδος ἐν δικῇ κακούμενον.

Iam. " soon."

24. *gentes . . . miserias*. This fine verse springs from an inspiration lacking to the original, which has only πολλοῖσιν οἰκτρόν. The feeling of universal pity, aroused by heroic suffering, was more marked in Cicero's day than in the time of Sophocles. The advance of civilisation brought with it a more kindly and humanitarian spirit. As another writer expresses the same idea : " Flebunt Germanicum etiam ignoti."

25. *me edere*. " to think that I should utter ! "

26. *quem . . . malo*. As in verse 22, the original which lacks the terse pathos of the Latin has been much shortened. T. 1072–4 :

καὶ τόδ' οὐδ' ἂν εἷς ποτε
τόνδ' ἄνδρα φαίη πρόσθ' ἰδεῖν δεδρακότα,
ἀλλ' ἀστένακτος αἰὲν ἑσπόμην κακοῖς.

27. *Sic feminata.* 'Effeminata' is the emendation of Klotz. 'Feminata' vulgo : the word is ἅπαξ λεγόμενον.

28. After verse 1076 of the original, there occurs in the Latin translation a lacuna. Below is printed Jebb's translation of the passage in question. "*Approach, stand near thy sire,* and see what a fate it is that hath brought me to this pass ; for I will lift the veil. *Behold !* *Look, all of you, on this miserable body ;* see how wretched, how piteous is my plight !

" Ah, woe is me !

" The burning throe of torment is there anew, it darts through my sides—I must wrestle once more with that cruel, devouring plague ! O thou lord of the dark realm, receive me ! *Smite me, O fire of Zeus !* "

The words italicised are those verses which appear in the Latin translation.

31. *caelestum.* Written, as often, for 'caelestium' on metrical grounds. Cf. Lucret. vi. 1274 and *Aen.* vii. 432. For the use of 'sator' thus, cf. *Aen.* i. 254 : "hominum sator atque deorum " ; and again in xi. 725.

33-4. *Nunc . . . ardor.* A dramatic rendering of T. 1088-9 :

Δαίνυται γὰρ αὖ πάλιν,

ἤνθηκεν, ἐξώρμηκεν.

35. *O lacertorum tori !* " sinewy arms." T. 1090 : ὦ φίλοι βραχιόνες.

From amongst all the poems, original or translated, this apostrophe of Hercules to his tortured body contains some of the best verses in Cicero. Here, as frequently, the translator turns the Greek into five successive questions—an effective device. He becomes very free, omitting or adding at will. For example, T. 1092-3 :

Νεμέας ἔνοικον, βουκόλων ἀλάστορα,

λέοντ', ἄπλατον θρέμμα κ' ἀπροσήγορον·

is translated simply by ' Nemaeus leo.'

255

37. *frendens . . . halitum.* This verse is represented by βίᾳ κατειργάσασθε, whilst for the succeeding verse Sophocles has only Λερναίαν θ' ὕδραν.

38. *excetra.* "snaky monster." Servius derived this from 'excresco,' because "uno caeso tria capita excrescebant"; but Orelli supposes it to be a corruption of ἔχιδνα. If originally borrowed by ear, the greatly altered form might have arisen thus.

39. *bicorporem . . . manum.* This epithet is extremely rare : it is found in Naevius, *Bell. Pun.* 2. 14 (*ap.* Prisc.) in the phrase "bicorpores Gigantes." Trans. "the host of double form," alluding to the Centaurs. Note the omissions in the Latin version. T. 1095-6 :

διφυῆ τ' ἄμικτον ἱπποβάμονα στρατὸν
θηρῶν, ὑβριστὴν, ἄνομον, ὑπερόχον βίαν.

40. *vastificam abiecit beluam.* For 'vastificam' cf. note *Prog.* iii. : 'abiecit,' 'overthrew,' i.e. 'flung to earth.' The reference is to the wild boar of Mount Erymanthus in Arcadia.

42. *Hydra generatum.* T. has δεινῆς Ἐχίδνης θρέμμα. As editors have pointed out, Cerberus and the Lernean Hydra were both sprung from Echidna (Hes. *Theog.* 295 *et sqq.*), in which case Cicero seems to have confounded the Hydra with Echidna, as Ovid has "Lernaeae Echidnae," *Met.* ix. 69 and 158 (note Dougan ed., *ad loc.*).

The description of Cerberus as being ἀπρόσμαχον τέρας, T. 1098, is omitted. In the next verse, however, is inserted 'tortu multiplicabili,' which is not represented in the original. T. 1100 also has ἐπ' ἐσχάτοις τόποις in reference to the place where the Dragon lived. This, too, is not present in the Latin.

For 'tortu Draconem,' cf. Hom. *Il.* F. i. 11, 'tortuque draconem,' and for the epithets, 'multiplicabili' and 'auriferam,' cf. note *Prog.* iii.

45. *lustravit.* A curious translation of ἐγευσάμην. It presumably means 'encountered,' perhaps an extension

of ' pass through,' as in *Aen.* ix. 96, " incerta pericula lustret Aeneas ? "

46. *spolia cepit.* The military metaphor of T. 1102,

κ' οὐδεὶς τροπαῖ' ἔστησε τῶν ἐμῶν χερῶν.

is retained.

By ancient writers this story of Hercules was held in high esteem. Amongst the more familiar passages relating to it are : Lucret. v. 22 *et sqq.* ; *Aen.* viii. 287 *et sqq.* ; Ovid *Met.* ix. 182 ; Seneca, *Trag. Herc. Oet.* 1235.

TRANSLATIONS OF EURIPIDES

F. I.

Emotional excess of any kind—even that which may arise from wisdom herself—is to be condemned. An examination of human nature reveals many ways by which the mind may find rest. " . . . and so Socrates, with good reason, is said to have encored the first three verses of the Orestes, when Euripides was exhibiting this play " :

οὐκ ἔστιν οὐδὲν δεινὸν ὧδ' εἰπεῖν ἔπος
οὐδὲ πάθος οὐδὲ ξυμφορὰ θεήλατος,
ἧς οὐκ ἂν ἄραιτ' ἄχθος ἀνθρώπου φύσις.

Neque . . . est. Cicero has mistaken the sense of the original. The meaning is that there is nothing dreadful, be it suffering or any other heaven-sent disaster, the burden of which the human mind cannot endure. He has translated the phrase ὧδ' εἰπεῖν ἔπος, ' so to speak,' as if it were ἔπος οὕτω δεινὸν εἰπεῖν.

ira . . . malum. An accurate, but clumsy, rendering of θεήλατος.

patiendo. The transference of the Greek ἧς . . . ἄχθος into the Latin gerund gives a slightly different turn to the sentence.

257

F. II.

Power acquired by unjustifiable means is of no advantage to a man. This is so in the case of Julius Caesar, who was constantly repeating Greek verses from the *Phoenissae*, " which I will express as well as I can, it may be awkwardly, but still so as to make their sense intelligible " :

Εἴπερ γὰρ ἀδικεῖν χρή, τυραννίδος πέρι
κάλλιστον ἀδικεῖν, τ' ἄλλα δ' εὐσεβεῖν χρεών.

Cicero's interpretation of the verses is not quite the meaning of the original. Note the omission of κάλλιστον. His own opinion on this precept follows immediately in the *De Officiis*. He says : " Capitalis (i.e. criminal) Eteocles vel potius Euripides qui id unum quod omnium sceleratissimum fuerit, exceperit ! "

F. III.

The opinion here expressed is similar to that found in F. v. of the *Misc. Vv.* (cf. intro. to that Fragment). Only a few fragments of Euripides's *Cresphontes* remain. The story goes that Cresphontes, king of Messenia, was murdered, together with his sons, by the nobles of the country who were jealous of his popularity :

῎Εδει γὰρ ἡμᾶς σύλλογον ποιουμένους
τὸν φύντα θρηνεῖν, εἰς ὅσ' ἔρχεται κακά.
τὸν δ' αὖ θανόντα καὶ πόνων πεπαυμένον
χαίροντας εὐφημοῦντας ἐκπέμπειν δόμων.

Nam nos . . . There seems to be no reason for punctuating at the end of this verse and changing ' coetus ' to ' coetu,' as in the earlier editions of the *Tusc. Disp.* Cf. *Aen.* i. 739 : " Et vos O coetum Tyrii celebrate frequentes."
coetus celebrantes. " assembling in great numbers." ' Coetus ' here stands for ' conventus,' the phrase being equivalent to " frequenter convenientes." Servius, however, interprets the word in Virgil to mean " convivium."

ubi . . . editus. An unnecessarily involved rendering of τὸν φύντα. ' *Ubi*,' " in which."

graves. An addition of Cicero's.

omni. For this emendation of Davisius in place of MS. ' omnes ' which the metre rejects, cf. Livy x. 29. 20, where a similar sentence occurs : " Funus omni honore . . . celebrat."

amicos. Sc. ' decebat.'

hunc . . . exsequi. A paraphrase which closely preserves the sense of the original. ' *Exsequi*,' the customary term for ' accompany to the tomb.'

F. IV.

If an oath were taken, the facts of the case being only imperfectly known, the oath could not be considered valid. So Euripides. Cicero is showing that perjury is not committed merely by swearing what is false, but by failure to perform acts, the performance of which one has undertaken by oath :

Ἡ γλῶσσ' ὀμώμοχ', ἡ δὲ φρὴν ἀνώμοτος.

Plautus, *Rudens* 1355, translates : " meus arbitratust lingua quod iuret mea."

F. V.

The conditions under which man is born make it impossible for him to be free of evil and misfortune. An acceptance of the inevitable is the only course if a man would learn how best to endure suffering. Carneades was one who used to blame Chrysippus for commending these verses of Euripides : Cicero entirely disagrees with Carneades.

Ἔφυ μὲν οὐδείς, ὅστις οὐ πονεῖ, βροτῶν
θάπτει τε τέκνα, χ' ἄτερ' αὖ κτᾶται νέα,
αὐτός τε θνῄσκει· καὶ τάδ' ἄχθονται βροτοὶ
εἰς γῆν φέροντες γῆν· ἀναγκαίως δ' ἔχει
βίον θερίζειν ὥστε κάρπιμον στάχυν.

quem . . . morbusque. An extension of ὅστις οὐ πονεῖ. The use of the indicative ' attingit ' is doubtless due to Greek influence, being a conscious imitation of the original.

finita est. " is destined." Cf. *De Legg.* ii. 26. 66, " Sepulcris autem novis finivit modum."

quae . . . afferunt. A verse which is too far from the original to be called a translation.

ut fruges. Note the omission of κάρπιμον : the force of ἀναγκαίως δ' ἔχει is reproduced by the gerundive, ' metenda,' whilst the final sentence of three words, containing the personification of Necessity, makes an ending more effective than that of the original.

F. VI.

" To ponder beforehand upon those evils which you see afar off," says Cicero, " makes their approach more tolerable. Therefore we praise the words of Theseus, as found in Euripides. Let me translate into Latin, as I so often do."

> Ἐγὼ δὲ τοῦτο παρὰ σοφοῦ τινος μαθών,
> εἰς φροντίδας νοῦν συμφοράς τ' ἐβαλλόμην,
> φυγάς τ' ἐμαυτῷ προστιθεὶς πάτρας ἐμῆς,
> θανάτους τ' ἀώρους, καὶ κακῶν ἄλλας ὁδούς,
> ἵν', εἴ τι πάσχοιμ', ὧν ἐδόξαζον φρενί,
> μή μοι νεωρὲς προσπεσὸν μᾶλλον δάκη.

meminissem. The subjunctive is generic, the antecedent being ' (ego) qui.' μαθών is rendered by ' audita . . . meminissem.'

futuras. An addition.

aut semper . . . mali. " or ever did I ponder some grievous affliction."

diritas. " misfortune," is ἅπ : λεγ : it occurs once again in Cicero *In Vat.* 3 meaning " cruelty." The verb ' meditabar ' in the preceding verse makes the further translation of ὧν ἐδόξαζον φρενί unnecessary.

ut . . . ne. This use of 'ut ne' is found at all periods, but not in Caesar, Sallust, or Livy. Here it is a conscious imitation of the Greek. Cf. *Pro Ros. Amer.* xx : " Accusatores multos esse in civitate utile est ut metu contineatur audacia : verum tamen hoc ita est utile ut ne plane illudamur ab accusatoribus."

F. VII.

Sorrow and grief can be laid aside when it is seen how little they benefit one. Hence it follows that mourning can be assumed at will. Some, there are, who have patiently endured sorrow and, better able to withstand whatever ills befall them, suppose themselves inured to misfortune, as that character in Euripides. . . .

Some editors attribute these verses to Ennius, and it should be noticed that here Cicero does not refer to himself as having translated the passage, but Orelli (*Onom.* vii. 1, p. 234) says : " . . . ut totum genus dicendi et versiculorum tenor docet a Cicerone ipso in Latinum conversi sunt, non ex Enii aliqua tragoedia desumpti." Indeed an inadequate reason, but there seems no evidence sufficient to warrant the exclusion of this Fragment from the poems.

The verses of Euripides are from a lost play *Aeolus*.

'Ει μὲν τόδ' ἦμαρ πρῶτον ἦν κακουμένῳ
καὶ μὴ μακρὰν δὴ διὰ πόνων ἐναυστόλουν
εἰκὸς σφαδάζειν ἦν ἄν, ὡς νεόζυγα
πῶλον, χάλινον ἀρτίως δεδεγμένον·
νῦν δ' ἀμβλύς εἰμι, καὶ κατηρτυκὼς κακῶν.

equulei. A rare word. Cf. Livy xxxi. 12.

tractu . . . novo. Not represented in the original.

subactus miseriis. Cf. κατηρτυκὼς κακῶν. Both versions retain the simile of the colt, ' subigo ' being used in Latin for ' to bring under the yoke,' as καταρτύω in Greek. For ' subigo ' in this sense, cf. Sen. *Hipp.* 1002 ; Cic. *De Rep.* ii. 40.

F. VIII.

Cicero, speaking of Jupiter, "the helpful father" ('iuvans pater'), says that the Romans, changing the cases, call the god Jove from 'iuvando.' To their ancestors he was known as 'the best and greatest,' while poets styled him 'father of gods and men.' Euripides, who said many things excellently, thus put the matter briefly. . . .

Varro (*De L.L.* 66) gives a better etymology: "olim Diovis et Diespiter dictus, id est dies pater."

ὁρᾶς τὸν ὑψοῦ τόνδ' ἄπειρον αἰθέρα
καὶ γῆν πέριξ ἔχονθ' ὑγραῖς ἐν ἀγκάλαις·
τοῦτον νόμιζε Ζῆνα, τόνδ' ἡγοῦ θεόν.

fusum. An addition, 'immoderatum' translating ἄπειρον. Cf. Lucret. i. 1013: "simplice natura pateat tamen immoderatum."

tenero circumiecto. This takes the place of ὑγραῖς ἐν ἀγκάλαις. 'Circumiectus' is a rare word, found elsewhere in Cicero only once, *De Rep.* ii. 6, where it is used of the rampart of the arx. The happy addition of 'tener' should be noted. Cf., too, Lucret. i. 207, ii. 106.

hunc perhibeto Iovem. The ancients were fond of deifying the sky. Herod. i. 131 says of the Persians: τὸν κύκλον πάντα τοῦ οὐρανοῦ Δία καλοῦσιν. Cf. with this verse 'Verses of Doubtful Authenticity' 3. And Ennius, *Scen.* Vahlen 345: "Aspice hoc sublime candens quem vocant omnes Iovem." Pacuvius (86 Ff. Ribbeck) has:

"Hoc vide, circum supraque quod complexu continet/
   terram ;
Solisque exortu capessit candorem occasu nigret/
id quod nostri caelum memorant, Grai perhibent
   aethera."

F. IX.

Cicero is referring to the remembrance of past events, good and bad, so far as they affect a man's present state. " Generally one says : ' Past toils are pleasant.' Euripides speaks well about this. I will finish, if I can, in Latin ; for you all know this Greek verse " :

$$\text{'Αλλ' ἡδύ τοι σωθέντα μεμνῆσθαι πόνων.}$$

praeteritorum. The sentence has been re-cast, this word taking the place of σωθέντα.

APPENDIX

BIBLIOGRAPHY

1. Texts. 2. Cicero's Poems. 3. General.
4. Astronomy. 5. The Hexameter.

The following lists are by no means exhaustive, but are intended to indicate works which have been of most use in the preparation of this edition.

1. Texts

De Natura Deorum. *J. B. Mayor*, 1891.
De Divinatione. *A. S. Pease*, 1920–23.
Tusculan Disputations. *T. W. Dougan*, 1905.

In addition to the above commentaries (see, too, pp. 72–4) and Frag. Poet. Lat., *W. Morel*, 1927, reference has also been made to the earlier editions of Cicero, namely, those of *Orelli*, 1845–63; *Nobbe*, 1850; *Baiter and Kayser*, 1861–9; *C. F. W. Müller* and others, 1890–96.

Poetae Latini Minores. *A. Baehrens* (Teubner), 1886.
Aratus, Text and Translation. *A. W. and G. R. Mair*, 1921.
Aratus, Text. *A. Breysig*, 1882.
Aratus (Hermes, xix. pp. 92–122). *E. Maass.*
Aratus, A dissertation, with facsimiles of H. Cod. Harl. 647. *W. Y. Ottley*, 1834.
Aratus, Phaen. and Dios. *P. Buttmann*, 1826.
Aratus, Phaen. and Dios. *J. H. Voss*, 1824.
Aratus, Les phénomènes. *L'Abbé Halma*, 1821.
Aratus, Phaen. and Dios. *J. H. Buhle*, 1801.
Aratus, Syntagma Arateorum. *H. Grotius*, 1600.
Germanicus and Avienus. *A. Breysig*, 1899, 1882.

2. CICERO'S POEMS

Ciceronis carmina historica, Diss. Greifswald. *E. Koch*, 1922.

De Cicerone interprete Graecorum. *C. Atzert.* Göttingen, 1908.

De Cicerone Lucretioque Enii imitatoribus. *R. Wreschniok.* Breslau, 1907.

Lucretius and Cicero's Verse. *W. Merrill.* (Univ. of California Publ.)

De Ciceronis poetae arte. *M. Guendel.* Leipzig, 1907.

De Cicerone poeta. *M. Grollmus.* Königsberg, 1887.

De poetica M. T. Ciceronis facultate *V. Faguet*, 1856.

See also :

A. Drachmann in Hermes xliii. 415.

F. Leo in Hermes xlix. 191.

Ciceros Aratea. *E. Moll*, 1891.

Zu den Fragmenten der Sprache Cic. *F. Hoppe.* Gumbinnen, 1875.

De M. T. Cicerone Graecorum interprete. *V. Clavel*, 1868.

Cf. Beiträge z. Berichtigung der Cic. Fr. *K. Halm.*

Phaenomena :

De Cicerone, Germ., Avieno, Arati interpretibus. *G. Sieg.* Halle, 1886.

De Cicerone et Germanico Arati interpretibus. *J. Maybaum.* Rostock, 1889.

Riv. di Storia ant. iii. 135. *A. Oliveri.*

Prognostica :

Clas. Phil. xii. 302. *A. S. Pease.*

De Consulatu :

Adversaria ad Cic. de Cons. suo poema. *E. Heikel.* Helsingfors, 1912.

3. GENERAL

Cicero and his influence. *J. C. Rolfe*, 1923.

De M. T. Ciceronis poetarum lat. studiis. Diss. phil. Vindobonenses, vol. 1, 1887.

Oeuvres complètes de M. T. Cicéron. *J. V. Le Clerc.* Paris, 1827.

A History of Criticism. *G. Saintsbury.* Lond., 1908.

Roman Poetry. *E. E. Sikes.* Lond., 1923.

Lectures and Essays. *H. Nettleship.* Oxon., 1895.

A Literary Hist. of Rome. *J. Wight Duff.* Lond., 1920.

Greek Life and Thought. *J. P. Mahaffy.* Lond., 1887.

History of Greek Literature. *G. Murray.* Lond., 1917.

Numerous translations of Cicero's works, including:

Ep. ad Fam. *W. Glynn Williams.* Lond., 1927.

Ep. ad Att. *E. O. Winstedt.* Lond., 1919.

Also:

Plutarch trans. by *J. and W. Langhorne.* Lond., 1805.

Servius Comm. on Virgil, 1881.

Aulus Gellius. Leipzig, 1871.

4. ASTRONOMY

From amongst a great number of books on this subject, the following are useful:

The Stars in their Courses. *J. Jeans.* Camb., 1931.

The Mysterious Universe. *J. Jeans.* Camb., 1930.

How to enjoy the Starry Sky. *M. Woodward.* Lond., 1928.

Astronomy for Young Folks. *I. M. Lewis.* Lond., 1924.

Astronomy for Everybody. *S. Newcomb.* Lond., 1903.

The Starry Heavens. *H. M. Metcalfe.* (Philips' Publication.)

Elements of Descriptive Astronomy. *H. A. Howe.* Lond., 1897.

The Story of the Heavens. *R. S. Ball.* Lond., 1892.
Popular Astronomy. *S. Newcomb.* Lond., 1890.

Star Atlases :

The Kullmer Constellation Finder. (Philips' Pub-
lication.)
Philips' Revolving Planisphere. (Philips' Publication.)
An Atlas of Astronomy. (72 plates.) *R. S. Ball.*
Lond., 1892.
Star Groups. *J. E. Gore.* Lond., 1891.

5. THE HEXAMETER.

Apart from standard works by L. Müller, Rönström,
Christ, Haupt, Quicherat, and others, the following
works have been consulted :

Latin Hexameter Verse. *S. E. Winbolt.* Lond., 1903.
Traité de Métrique grecque et latine. *F. Plessis.* Paris,
1889.
Prosodia Latina. *J. P. Postgate.* Oxon., 1923.
Pamphlet. *S. Lederer.* Leipzig, 1890.
Amer. Phil. Assoc. Transactions and Proceedings, vol.
xxviii. 60. *T. Peck.* 1897.
Res Metrica. *W. R. Hardie.* 1921.
Statistics are available in :
Ein Statist. Versuch über die Formen des latein.
Drobisch.